Hells Canyon

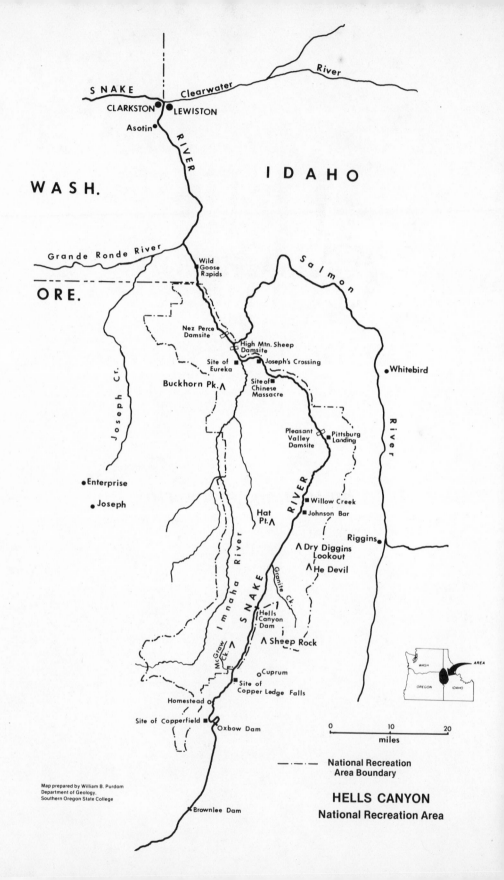

SNAKE

Clearwater River

CLARKSTON • LEWISTON

Asotin •

RIVER

WASH.

IDAHO

Grande Ronde River

ORE.

Wild Goose Rapids

Salmon

Nez Perce Damsite

High Mtn. Sheep Damsite

Site of Eureka

Joseph's Crossing

• Whitebird

Joseph Cr.

Buckhorn Pk. ∧

Site of Chinese Massacre

Pleasant Valley Damsite

Pittsburg Landing

River

• Enterprise

• Joseph

Hat Pt. ∧

RIVER

Willow Creek

Johnson Bar

Riggins •

∧ Dry Diggins Lookout

∧ He Devil

Imnaha River

SNAKE

Granite Cr.

Hells Canyon Dam

∧ Sheep Rock

McGraw Cr. ∧

Cuprum

Site of Copper Ledge Falls

Homestead

Site of Copperfield

Oxbow Dam

0   10   20
miles

Map prepared by William B. Purdom
Department of Geology.
Southern Oregon State College

Brownlee Dam

—··— National Recreation
Area Boundary

HELLS CANYON

National Recreation Area

WASH

OREGON   IDAHO

AREA

Hells Canyon

THE DEEPEST GORGE ON EARTH

by William Ashworth

Hawthorn Books, Inc.
Publishers/NEW YORK

Acknowledgment is gratefully made to the University of Washington Library, Seattle, Washington, for permission to reprint quotations from the Northwest Public Power Association Records appearing on pp. 91, 92–93, and 122 of this book; and to the University of Washington Library and M. Brock Evans for permission to reprint quotations from the Brock Evans Papers appearing on pp. 147 and 154 of this book.

Excerpts from this book appeared in *American Heritage,* April 1977.

HELLS CANYON

Library of Congress Catalog Card Number: 76–56528

ISBN: 0–8015–2007–X

1 2 3 4 5 6 7 8 9 10

To the ghost of Benjamin Bonneville

Contents

PART II:

The Politics of Power

69

PART III:

The Politics of Preservation

141

EPILOGUE:

Return to the River

212

APPENDIX:

Your Visit to Hells Canyon

219

Acknowledgments

This book owes an enormous debt to two remarkably similar men who happen to be on opposite sides of its central issue: Doug Scott of the Sierra Club and Hugh Smith of the Pacific Northwest Power Company. In terms of their ability to grasp and to sort facts; to understand and apply the intricate and often convoluted procedures of congressional politics; to analyze the past actions and motives of themselves and of others; and to communicate all this to the listener, they have no peers except each other. This book draws on all those qualities far more than I care to admit. To both I offer my thanks. I hope nothing in these pages betrays your trust in me.

Almost as important are three others, whose names not only appear often in the course of the narrative but who also helped considerably during the long months of research. They are John A. K. Barker of the Coalition to Save the Snake; Clem Stearns of the Pacific Northwest Power Company; and Floyd Harvey of Hells Canyon Excursions, Inc., the acknowledged father of the Hells Canyon preservation effort. John Barker, in addition to providing me with one of the meatiest single interviews I had, arranged for an eye-opening tour of the canyon and reviewed various parts of the manuscript prior to publication; Clem Stearns generously made available to me large portions of his time and of his file materials and responded with alacrity to my frantic long-distance cries for help, to fill a glaring gap in the manuscript, caught by an alert editor at Hawthorn Books; and Floyd Harvey proved to be not only a gold mine of information on early preservation efforts but an eagle-eyed manuscript reviewer and a remarkably warm companion over a bottle of Coors's finest.

So many others contributed so much to this project, over such a long period of time, that it is difficult to know where to begin thanking them all. Owen Hurd of the Washington Public Power Supply System; Don Warman of the Forest Service Regional Office staff in Portland, Oregon; Larry Williams of the Oregon Environmental Council; Senator Bob Packwood; and Pete Henault, Ken Witty, Dick Farman, Cyril Slansky, and Jerry Jayne of the Hells Canyon Preservation Council, donated, collectively, close to a fortnight of taped interviews. In addition, Mr. Warman provided a generous selection of photographs to assist in choosing the book's illustrations, and Mr. Witty very kindly opened his home to me as an overnight guest on the occasion of the dedication of the Hells Canyon National Recreation Area in July 1976. Representatives Al Ullman and Lloyd Meeds were very helpful in providing answers to certain questions, as were Mike Wetherell and Bill Hall of Senator Frank Church's staff, and Bob Moore of Senator Packwood's. Bill Pitney of the Oregon Fish and Wildlife Commission sent along several reams of information on the Oxbow Incident and on fisheries problems in general; Frank Parsons of the Walla Walla District, U.S. Army Corps of Engineers, came through with data I could not find elsewhere on the corps' "308 Report"; and Judith Austin of the Idaho State Historical Society ran down some valuable materials on the early days of electric power in Idaho, as well as an excellent selection of photographs. Frederic J. Cochrane and Bob Brown of the Idaho Power Company, a corporation that I have been forced to criticize rather heavily in this text, were generous and helpful despite my admitted bias, patiently answering some rather impertinent questions and throwing open their files of data and photographs. David McCraney of the Bureau of Outdoor Recreation and Frank Howard of the Oregon State Highway Division also contributed pictures. Roy Bessey and Tony Netboy provided me with several valuable leads; and my good friend Frank Mac-

Graw, professor of geography at Southern Oregon State College and former member of the Oregon Water Resources Board, gave me a number of interesting stories relating to the board's actions on Hells Canyon (most of which, alas, had to be sacrificed for brevity), as well as reviewing the entire final form of the manuscript prior to publication.

In a different category was the extremely valuable assistance of Dave Spencer and Ernie Duckworth, who took me into Rush Creek Rapids via jet boat and in the process gave me a whole new view of the canyon and its environs.

Among libraries and librarians (what would we do without them?), the star is probably Liisa Fagerlund of the Manuscripts Division of the University of Washington Library in Seattle, who kindly gave me access to and permission to quote from the division's extensive files of Northwest Public Power Association documents, as well as back archives of the Northwest Office of the Sierra Club (thanks also to Doug Scott and Brock Evans for approving use of the Sierra Club materials). But Cliff Wolfsehr and others at the Southern Oregon State College Library in Ashland— with its complete microfilm files of the Portland *Oregonian* and the *New York Times*, and its extensive collections of government documents and maps—would have to run a close second. Bob Wilson and his staff at the Ashland Public Library were also very helpful, as were the staffs and collections of at least the following: the Medford (Oregon) Public Library, the Oregon State Library in Salem, the Washington State University Library in Pullman, the Library of the University of Idaho in Moscow (for its collection of early Idaho newspapers), and the Seattle Public Library.

Finally, a great big thank you to all who provided me with the encouragement and moral support necessary to complete a project of this scope, especially Max Gartenberg, Sandra Choron, Bryan Frink, Larry and Karen Chitwood, Warren James and Jack Abele, and my wife Melody.

Prologue: The Place

In the northeast corner of the state of Oregon, lapping over into Idaho and Washington, lies a badly broken basalt upland that geographers call the Snake River Plateau. Scarcely anyone but a geographer would recognize it as a plateau. Great chunks of it have been lifted up to form mountain ranges; deep canyons have been incised into it, carving away much of the original surface and leaving behind a bewildering jumble of echoing depths and long, level ridges. One of these canyons—the canyon of the Snake River itself—is the deepest known gorge on this planet. It is called Hells Canyon, and it forms the boundary between Oregon and Idaho for slightly more than one hundred spectacular miles.

Gazing down into the canyon from the rim, or floating through it on the surface of the river, the visitor is struck first by the great barrenness of the place and only later by the overwhelming immensity of its size. Hells Canyon offers none of the colorful exhibitionism of the Colorado. The canyon walls are somber, monochromatic, and austere. In many places, great black cliffs rise almost vertically from the water for thousands of feet, often no more than 200 feet apart. These form what is known as the Inner Gorge of Hells Canyon. At other places, benches have developed. Here the canyon bottom may spread out as wide as a mile or more, and some cultivation is possible; ranching has been carried out in these depths for more than a century. Above the cliffs, or the benches, the canyon face sweeps upward in a series of huge terraces, mountain-steep and covered with bunchgrass. At the top of these slopes is the Rimrock, a stairstepped wall of basalt varying in height from several hundred to several thousand feet, reaching up to the level surface of the old plateau. The Rimrock is in turn capped for some distance on the Idaho side by the serrated metavolcanic peaks of the Seven Devils Mountains, whose western slopes plunge directly into the canyon and whose summits are therefore classed as a part of the rim. The Rimrock and the Devils stand an incredible distance above the canyon floor. For forty miles, the average depth of the canyon is better than 5,500 feet. For fifteen miles, from Hat Point south along the Oregon rim to Saulsberry Saddle, the average exceeds 6,000 feet. From one point on the Idaho rim it is fully 7,900 feet down to the river—a mile and a half of vertical distance, more than a third of a mile greater than at the deepest spot in the Grand Canyon of the Colorado.

Hells Canyon is not only amazingly deep; it is also amazingly narrow. The average width, rim to rim, is only ten miles, and at times it shrinks to considerably less. Where the canyon is narrowest, from Black Mountain on the Oregon rim to Dry Diggins Point in Idaho, the width is scarcely five miles. And it is five miles of thin air. Black Mountain stands 6,900 feet above sea level; Dry Diggins, 7,800. Between them flows the Snake, its surface at an elevation of just 1,350 feet.

The canyon is full of surprises. Here the fisherman can, if he is lucky, catch a fish twice as long as a man is tall. Here the lover of rare plants may find a veritable feast: At least twenty-four species grow here which can be found nowhere else in the world. Here are ruins that appear to have been lifted out of a picture book of the Andes as well as Indian pictographs that may go back 6,000 years. Near Buffalo Eddy, in the lower canyon, a friend once pointed out to me the image of a snake fifty feet long, carved by Indians into the middle of a basalt cliff where it would seem impossible for a person to even cling, let alone work. It can be seen only when the light is exactly right, and many frequent visitors to the canyon are unaware of its existence. At Deep Creek, Chinese numerals may be seen painted on a cliff wall at the back of a rude shelter, which seems much too small to hold the thirty-two men who were murdered there in 1887. Just below the Imnaha Rapids, near the heart of the canyon, there is, of all things, a steamboat landing. And one day, scrambling about the site of the proposed Pleasant Valley Dam near Pittsburg Landing, my wife and I came upon a very strange sight—a talisman made of magpie feathers, bits of herb, and pieces of string, tied onto some rusty machinery at the head of a long-abandoned mine shaft. It was obviously recent, obviously traditionally made, and obviously meant to exercise some undefined power over the site. Who put it there? When? Why? The questions continue to haunt me. I suppose they always will.

The floor of Hells Canyon is formed by the Snake River. It is a big river, big and powerful: more than three times the length of the Hudson, almost twice the volume of the Colorado. To a visitor on the rim, this may not be readily apparent. To a visitor at water level, drifting down the canyon in a rubber raft or ascending it in a powerful, specially built jet boat, it is inescapable. The river seems mostly white. Rapids follow rapids in stupefying succession, so many that even those who run the river regularly do not know the names of them all. Most are small. Some are not. One, Granite Creek Rapid, is exceeded nationally only by Lava Falls on the Colorado. Running such a rapid is an electrifying experience: Above, there is a smoothness and a sense of impending doom, of being drawn into the vortex of a maelstrom over which you will have no control. Acceleration is swift and silent. In the rapid itself, everything seems to happen in slow motion. The raft conforms itself to the water, bending and yawing. The river thunders and breaks and pours. You become a part of it. There is a pounding and a surging and an overwhelming sensation of irresistible, brute strength. And when the rapid is behind and the stream flows calmly once more, there is a mingled sensation of relief and regret—and an anticipation of the next rapid, just around the bend.

To the whitewater rafter, the power of this river seems immeasurable. To the engineer it is not: It can, in fact, be calculated with considerable precision. Between the two Idaho communities of Weiser and Lewiston—a distance of some 200 miles—the river drops 1,400 feet. Dam builders refer to such a drop as a head. A head of 1,400 feet, on a river the size of the Snake, has a theoretical potential energy of nearly 2.85 million horsepower, enough to generate an astounding 18 billion kilowatt hours of electricity annually. Not all of this power is recoverable, but a surprisingly large proportion of it is—providing that a combination of dams can be built in such a way as to utilize the entire head. Hells Canyon, with its deep, narrow Inner Gorge, was long ago recognized as an ideal location for such a combination of dams. And because of this singular characteristic, Hells Canyon—ruins, Indian relics, rare plants, rapids, and all—was eventually destined to become the location of one of the longest and most intense political whirlwinds in the history of resource management in the United States.

But controversy is only part of the story of Hells Canyon. Before the dam builders came the miners and stockmen; and before them, the explorers and the fur traders and the Indians; and before *them*. . . .

PART I:
THE HISTORY

"A high broken mountainous country . . ."
—Captain Meriwether Lewis, 1806

1

The Deep Past

The Nez Perce Indians believed that Coyote dug Hells Canyon with a big stick in one day in order to contain the Seven Devils in Idaho and keep them from coming over to eat people in the Blue Mountains. Early white observers, tied to the time scale of Noah and his ark, postulated that some great cataclysm—a huge earthquake, perhaps, or a volcanic explosion—must have rent the earth here and that the Snake was merely following a path laid down for it by some other means. Modern scientists, not surprisingly, tend to discount both theories; but—less predictably—their own account, when pieced together and stripped of scientific jargon, is also cataclysmic in nature. Hells Canyon was dug rapidly and fairly recently. And the Snake did not do it.

Geologists tell us that the present-day landforms of the Hells Canyon region began to take shape about the middle of the Miocene epoch, fifteen to twenty million years ago. At that time the land in this area was low and rolling, with a local relief—a hilltop-to-valley vertical distance—of less than 2,000 feet. Rivers came down from the central Idaho mountains and meandered westward among the hills; their beds have been found, buried beneath thick layers of basalt, in the west-lying Wallowa Mountains. To the north lay the Columbia; to the south, the ancestral Snake, flowing placidly to meet the Pacific somewhere along the coast of what is now California. Forests probably clothed the hills. The landscape was peaceful, unspectacular, and serene.

Then, in the north, violent things began to happen. Huge rifts opened in the earth's surface; great quantities of lava spewed forth, surging across the landscape like a stone sea. The first flow cooled and hardened; another poured out on top of it, and another, and another, until ultimately there were more than a hundred, reaching a total thickness of at least six thousand feet, spreading a vast, level tableland from the Cascade Mountains to the Rockies. One arm had reached south and covered the peaceful landscape, which now lay several thousand feet underground. It did not touch the Snake, which still flowed quietly to the sea.

But now, deep in the earth, new forces were at work. The land groaned and shifted; the southeast corner of the new plateau rose and tilted, developing a small but distinguishable slope to the northwest. The forces continued to push, but the plateau could take no more. It broke. Up through it thrust the Wallowas and the Seven Devils, great masses of rock, not yet carved into mountain shapes. At the same time, further south, the Owyhee Range rose, directly across the path of the Snake. The river was blocked: It had no place to go. It began ponding behind these new barriers, creating a lake. Gradually, steadily, the lake grew.

Now the drainage patterns we know today were beginning to become established in the Wallowa and Seven Devils mountains. Southward flowed Indian Creek and Pine Creek and the Powder and Weiser rivers, pouring into the still-rising waters of the great Idaho Lake. Northward flowed the Salmon and the Imnaha and the Grande Ronde, cutting their way down through thick basalts on their way to join the Columbia. And northward, too, flowed a small, unsung, unnamed tributary of the Salmon—no longer there today—which had found a weak spot in the mountain barrier.

This weak spot was a series of deep fractures in the basalt and the underlying granitic rocks, probably caused by deformation during the building of the nearby mountains. Here the rock was already cut to pieces; the water had merely to move it out of the way. Eroding rapidly downward along this ready-made pathway, the small tributary began moving its headwaters south, paralleling the Imnaha, curling around the base of the Seven Devils, until—early in the Quaternary, approximately one million years ago, barely an eyewink removed from us by geologic time—the rapidly downcutting stream met the slowly uprising waters of Idaho Lake, at a place now called the Oxbow. The results were predictable, and catastrophic. Spilling into the stream, the lake began draining northward. The already weakened lip gave way almost immediately, and a great flood of water surged down the channel as Idaho Lake emptied. When it was over, Hells Canyon as we know it today was essentially complete. The small tributary had been obliterated, and in its place, at the bottom of a ragged chasm, the mighty Snake roared and foamed and bulled its way north to the Columbia and onward to the sea.

ii

There were no humans around to witness the deluge that finished the creation of Hells Canyon; the first inhabitants did not enter the area until much later, most likely approximately fifteen thousand years ago. These early peoples left few traces of their passage, and little is known about them. They appear to have been nomads, living in the canyon only in the winter, summering in the high valleys nearby. At several places—Buffalo Eddy, Willow Bar, Nez Perce Shelter—they carved petroglyphs, pictures in stone that the Indians of the area at the time of first white contact had long since lost the ability to interpret. At other places they left tools, fish walls, and building foundations. It has been estimated that there are between 160 and 200 significant archaeological sites between the mouth of the Salmon River and Hells Canyon Creek, sixty miles upstream. Most have never been excavated. When and if study is ever carried out, the results should prove extremely valuable; it was near here, at the mouth of the Palouse River on the lower Snake, that Washington State University anthropologist Roald Fryxell discovered in 1965 what were then—and may still be—the oldest human skeletal fragments ever found in North America.

The Indians whom the first explorers found living in the canyon and the surrounding mountains were probably not descendants of the earliest inhabitants, though their life-style appears to have been much the same. The two principal contact tribes belonged to two separate and distinct cultural stocks. At the south end of the canyon lived the Western Shoshone, a Basin Culture tribe; to the north, and claiming most of the canyon itself, were the Nez Perce, who belonged to what is known as the Plateau Culture. There was open antagonism between the two tribes, as well as constant—if usually undeclared—warfare, in which the more powerful Nez Perce normally had the upper hand. Hells Canyon formed one of the principal contact points between the two peoples, and skirmishes often took place in its depths; the site of one such encounter, in which a group of Nez Perce warriors obliterated a Shoshone village set in the deepest part of the canyon, has been immortalized in the name of Battle Creek, a small stream that enters the Snake from the Oregon side just north of Barton Heights.

The Shoshone—also referred to as Snakes or, somewhat contemptuously, Diggers—were a weak, poverty-stricken people who lived a strictly nomadic existence, subsisting on roots, small seeds, insects, and the sparse game animals that roamed the deserts and mountains of their dry, hostile territory. The Nez Perce, by way of contrast, were one of the most powerful tribes in the west; they lived in permanent winter villages—taking up the nomadic life only in the summer—and had a strong economy, based on the abundant runs of salmon that come up the Snake River during the spring and fall months. When in the not-too-distant past buffalo had ranged the rolling grasslands of eastern Washington, the Nez Perce had hunted them there; after these herds, which had never been very numerous, were driven to extinction, Nez Perce buffalo parties began making yearly treks over the Rockies to the plains of eastern Montana and Wyoming, where they became one of the few tribes to compete successfully with the powerful Blackfeet for hunting rights. They practiced selective breeding of horses and had a method of gelding stallions superior to that practiced by the whites who conquered them. Samuel Parker, the first Protestant missionary to travel among them, summed up their character in words that positively glowed: "Probably there is no government upon earth," he wrote later in his *Journal of an Exploring Tour Beyond the Rocky Mountains* (1838), "where there is so much personal and political freedom, and at the same time so little anarchy; and I can unhesitatingly say, that I have no where witnessed so much subordination, peace, and friendship as among the Indians in the Oregon Territory. The day may be rued when their order and harmony shall be interrupted by any instrumentality whatever.''

Neither the Shoshone nor the Nez Perce had much in the way of formal tribal unity before the coming of the white man. The Shoshone never developed any. The Nez Perce did—a circumstance which would constitute a deep interruption in the ''order and harmony'' that Parker had praised so thoroughly, and which would eventually have a profound and moving effect on the human side of the story of the deepest gorge on earth.

2
The Explorers

The contact of white civilization with Hells Canyon began—as did so many things in the Pacific Northwest—with the Louisiana Purchase and the explorations of captains Meriwether Lewis and William Clark, in the opening years of the nineteenth century.

It is sometimes difficult to realize just how recent our knowledge of this northwestern corner of America actually is. By the time the Louisiana Purchase was negotiated in 1803, the modern era was already well under way. It had been almost one hundred years since the beginning of the Industrial Revolution. Steam power had been used to propel carriages for more than forty years, and regular steam passenger service was under way on the roads of England; manned flight in lighter-than-air craft was twenty years old; photography and the telegraph were barely thirty years in the future. Yet when Lewis and Clark set out up the Missouri River from St. Louis in the spring of 1804, the part of the world they were headed into was so little known that President Thomas Jefferson predicted encounters with woolly mammoths and giant ground sloths, and the two explorers fully expected to be able to portage canoes across the Continental Divide. This was a comforting assumption, but it was dead wrong. Between the point on the upper Missouri where they were forced to abandon their boats and the start of the first navigable stretch of the Columbia River system lay more than 250 miles of the roughest kind of country. Wandering almost at random among the rugged and trackless Bitterroot Mountains at the headwaters of the Salmon and Clearwater rivers, it took the Corps of Discovery more than a month to make the crossing. The weather was foul: rain mixed with hail in the valleys, snow on the high ridges, though the calendar still said "summer." On September 18, 1805, "verry cold and much fatigued," the men finally came down out of the mountains; on October 7, near the present-day site of Orofino, Idaho, they launched forth upon the Clearwater in hastily constructed dugout canoes, and three days later, at what would someday be the city of Lewiston, they floated out onto the main stem of the Snake, which they called Lewis's River and the local Indians called Ki-moo-e-nim. Thirty miles to the south, though they were not aware of it at that time, was the lower end of Hells Canyon.

That was on the way west. In May 1806, on the way east, they were back, anxious to be home and powerfully frustrated by the many delays they were experiencing in the process of getting there. Here on the Clearwater, the principal source of that frustration was the Bitterroot Range, which was still covered with snow and impassable to all reasonable travel. On May 14, at the mouth of Kamiah Creek—twenty-five miles above the site on the Clearwater where they had built their canoes the previous fall—they were forced to a halt. They would remain at that location for nearly a month.

It was a long, boring month. The men repaired their gear, rambled the nearby countryside, and traded visits with the Indians. The two captains caught up on their journals. A bower was built along with a sweat lodge, in which Captain Clark—the physician of the party—treated white and red men alike for various ailments. Supplies became low; hunting parties were detailed, and some of the men were sent to trade for food at the native villages. The departure of one such party was briefly noted in Clark's journal entry for May 27, 1806:

> Serjt Ordway and two men are ordered to cross this river and proceed on through the plains to Lewis's and precure some salmon on that river, and return tomorrow if possible he set out at 8:00 AM.

Five days later, June 1, the men had not returned, and the two captains were beginning to be concerned about their absence. There is a brief, anxious note from Lewis:

> We begin to feel some anxiety with rispect to Sergt Ordway and party who were sent to Lewis's river for salmon; we have received no inteligence from them since they set out.

The next day was Monday, June 2. Lewis was evidently feeling garrulous; his journal for that day contains a long, tedious description of the recovery of a stolen hatchet and another concerning burial practices among the local Nez Perce Indians. And then, quite suddenly, with no visible preamble, he begins an almost offhand account of the return of the overdue party:

> The Indians inform us that there are a plenty of Moos to the S. E. of them on the East branch of Lewis's river which they call Tommanamah R. about Noon Sergt Ordway Frazier and Wizer returned with 17 salmon and some roots of cows; the distance was so great from which they had brought the fish that most of them were nearly spoiled. these fish were as fat as any I ever saw; sufficiently so to cook themselves without the addition of grease; those which were sound were extremely delicious; their flesh is of a fine rose colour with a small admixture of yellow. these men set out on the 27th ult and instead of finding the fishing shore at the distance of half a days ride as we had been informed, they did not reach the place at which they obtained their fish untill the evening of the 29th having travelled by their estimate near 70 miles. the rout they had taken however was not a direct one; the Indians conducted them in the first instance to the East branch of Lewis's river about 20 miles above its junction with the South branch, at a distance of about 50 Ms where they informed them they might obtain fish; but on their arrival at that place finding that the salmon had not yet arrived or were not taken, they conducted them down that river to a fishery a few miles below the junction of the forks of Lewis's river about 20 Ms further, here with some difficulty and remaining one day they purchased the salmon which they brought with them. the first 20 Ms of their

rout was up Commeap Creek and through a plain open country, the hills of the creek continued high and broken with some
timber near it's borders. the ballance of their route was
through a high broken mountanous country generally well
timbered with pine the soil fertile in this quarter they met with
an abundance of deer and some bighorned animals. the East
Fork of Lewis's river they discribe as one continued rapid
about 150 yds wide it's banks are in most places solid and perpendicular rocks, which rise to a great hight; it's hills are
mountains high. on the tops of some of those hills over which
they passed the snow had not entirely disappeared, and the
grass was just springing up. at the fishery on Lewis's river
below the forks there is a very considerable rapid nearly as
great from the information of Sergt Ordway as the great falls
of the Columbia the river 200 yds wide. their common house at
this fishery is built of split timber 150 feet long and 35 feet
wide flat at top. The general course from hence to the forks of
Lewis's river is a little to the West of south about 45 ms. The
men at this season resort their fisheries while the women are
employed in collecting roots. both forks of Lewis's river above
their junction appear to enter a high Mountainous country. my
sick horse being much reduced and appearing to be in such an
agoni of pain that there was no hope of his recovery I ordered
him shot this evening. The other horses which we casterated
are all nearly recovered. . . .

And in this manner, between a moose and a castrated horse, the
deepest gorge on earth entered written history.

iii

Our knowledge of the next few years is sketchy at best. It is
known that Peter Weiser (the "Wizer" whom Lewis records as having been with Ordway) came west again in 1807; since the Weiser
River, which falls into the Snake at the south end of the canyon,
was named for him, we can assume that he penetrated the canyon
country at least that far. The mysterious "Zachary Perch" expedition the same year may have visited the gorge, and it is almost cer-

tain that the east rim was traversed three years later by Archibald Pelton, a teen-ager from Northampton, Massachusetts, who was discovered living with the Nez Perce by a party of fur traders in the winter of 1811–1812.

By far the best-recorded of the early expeditions was that commanded by Wilson Price Hunt, a partner in John Jacob Astor's ill-fated Pacific Fur Company, who spent most of the month of December 1811 trying to force a passage through the canyon from the south. Astor was attempting to wrest control of the lucrative western fur trade from the monopoly held by two British Crown Corporations, the North-West and the Hudson's Bay companies. To do this, he had proposed the establishment of a major trading post at the mouth of the Columbia and smaller subsidiary posts along the inland waterways of the Columbia system, the whole thing to be supplied both by sea—around Cape Horn—and by land, through the establishment of a new cross-country trade route. It was a bold, sweeping, brilliantly conceived plan, but it contained a major flaw: It depended for its success on a concept of geography that Lewis and Clark had shown to be false but which nevertheless was proving difficult for educated men to abandon. This was the idea that somehow a navigable tributary of the Missouri should prove to lie within easy portage distance of a navigable tributary of the Columbia. The Snake came nearer to answering that description than any other; but the Snake was not navigable, a fact that unfortunately had to be learned the hard way.

Leaving the Missouri somewhat lower on its course than had Lewis and Clark, Hunt and his party of sixty men—including another Astor partner, Donald McKenzie—traveled across the upper Great Plains by horseback, striking the Continental Divide near the headwaters of Wyoming's Wind River on the sixteenth of September, 1811. A week later, following a short detour down the Green River toward the Gulf of Colorado, they crossed the Snake River Range along the route now followed by U.S. Highway 189 and found themselves on the Hoback, a tributary of the Snake which enters the main stem not far below Jackson Hole. Elated, they immediately began building canoes to be launched onto the swift, westward-flowing waters. Fortunately, however, Hunt was prudent enough to send a scouting party downstream to look at the river. They returned shaking their heads, and the sobered expedition got back on its horses. Two weeks later and sixty miles further along they tried again, this time on the Henry's Fork, near an abandoned Hudson's Bay Company outpost called Fort Henry. This attempt was a little more successful; they actually made the launch and were able to keep to the water for ten days before losing the canoes—and one of the men—in a boiling black rapid they called Caldron Linn. The horses were back at Fort Henry; there was nothing to do but proceed on foot.

Sending McKenzie and two others ahead as a scouting party, Hunt divided his remaining men into two groups, one under the command of Ramsey Crooks to proceed along the left bank of the Snake, and the other, under Hunt's own command, to proceed along the right bank. In this manner—divided, footsore, and low on provisions—Hunt's half of the party reached the mouth of the Boise River, near the upper end of Hells Canyon, on the twenty-fourth of November, 1811. They had long since lost track of the others.

The following month was one of severe privation, suffering, and despair. Clinging to the notion that the Snake River would somehow prove to be the best route, Hunt followed it stubbornly as it entered the canyon at the base of what his contemporary, the novelist Washington Irving, who would write a chronicle of the expedition from Hunt's journal (*Astoria*, 1836), eventually termed a "wintry-looking mountain covered with snow on all sides." Rations were short. Two horses that they had managed to purchase at a Shoshone village along the route from Caldron Linn were slaughtered for food, and one of the men managed to shoot a blacktail deer, but there were thirty people in the party, and a deer and a couple of skinny horses didn't go very far. Travel was appallingly difficult: The river "passed through rocky chasms and under steep precipices," forcing them to make long detours away from it up the canyon sides. For the first time, Hunt began to feel that the river route might be a mistake. Taking a few men with him, he climbed partway out of the canyon, probably in the vicinity of the Oxbow. The prospect he achieved that way was not encouraging. "In every direction," wrote Irving, "they beheld snowy mountains, partially sprinkled with pines and other evergreens, and spreading a desert and toilsome world around them. The wind howled over the bleak and wintry landscape. . . ." Considerably shaken, they rejoined the main party. There would be no escape *that* way. Perhaps a little further downstream. . . .

On December 6, twelve days into the canyon, they noticed movement on the opposite bank of the Snake. It was Crooks and his half of the party—going upstream. Hails were exchanged across the water, and the skin of one of the slaughtered horses was hastily made into a bullboat in which, with considerable difficulty, Crooks and one of his men were brought across for a conference. Their report was not calculated to raise Hunt's level of confidence very far. They had been, they said, three days' march further down the river, feeding their party on "a single beaver, a few wild cherries, and the soles of old mocassins, and the carcass of a dog." Despite the inadequacy of this diet and the increasing difficulty of the terrain, they had kept slowly on, until "at length they had arrived to where the mountains increased in height, and came closer to the river, with perpendicular precipices, which rendered it impossible to keep along the stream. The river here rushed with incredible velocity through a defile not more than thirty yards wide, where cascades and rapids succeeded each other almost without intermission. . . ."

And so, approximately at the future Hells Canyon damsite, they had turned back. Crooks advised Hunt to do the same. Under the circumstances, Hunt had little choice but to accept the advice.

The journey out was at least as bad as the journey in. The two parties moved slowly, keeping pace with one another on opposite sides of the river. For four days they were without provisions of any kind; then, coming upon an encampment of Shoshone Indians, Hunt's half of the party managed to steal several horses. These were immediately butchered and their skins made into canoes to fetch Crooks's party across the river. One of Crooks's men, Jean Baptiste Prevost, became delirious at the smell of cooking meat as the boat he was in approached the east bank; jumping to his feet in a whirling, clapping dance of joy, he upset the ungainly little craft and was swept away by the swift water. Hells Canyon had claimed its first victim.

On December 15, the reunited party, less Prevost—and less Mc-

Kenzie and his two companions, whom they would not see again until they reached the mouth of the Columbia several months later—tottered out of the southern end of the canyon; and on December 24, Christmas Eve, having spent the intervening week recuperating in a village of friendly Shoshone (who evidently had not heard about the horse theft), they rafted across the river amid floating ice floes and headed westward into the Blue Mountains. They had left that "Accursed Mad River," the Snake, well behind. Most of them—with a few notable exceptions—would never go back.

iv

Donald McKenzie was one of the exceptions. Like Hunt, he had undergone the most intense difficulties, privations, and hardships in the neighborhood of Hells Canyon (in McKenzie's case, along the east rim); unlike Hunt, he had apparently had his imagination captured by the ruggedness, the stark beauty, and the magnificent challenge of this incredibly deep hole in the earth. And—also unlike Hunt—he was soon back. In the spring of 1819 he poled his way into history by taking a loaded barge from Fort Nez Perces, near the mouth of the Snake, all the way upstream to the Shoshone country—right through the mad, foaming "Narrows" of Hells Canyon.

This would be a remarkable feat in any age; but then McKenzie was, by all accounts, a most remarkable man. A gargantuan Scotsman, standing well over six feet tall and weighing in at a solid 312 pounds, he was a born leader whose firm but fair treatment of the Indians, ability to make lightning decisions in difficult situations, and total and contagious fearlessness were soon legendary throughout the fur country. When Astor's enterprise folded, McKenzie switched his allegiance to the North-West Company, where he soon became chief factor in charge of the Interior Division of the Columbia District—much to the disgust of the bureaucrats he had been promoted past, who disdained him as one fit only, in the words of his contemporary and friend Alexander Ross, "to eat horse flesh and shoot at a mark." Never a desk-bound administrator, McKenzie was everywhere in his vast territory, but mostly in those spots where trouble was to be found. When the Cayuse and Palouse Indians of the lower Snake closed their stream to commerce and began firing on all parties of whites who approached its mouth, McKenzie personally supervised the building of Fort Nez Perces near the confluence of the Snake and the Columbia, quelling the trouble at its source. When an expedition was proposed to explore trapping and trading possibilities in the country of the increasingly hostile Shoshone, McKenzie unhesitatingly led the party himself, detouring long enough to take another look at the southern end of Hells Canyon and to establish a trapping party on Indian Creek, which falls into the Snake at the Oxbow. This trip occupied six months; yet he had been back barely a week when he was off again, in late February 1819, on the trip that was to assure his place in history. Our best description of that journey has come down from Ross, in his *Fur Hunters of the Far West* (1855), who was there to see him off, and as it reads far better than any paraphrase possibly could, we will quote it in its entirety:

After a short respite of only seven days at Nez Perces allowing him scarcely time to repose himself and recount his adventures, this indefatigable man set out anew through ice and snow to examine that state of the navigation into the Snake country by the south branch. For this purpose he and his handful of Canadians, six in number, embarking on board of a barge, left Fort Nez Perces and proceeded up Lewis River. The turbulent natives on both sides the stream, notwithstanding his late return from their foes, suffered him to pass through this channel unmolested. After a voyage of two months the boat with four of the men returned to this place, while McKenzie and the other two set out on the prementioned adventure of reaching the hunters, a distance of twenty days' travel through a country where it had often been asserted that ''less than fifty men could not set foot with safety!''

McKenzie's letter by return of the boat was elated. ''Point Successful, head of the narrows, April 15th, 1819.'' He then stated that ''The passage by water is now proved to be safe and practicable for loaded boats with one single carrying place or portage. Therefore, the doubtful question is now set at rest forever. Yet from the force of the current and the frequency of rapids, it may still be adviseable and perhaps preferable to continue the land transportation while the business in this quarter is carried on upon a small scale." He then goes on to observe that "We had often recourse to the line," and then adds, "There are two places with bold cut rocks on either side of the river where the great body of water is compressed within a narrow compass, which may render those parts doubtful during the floods, owing to rocks and whirlpools; but there are only two and neither of them are long. . . ."

Two points need to be made concerning this remarkable voyage. The first is the astonishing fact that it was ever attempted; and the second is the even more astonishing fact that it was a success. A comparison is in order here. At the time of McKenzie's trip, the Grand Canyon of the Colorado had been known for 300 years, Hells Canyon for scarcely 13. Yet nobody had taken a boat through the Grand Canyon, and those who even considered such a feat possible were thought mad. The Grand Canyon, it was widely believed, contained waterfalls hundreds of feet high; it contained raging whirlpools that would swallow a boat whole; it contained spots where the entire Colorado disappeared into the earth, to be spewed forth ten, twenty, even a hundred miles further along. So firmly were these myths held to that when someone *did* finally float through the canyon—one James White, in 1867—the settlers who met him at the lower end called him deranged and refused to believe his story. Furthermore, when Major John Wesley Powell made his well-publicized trip a few years later, he emerged from the western mouth of the gorge to find those same settlers dragging the river for his bones. Why were similar beliefs not held about Hells Canyon, which is deeper and at least as rugged, has as many rapids, and passes through far more difficult terrain?

There are three possible reasons, all of which probably contain some truth. The first is that Hells Canyon was not yet widely known and had not had time to develop an extensive mythology; the second is the tenacity with which the theory that the Snake-Columbia system *had* to be navigable was clung to; and the third is the physical means of approach to the two canyons, which are vastly different. The Grand Canyon was discovered and first described from its two rims, and for many years this was the only way that it was known at all. Hells Canyon was discovered from its two ends, approaching along the river, and only the haziest notions about its extent and awesome depth were yet current. And it was therefore not too unusual that men would continue to seek a water-level route through it.

The outcome of that search is another matter entirely. McKenzie's "Point Successful" has never been properly identified. Did he actually make it all the way through the canyon? He was, as has already been pointed out, a gigantic man with a reputation for prodigious feats of strength. But poling a loaded barge upstream through Hells Canyon would seem to require more than prodigious strength—something more in the nature of a miracle. An acquaintance of mine, an experienced Snake River pilot who operates a boatbuilding shop near the downstream end of the canyon, is highly dubious about the whole affair. The river is so swift in many places that powerful jet boats have trouble ascending it; what chance, therefore, would a loaded barge have under strictly human power? At other places the water is so confined that it becomes deeper than it is broad, literally "turning on edge," and requiring, as my friend puts it, "a mighty long pole." Some of these places are also very swift, and there is little room for lining along the bank. This is hardly the "safe and practicable passage" of which McKenzie paints such a rosy picture!

Yet, with all this, there seems little reason to doubt that the voyage actually took place. McKenzie had a high reputation for honesty, and there is nothing tentative about his claim. It is also unlikely that he stopped partway through and merely thought he had made it all the way. He was well acquainted with the geography at the south end of the canyon, having been there at least twice, the last time less than six months before. There is little likelihood that he could have mistaken Pittsburg Landing—the one spot where the canyon opens out wide enough to make a person traveling through it think he might have reached the end—for the actual end, another fifty miles south. Thus McKenzie's place in history as the first man to pass all the way through Hells Canyon must remain secure.

His glowing account of the navigability of the place failed to turn any heads, however. The next boat did not descend the stream for more than forty years, and no one has ever duplicated the feat of boating through the canyon upstream.

v

McKenzie's voyage is almost the last event in the history of Hells Canyon that can properly be called an exploration, for by this time—and certainly before another ten years had passed—most of the American West was already quite thoroughly known. Hundreds of anonymous fur trappers and mountain men had fanned out over the map, filling in the blank spots, naming the natural features, and correcting the mistakes of imaginative cartographers who had never gotten any further west than Philadelphia. When Jedediah Smith reached the Columbia River overland from California in the summer of 1828, the last major gap was filled in. Some men would be called explorers after this, but it would be a misleading use of the term. Most would more accurately be called surveyors, their task being to fix with precision the locations of landmarks whose names, general characteristics, and physical whereabouts were already common knowledge.

A smaller and generally noisier group were merely adventure-seekers. Too late to be trailblazers and too impatient to be accurate surveyors, these men came west with great fanfare, made journeys through terrain that more reasonable men knew about but had sense enough to avoid, and then went home and wrote books about them. And it is in this latter category that we must place one of the most remarkable expeditions ever to enter the Hells Canyon country: a four-man party under the leadership of Capt. B. L. E. Bonneville, U.S. Army, in the winter of 1833–1834.

Benjamin Louis Eulalie de Bonneville was born in Paris, France, on April 14, 1796. His father was a friend of Thomas Paine, and the family came to the United States in 1803, when Benjamin was seven years old. A shy, bookish youth with a strong romantic streak, the young Bonneville had an imagination that was easily captured by thoughts of distant adventures and uncharted pathways, and this imagination drove him into an unbookish occupation. He enrolled at West Point on his seventeenth birthday, and upon graduation two years later set out on a career as an army officer. For fifteen years he moved from post to post along the American frontier, which at that time was still the Mississippi Valley. This brought him into contact with a motley milieu of trappers, fur traders, and Indian fighters, whose tales of the Rocky Mountains fanned his desire for romance and adventure to new heights; by the early 1830s he was ready to do something about it. He wangled a two-year leave of absence from the army by promising to write a report of his journey for the War Department; he sought, and found, financial backing among the barons of the American fur industry, who were still grasping at any means presented that might serve to drive an American wedge into the British fur monopoly in the watershed of the Columbia River. In May of 1832, with 110 men at his back, Bonneville left civilization behind and rode blithely off into the Great Unmapped.

For the first year and a half Bonneville followed mostly well-blazed routes, ascending the Missouri and the Platte, penetrating the Wind River Range—where a peak has since been named in his honor—and crossing South Pass to the headwaters of the Green, where he participated in the annual summer fur rendevous in 1833. The winter of that year found him camped on the Portneuf River, a tributary of the Snake that falls into it early in its course through Idaho, on the eastern margin of the Snake River Plains. But the enforced idleness of the winter camp soon bored him, and it was not long before he had conceived a plan to put a little life into things. He would take a small party of men and make a little journey over to the Columbia to see how the British were doing. It shouldn't be too difficult, he reasoned. They were almost there already. So on Christmas Day, 1833, Bonneville and three hand-picked companions left the Portneuf and headed west toward the distant, perilous Blue Mountains.

After three weeks of difficult, cold, but not unduly hazardous travel, Bonneville and his men reached the vicinity of Farewell Bend, where the town of Ontario, Oregon, now stands. Here the standard trail pioneered by Wilson Price Hunt left the Snake and climbed westward over a low divide into the Powder River Valley and beyond it, into the Blues. Bonneville was not too anxious to go that way. He had heard tales of what to expect from the Blues; besides, it was too well known to make a real adventure. Still, he probably would not have had the courage to try anything different had he not run into a party of Shoshone who gave him a piece of advice that, in retrospect, seems to have been calculated to rid the neighborhood of this particular band of troublesome whites. Too much snow in the mountains, they said. Better stay by the river. They would even provide a guide.

The guide stuck with them for two days, just long enough to lead them to the upper threshold of Hells Canyon. Then he deserted. And there were Bonneville and his men, guideless, heading innocently forward into the extraordinarily rugged terrain of the deepest gorge on earth.

At first, following the Indians' advice, they tried to stay with the river. Washington Irving, whose *Adventures of Captain Bonneville* (1837), written from Bonneville's notes, remains our best source of information about the expedition, describes the fate of that attempt in vivid detail:

> For a short time they jogged along the bank with tolerable facility, but at length came to where the river forced its way into the heart of the mountains, winding between tremendous walls of basaltic rock, that rose perpendicularly from the water's edge, frowning in bleak and gloomy grandeur. Here difficulties of all kinds beset their path. The snow was from two to three feet deep, but soft and yielding, so that the horses had no foothold, but kept plunging forward, straining themselves by perpetual efforts. Sometimes the crags and promontories forced them upon the narrow ribbon of ice that bordered the shore; sometimes they had to scramble over vast masses of rock which had tumbled from the impending precipices; sometimes they had to cross the stream upon the hazardous bridges of ice and snow, sinking to the knee at every step; sometimes they had to scale slippery acclivities, and to pass along narrow cornices, glazed with ice and sleet, a shouldering wall of rock on one side, a yawning precipice on the other, where a single false step would have been fatal. . . . In this way they struggled forward, manfully braving difficulties and dangers, until they came to where the bed of the river was

narrowed to a mere chasm, with perpendicular walls of rock that defied all further progress.

Since Irving destroyed Bonneville's notes after he was through with them, it is impossible to pin down exactly where that "mere chasm, with perpendicular walls of rock" actually was; but it would have been in the neighborhood of what is now Hells Canyon Dam or a little above, most likely just below Vermillion Bar, about the same spot where Ramsey Crooks had turned back twenty years earlier. Wherever it was, it presented the explorers with a dilemma. They appeared to have but three choices: They could go back the way they came; they could climb out of the canyon; or they could slaughter their horses, make boats of the skins, and float down the river to whatever fate might await them. After serious consideration, they tried the second of their choices, scaling the canyon wall directly in front of them with considerable difficulty, pulling the horses and the one pack mule up after them; but when they had been at it for most of a day, a series of precipices around which they could find no path forced them to give up. They lowered themselves and their animals back into the canyon. No progress that day.

Several miles back the way they had come there was what Irving calls "a small ridge of mountains approaching closely to the river"—most likely what is known today as the McGraw Creek Divide. Perhaps *that* would be a way out. Working their way upstream to its base, they began scrambling up, dragging the horses and the mule once more. It was slow work. "The only chance of scaling it," reports Irving, "was by broken masses of rock, piled one upon another, which formed a succession of crags, reaching nearly to the summit." They wound back and forth across the canyon face, looking for the easiest path. Darkness caught them far below the summit; still they struggled on, until, long after nightfall, they finally reached a large windy platform which they presumed to be the top of the ridge. Here they encamped. But the next morning they were in for a disappointment, for their lofty platform was only a shoulder halfway up the side of "a great sierra, or ridge, of immense height, running parallel to the course of the river, swelling by degrees to lofty peaks, but the outline gashed by deep and precipitous ravines.'' They were looking at Summit Ridge, the 7,000-foot-high west rim of Hells Canyon, a remnant of the old Snake River Plateau.

The platform that Bonneville and his men were now on, halfway up the McGraw Creek Divide, is the south end of a great bench or terrace nearly a mile wide which, though broken by numerous tributary canyons, is traceable northward for some thirteen miles along the canyon face. Geologically, it is a remnant of the land surface that existed in this region before the southern lobe of the Columbia basalt flows came pouring in to form the Snake River Plateau, back in the Miocene. Over this ancient ground the little party now moved painfully forward, burdened by snow—it was somewhere around the first of February—and forced to make long detours into the head of gulch after tributary gulch. After a week of this, during which time he had to slaughter the pack mule for food, Bonneville sent the strongest of his three companions forward on a scouting trip. Moving much more rapidly than the rest of the party, the scout reached and scaled Barton Heights at the north end of the bench. From this point it is possible to get a long look forward down the deepest part of the gorge. The scout didn't like what he saw; he went back and reported to Bonneville, who didn't much like the sound of it either. They abandoned the bench, and, someplace between the head of Thirty-two Point Creek and Hells Canyon Creek, climbed up and over the west rim. It took them two days. Another week was required to descend the other side. Finally, just at sunset on the fifteenth of February, they reached the Imnaha Valley. A breath of spring was blowing, and the new grass was just springing up.

Difficult and hazardous as the passage of the canyon had been, it was the overwhelming magnificence of its scenery that most impressed Bonneville. "The grandeur and originality of the views presented on either side," he wrote, in a passage given to us verbatim by Irving and later widely quoted by environmentalists trying to keep dams off the Snake, "beggar both the pencil and the pen. Nothing we had ever gazed upon in any other region could for a moment compare in wild majesty and impressive sternness with the series of scenes which here at every turn astonished our senses and filled us with awe and delight." And so it was only natural that, on his return trip three months later, Bonneville would avoid the Blue Mountain route once more, choosing instead to retrace his steps through Hells Canyon. This time, however, he came prepared. In fact, only one small adventure took place. Crossing over from the Imnaha to the Snake, probably through the saddle at the head of North Pine Creek, he was baffled for a time by snow that one of his men insisted was "a hundred feet deep up there!" But a light, drizzly rain—and Bonneville's ingenuity—came to his rescue. Loading most of their gear onto hastily constructed sledges, he and his men dragged them back and forth through the pass until they had compacted a broad roadway in the snow. The rain and a cold, clear night did the rest, giving the "roadway" a frozen surface that was strong enough to bear the weight of their horses. By morning they were on the Snake side of the ridge, and a month later they were back at the Portneuf. Bonneville returned to the east coast and eventually served his adopted country for thirty more years. On June 12, 1878, at the age of 82, he died, in Fort Smith, Arkansas. One would have hoped that he died unaware of the Nez Perce War, the Oregon Steam Navigation Company, and all the other drastic changes that had come to the canyon he had loved and left a howling wilderness just over forty years before.

3

Steamboats and Indians

The changes that came to the canyon after Bonneville had left it were not immediate. For more than a quarter of a century, in fact, little happened. Outside, the fur trade collapsed; the great western migration began; gold was discovered in California; Oregon was admitted to the Union; and a nation gone mad grimly began tearing itself to pieces over the issue of slavery. None of this, however, had more than a peripheral effect upon Hells Canyon. Elsewhere, Indians were exhorted by missionaries and harried by settlers; here in the canyon they continued to live as they had for generations, fishing and hunting, moving with the seasons, emerging for yearly treks to the buffalo country. In its black chasm the river thundered and growled; salmon ascended it as they had for millennia, hawks and eagles wheeled slowly above it, while high and distant on the plateau's edge the Rimrock frowned down. Fifty miles to the south the emigrant wagons were passing; thirty miles to the north, near the junction of the Snake and the Clearwater, the Reverend H. H. Spalding built his school and his chapel, planted his crops, and began the work of converting the northern bands of Nez Perce to his austere and unforgiving New England God. Sixty miles to the west the fertile Grande Ronde and Powder River valleys felt the first kiss of the plow. These events swirled about the canyon, but they did not touch it. Locked behind rugged ranges, the great gulf waited.

In June of 1844, the German botanist Karl A. Geyer visited the area, penetrating the lower end of Hells Canyon as far as the junction of the Snake and the Salmon. His description, the first ever by a trained scientist, appeared only in an obscure European publication and had no effect whatsoever on the region's destiny.

Sometime during the summer of 1852 a man named Henri Chase found a few flakes of gold in an upper tributary of the Grande Ronde. This caused a flurry of speculative excitement, and from all around prospectors began converging on the Blue Mountain region. None are known to have immediately entered the canyon.

In 1855, partly as a result of the nearby Cayuse War—which they had not participated in—a huge reservation was set aside for the Nez Perce nation, running from the Bitterroot Mountains west to the Grande Ronde Valley and from the Palouse River south to Payette Lake, an area of several thousand square miles. Hells Canyon was included within these boundaries, but it was not otherwise affected.

And then, in 1860, as the first guns of the Civil War boomed, an event took place that *did* directly affect the canyon. Elias D. Pierce reported the discovery of a major gold strike on the upper Clearwater River.

The Pierce strike was the beginning of a full-scale gold rush that spread rapidly to encompass the entire northern end of the Rocky Mountains. Within a year the search had spilled southward into the Salmon River Breaks and westward through the Seven Devils. The newly formed Oregon Steam Navigation Company, operating out of Portland, Oregon, was soon running steamboats filled with supplies up the Columbia and the Snake, directly into the heart of the Nez Perce domain; by October of 1861 these supply runs had spawned the city of Lewiston at the junction of the Snake and the Clearwater, in brazen violation of Indian treaties that technically had been reaffirmed as late as April of that same year. By 1862 the miners were agitating for territorial status of their own; in 1863 they got it. The new Idaho Territory was formed, taking in all of present-day Idaho and parts of what would someday become Montana and Wyoming. Hells Canyon had become a political boundary.

Meanwhile, the search for gold was expanding southward to the headwaters of the Salmon and beyond. In August 1862, the "biggest strike of all" was discovered in the Boise basin. Idaho City grew up on the spot; almost overnight, it boasted a population of 30,000. Supplies for this mass of humanity quickly became a major problem. Overland routes stretched to tenuous lengths and were subject to spoilage, Indian attack, and raids by desperados such as the legendary Chief Bigfoot. This was the steamboat era. Was a water route practicable? Was the Snake navigable?

No one knew. Donald McKenzie's voyage through Hells Canyon had long been forgotten, and no one who knew anything about water transport had entered the canyon since. Any new investigation would have to start from the beginning.

Such an investigation was launched almost immediately. News of the Boise basin strike had scarcely reached Lewiston before the Army Corps of Engineers—then, as now, the agency mandated by the government to have jurisdiction over navigable waterways—dispatched a small party to determine whether or not steamboats could ascend the Snake to the new gold fields to the south. This team, consisting of what the *Golden Age*, Lewiston's neophyte newspaper, called "three reliable men," left for the Boise mines on September 20, 1862. By October 24 they were back in Lewiston with a report somewhat longer on optimism than it was on fact. "They found nothing in the river to impede navigation, whatsoever," crowed the *Golden Age*. "The examination of the river shows the fact that Snake River is navigable for steamers and will be much safer to travel than the river is from Lewiston to the mouth of the Snake. . . ."

In the light of current knowledge about the canyon, it is easy to doubt that those "three reliable men" were ever on the river at all. They estimated the distance to the mouth of the Boise as somewhere around one hundred miles; the true figure is closer to two hundred. And the Snake in Hells Canyon is something less than clearly navigable, as the Oregon Steam Navigation Company—much to its disappointment—would shortly discover.

ii

The OSNCo. did not attempt to check out the army's report right away; it had its hands full, temporarily, simply getting to Lewiston. More than two years passed, in fact, before the steamer *Colonel Wright* could be freed to attempt the upriver run. It was a trip that turned out to be considerably less than the picnic that had been predicted. Clawing, winching, and grinding his way upstream through rapid after angry rapid, the boat's pilot, Capt. Thomas Stump, managed to force his considerably battered craft to the mouth of the Salmon and some twenty-five miles above it. Here, in the neighborhood of what is now called Pittsburg Landing, Captain Stump attempted one rapid too many. The *Colonel Wright* smashed against a large rock, virtually destroying her paddle wheel and rudder. Out of control, the boat swung sideways, breaching against the current and nearly capsizing. The river carried them several miles downstream before a considerably shaken Captain Stump managed to run his bow aground and stop for a look at the damage and an attempt at repairs. When he got going again some time later, all thoughts of making any further headway upstream had been abandoned. Engineers' report or no engineers' report, there would be no steamboat traffic between Lewiston and the Boise basin.

It had taken five days to reach Pittsburg Landing from Lewiston. Going home, the log recorded an elapsed time of just over three and one-half hours.

But though the defeat of the *Colonel Wright* ended all serious attempts to establish regular steamer service through Hells Canyon, it did not mark the last of the Oregon Steam Navigation Company's involvement with the great gorge. There were, after all, other things to think about. For example, there was the 150-mile stretch of relatively calm water between the upper end of the canyon and Swan Falls, the next major steamboat barrier. Navigation on that section of the river looked as though it would be easy—and profitable. Besides the Boise basin gold claims, which had already produced nearly three million dollars worth of ore, there were silver deposits being worked in the Owyhees, just to the south, that looked nearly as rich as the Boise gold. There were rumors of copper finds in the Seven Devils. And the Transcontinental Railroad, which would pass a short distance to the south, was already under construction. A relatively minor connecting rail length from Swan Falls to the Transcontinental would make steamer traffic on the upper Snake part of a transportation network that would reach all the way to the populous East. And if you couldn't get a boat up there from Lewiston, well, there was another solution.

You could build a boat on the site.

Such a boat was built at Fort Boise the year after the *Colonel Wright*'s failure. A large, shallow-draft steamer, she was 136 feet long and weighed in at more than 300 tons. The company christened her *Shoshone* and put her to work.

The results proved disappointing. The boat lost money almost from the start. Not only were the cargoes carried well below payload, but the boat was also far more costly to run than had been predicted. There were few trees on the banks of the upper Snake, and the boat had to burn cordwood brought in from a distance, at considerable expense; coal deposits near the river, which had been counted on to stretch out the scarce supplies of firewood, proved too low-grade for use as fuel. After three years of sporadic service, in 1869 the upper Snake runs were abandoned. And this left the Oregon Steam Navigation Company with a serious problem. The *Shoshone* was too unprofitable to run and too expensive to abandon. What should be done with her?

To Capt. John Ainsworth, the flamboyant president of the OSNCo., the answer was obvious. If the *Shoshone* couldn't run at a profit where she was, why, take her where she *could* run at a profit. The *Colonel Wright* had proved you couldn't take a steamboat upstream through Seven Devils Gorge—as Hells Canyon was then called—but nobody had proved you couldn't take one *downstream*. Well, proof was about to be had—one way or the other. In the summer of 1869, Ainsworth ordered Capt. Cyrus Smith to bring the *Shoshone* down to Lewiston, or, failing that, as he bluntly put it, to "wreck her in the attempt."

Cy Smith did as he was told—up to a point. He cast off and headed downstream, past the Jacobs Ladder, around the Oxbow, and over Kerr and Cattle rapids, to Lime Point. Here he balked.

Just ahead was Copper Ledge Falls, a roaring, churning, thundering whitewater chute where the river dropped 18 feet down in barely 300 forward. To Cy Smith, it looked like an invitation to Hell. He tied the *Shoshone* to a convenient tree, left two crew members aboard her as watchmen, and walked out, sending a report down to Portland that nobody could run that thing and survive. John Ainsworth's reaction to this news went mercifully unrecorded; but within days, a new skipper was on his way to the beached *Shoshone*. His name was Sebastian E. Miller, and he carried explicit instructions from his chief. If Copper Ledge Falls could be run, he was to run it; if it couldn't be run, he was to burn the boat on the site and sink the remains.

Bas Miller had been pulled off a Willamette River run for this assignment, so he had some distance to travel, and it took him a while. Accompanied by engineer Dan Buchanan, he traveled up the Columbia on OSNCo. steamboats, transferred to a buckboard at Fort Walla Walla, and headed over the snow-covered Blue Mountains. The crossing was difficult; it was not until mid-April that the two men reached the *Shoshone*, wallowing gently in the still water just above the biggest and toughest rapid of the gorge. The watchmen were still on her, bored from the long winter and ready for a little excitement. Bas Miller signed them on as crew for the run. They wouldn't be bored much longer.

Six months of disuse had weathered the ship badly, and great cracks had opened between the boards of her hull. It would take weeks to caulk them properly. Dan Buchanan suggested that they simply attach a hose to the bilge pump and play water over the dried-up boards till the cracks swelled shut. This was done. The cracks didn't close down all the way but enough so that Miller and Buchanan thought they could chance it. With a full load of fuel and a full head of steam, they cast off from the bank and headed for the brink of Copper Ledge Falls. It was April 20, 1870.

An eddy at the top of the falls caught them almost immediately, spinning the 136-foot, 300-ton *Shoshone* around and around like a cork. They got free of that, but it spewed them out crossways to the current, and Miller didn't quite have them straightened out again when they went over the brink. The boat nosed down; the paddle wheel spun helplessly in the air, then slapped back into the water, splintering on impact. The bow struck a rock, hard, and the boat was suddenly eight feet shorter. Water poured in. Desperately, Miller fought the wheel. Somehow they got down to the quiet water at the base of the falls and managed to beach the damaged bow. Two days of nonstop work made them relatively shipshape again; they cast off once more on April 22. Five days later, having run the rest of the canyon—including the 60-foot-wide Mountain Sheep section, where they could practically reach out and touch both walls as the ship squeezed through—with little incident, they tied up at Lewiston. The OSNCo. agent there treated them as apparitions returned from the grave: Recognizable pieces of the *Shoshone* had been fished out of the Columbia at Umatilla four days before, and the boat and her crew had been given up for lost.

iii

The spectacle of a steamboat coasting through a mile-and-a-half-deep slot in the earth barely wide enough to contain her was more than incongruous; it was also, strictly speaking, illegal. The Treaty of 1855 had given Hells Canyon to the Nez Perce, and though renegotiations in 1863 had attempted to change that, the terms of this new treaty had not yet been accepted by the canyon's inhabitants. Technically, the Treaty of 1855 was still in force. But technicality did not jibe with reality—a situation which would shortly turn Hells Canyon into the deepest battlefield on earth.

The short-lived Nez Perce nation had been born in 1842, midwifed into existence by the Indian agent for Oregon, Dr. Elijah White. Before this, the tribe had existed as a series of autonomous villages, each with its own headman, bound together by ties of culture and language but with no central authority. However, the Nez Perce were quick to see the advantages of greater structure in dealing with the rapid onslought of white culture, and under Dr. White's guidance they had adopted a code of laws and elected a single chief to speak for the tribe as a whole. At first this position was passed around, but by the time of the Treaty of 1855 the chief's mantle had fallen on the person who was to wear it for the next twenty years. An unprepossessing-looking man of medium height and build, he was nevertheless known as a skillful warrior and an able administrator whose principal flaw was a too-great admiration for white culture. He had been born near Kamiah at about the time Lewis and Clark had passed that way and was now a leader in the Lapwai band, where he had been one of Henry Spalding's first converts to Christianity. White men called him Lawyer.

The Treaty of 1855 had given the Nez Perce most of their traditional tribal lands, and as a consequence it had been widely accepted by the Indians. The Treaty of 1863 was something else again. In the intervening eight years the whites had discovered just how valuable the Nez Perce lands were, and the government negotiators who came to the treaty conference had just one goal in mind: to shrink the Nez Perce reservation from its sprawling 6.5-million-acre size to a more "manageable" 768,000 acres, which just happened to be, from the white man's point of view, virtually worthless.

The Indians had come to the conference expecting to negotiate the sale of the gold fields and the area at the mouth of the Clearwater, which was then illegally occupied by the city of Lewiston, and they were appalled when they discovered how much more it was that they were expected to give up. Of the principal chiefs, only Lawyer—whose Lapwai territory would be unaffected by the reduction of the reservation—was favorably disposed toward the new treaty, and when he tried to persuade the others to follow him, most refused. Under the leadership of Toohoolhoolzote and Joseph, chiefs of the Hells Canyon and Wallowa bands, the twenty-one-year-old Nez Perce nation was formally dissolved.

This act, which took place at a private conference of the chiefs, was either unknown to or simply ignored by the government negotiators, and when Toohoolhoolzote and Joseph rode out of the conference to return to their homes no attempt was made to stop them. Negotiations continued. One by one the minor chiefs capitulated, and when the whites had the signatures of a majority of them, plus head chief Lawyer, on the new treaty, they declared it officially adopted and dispersed the conference.

For more than ten years afterward, little overt happened. Toohoolhoolzote and his people continued to live in the depths of Hells Canyon, paying little attention to the passage of the *Colonel Wright* and the *Shoshone* and sharing grazing rights amicably with settlers from the Powder River who came into the canyon seeking winter range. In the fertile and extraordinarily beautiful Wallowa Valley, Joseph and his band attempted to do the same. Scrupulously observing the terms of the 1855 treaty, the Indians surveyed the boundary set forth by that document, marking it with a series of large upright poles. When the settlers, attracted by the lush greenness of one of the most beautiful valleys of the West, ignored the poles and began a land rush into the Wallowa country, Joseph held his temper and with considerable patience sought relief through legal channels. After his death in 1871, his son Heinmot Tooyalakekt, whom the whites knew as Young Joseph, continued the course his father had set, and in 1873 he won what seemed like a major victory. The administration of President Grant recognized that Joseph, Toohoolhoolzote, and a few others (notably, Looking Glass of the Kamiah region and White Bird of the lower Salmon canyon), not having signed the Treaty of 1863, were not bound by it. Grant issued an edict declaring the contested Wallowa Valley the property of Joseph's people and ordering the whites to withdraw.

It was a sweet moment for the Nez Perce, but it was short-lived; almost at once it became obvious that the white settlers had no intention of following their own president's orders. Instead of withdrawing, more whites continued to pour into the valley. Across the mountains to the west, the La Grande *Mountain Sentinel* began urging its readers to begin a war of extermination against the Wallowa Indians, and Joseph needed all the diplomatic skill he could muster to keep his young men in check. Then, on June 10, 1875, his brand-new legal rug was pulled out from under him. President Grant—bowing, perhaps, to what he perceived as the inevitable—issued a new edict, reversing his 1873 declaration and ordering the nontreaty Nez Perce to move onto the Lapwai Reservation or face being placed there by force.

The nontreaty bands councited at Lostine, in the Wallowa Valley, and decided to ignore the new edict. Another delicate year went by.

The summer of 1876 brought the first violence; a young Nez Perce hunter named Wilhautyah was murdered by two settlers who accused him falsely of stealing their horses. It could have been the start of a major war, but cooler heads on both sides prevailed: The whites agreed to arrest the murderers, and the Indians settled for having them arrested, though there was considerable grumbling when an all-white jury let them off scot-free. Later that same year, spurred by the escalating tension in the Wallowa, the government called a new conference at Lapwai, and this time they set a specific deadline: The nontreaty bands were to be on the Lapwai Reservation by April 1, 1877, or the cavalry would put them there.

April 1 came and went; Joseph, Toohoolhoolzote, Looking Glass, and White Bird made no move toward the reservation, and the cavalry made no move toward them. Instead, still another Lapwai conference was called for May 4. Gathering just beforehand, the Nez Perce chose Toohoolhoolzote to speak for them. The tall, powerfully built old man from the harsh depths of Hells Canyon made an impressive figure as he rose at the council fire to express his contempt for the 1863 treaty. "The Great Chief made the world as it is," he insisted, "and as he wanted it, and he made a part of it for us to live upon. I do not see where you get the authority to say that we shall not live where he placed us." It was an effective speech—too effective. The government agents had no logical reply, and they responded not by answering Toohoolhoolzote's pointed remarks but by seizing him and throwing him in the guardhouse under threat of deportation to Oklahoma. Shocked and despondent, the remaining nontreaty chiefs agreed, at last, to the whites' demands. If Toohoolhoolzote were released, they would move onto the Lapwai Reservation. This condition was met; and on May 14, with the freed Hells Canyon chief among them, the nontreaty leaders rode sadly out of Lapwai toward the lands, no longer their homes, where their people waited. Sadly, but not slowly; they had been given thirty days to gather their people, their livestock, and their belongings and make the move. For White Bird, who had only to move up from the Salmon, that might be relatively easy; for Joseph, many times as far away and on the wrong side of the gorge, it would be virtually impossible.

A little over two weeks later, the Wallowa band of Nez Perce, some 400 strong—men, women, and children—together with several thousand head of cattle and horses, gathered forlornly on the Oregon bank of the Snake in the depths of Hells Canyon. Behind them in their beloved Wallowa Valley, now left behind for the last time, the gleeful settlers were busily appropriating the several hundred animals the Indians had not had time to round up. Bands of white marauders harassed the rear of the column, driving off large portions of the bawling, milling herds scattered along the narrow riverbank. The trek this far had been bad enough—down the hot, rocky Imnaha Canyon, over the low dividing ridge at its mouth, and down the short, steep draws on the other side to the river's edge. But what was ahead was worse. The Snake was at flood stage, a roiling, swollen yellow torrent a quarter of a mile wide. Joseph had expected this and had begged at Lapwai to be allowed to wait until September to come to the reservation so that the crossing could be made at low water. He had been met with a curt, brusque, and entirely adamant refusal. Hazardous as it was, the crossing would have to be made now.

Rafts were fashioned of hide bundles rolled and lashed tightly together. The rafts were heaped high with baggage and gear. Young men, stripped naked and riding bareback on horses known to be strong swimmers, entered the water in groups of four, one to each corner of a raft. Bobbing, yawing, and spinning helplessly in the powerful current, the little flotilla moved slowly out from the bank. Across the river, great black cliffs and fantastically shaped lava buttes loomed a vertical mile above them. Here and there rafts got away from their handlers, bobbling away downstream or upsetting and spilling their contents into the turbulent Snake. The sun beat down; the canyon air was still and oppressive. And while the Indians' full attention was occupied with the baggage rafts, thieves crept up to their herds and cut out several hundred head more to be driven back up the Imnaha and branded with white men's brands.

Next came the people themselves—the women and children, the old and infirm, the men with families, all except those responsible for the livestock. Mounted on the tribe's best horses, they rode apprehensively into the broad, swift river. The horses, the whites of their eyes showing, swam frantically, spinning and floundering in the current. Yet, amazingly—miraculously—all made the quarter-mile swim in safety.

The livestock were not no lucky. Driven off the bank into the swirling water, the herds milled about in a confused, bawling mass, unwilling to strike out toward the far shore until forced to do so.

Many were swept away and drowned before the remainder could be led, dripping and shivering with fatigue, up the Idaho bank and onto the small, crowded bar at the mouth of Divide Creek.

Now, joined by Toohoolhoolzote's people, the Wallowa Nez Perce drove their tired stock up the rugged canyon of Divide Creek to the plateau between the Snake and the Salmon. Here on this mile-high island between the two great canyons the cattle and horses were at last allowed to rest and recuperate. A few of the young men were left with the herds as guards; the remainder of the combined bands pushed on down Rice Canyon, across the Salmon, and up Rocky Canyon to Tolo Lake, near Grangeville. Here, just two miles from the reservation boundary and with twelve days remaining before the June 14 deadline, they halted and went into encampment for a "last council in freedom" before submitting to the imprisonment of the reservation.

Up to this point, the dominant force of Joseph's personality—and the excellent assistance of his younger brother Ollokot, a well-known buffalo hunter who had the respect of the younger and more belligerent men of the tribe—had managed to keep things peaceful. But now Joseph and Ollokot made a mistake. With things well under control—so they thought—they returned to the herds between the Snake and the Salmon to do some butchering. While they were gone, three young rowdies—Wahlitits, Red Mocassin Tops, and Swan Necklace—spurred on by the taunts of an old warrior who should have known better, slipped away from camp at night and murdered settlers in several nearby cabins. That small spark of violence illuminated, with startling clarity, just how close both sides had been to violence all along.

When Joseph and Ollokot returned from the herds, they found the camp in an uproar, shot through with rumors of approaching troops and filled with posturing and prancing young men in full war regalia. The two brothers continued to counsel patience and peace, but now they counseled in vain. Over their protests the camp was struck and moved south to the Salmon River, to the village of Chief White Bird. Joseph and Ollokot followed with heavy hearts. In the war councils that followed they took an active part, and they managed to win one concession: The troops would be met for the first time under a white flag. If war could be averted, it would be; if not, then the Nez Perce would be prepared.

On the morning of June 17, the troops were sighted, a hundred cavalrymen under the command of Capt. David Perry, their ranks swelled by volunteers from Grangeville, riding down White Bird Canyon in the gray light of early dawn. The camp stirred to action: Sixty-five armed warriors, led by Ollokot and a man named Two Moons, concealed themselves on either side of the canyon while beween them, unarmed and carrying the promised white flag, a six-man truce team waited calmly for the arrival of the troops. The lead soldiers rounded a corner suddenly and sighted the truce team. There was a moment of shocked surprise; then one of the volunteers raised his rifle and fired at the Indians holding the white flag. The last slim chance for peace had been destroyed; the war that Joseph had resisted for so long had finally begun.

This first battle ended in a stunning victory for the Indians, as Perry's command—a third of their number slain—fled in confusion back up White Bird Canyon toward Grangeville. The Nez Perce forces had lost not a single man and had only two wounded, neither seriously. But there was no time for celebration. At Lapwai, Joseph knew, was Gen. O. O. Howard, sitting beside a telegraph that could summon thousands of troops from all corners of the nation. Howard and Joseph had considerable respect for each other and were even, as far as was possible under these difficult conditions, friends. But though the friendship would outlast the war, causing Howard to become one of Joseph's staunchest and ablest defenders before the court of American public opinion and the heavy-handed bureaucrats of the Commission of Indian Affairs, it could not be counted on to bring an end to the hostilities. The Nez Perce would not be safe where they were. It was time to move.

Thus began one of the greatest and most courageous retreats in the history of warfare. Westward to the rim of Hells Canyon, northward along it a long day's march, then eastward for a thousand miles, across the Bitterroot Mountains, through the newly created Yellowstone National Park, and onto the plains of eastern Montana, Joseph led his people, dogged by Howard every step of the way. The Nez Perce conducted themselves superbly: They scrupulously avoided harming noncombatants, carefully obtained permission before passing over private lands, and insisted on paying for all the supplies they obtained along the way. Whenever Howard's forces attacked them, they fought brilliantly; at all other times they moved peaceably, refusing utterly to act like the popular image of a war party and in the process winning universal admiration and acclaim from the American public. When defeat came at last, four months from the outbreak of hostilities and a heartbreaking five miles short of permanent sanctuary in Canada, Joseph in captivity proved as noble as Joseph in warfare. His speech of surrender, delivered to Col. Nelson Miles and taken down verbatim by an alert junior officer, has become a minor classic: It was, as Alvin M. Josephy has called it, "one of the most touching and beautiful speeches of surrender ever made."

Tell General Howard I know his heart. What he told me before I have in my heart. I am tired of fighting. Our chiefs are killed. Looking Glass is dead. Toohoolhoolzote is dead. The old men are all dead. It is the young men who say yes or no. He who led the young men is dead. It is cold and we have no blankets. The little children are freezing to death. My people, some of them, have run away to the hills, and have no blankets, no food; no one knows where they are—perhaps freezing to death. I want to have time to look for my children and see how many I can find. Maybe I shall find them among the dead. Hear me, my chiefs. I am tired; my heart is sick and sad. From where the sun now stands, I will fight no more forever.

The people of Billings, Montana, turned out to give the captive Nez Perce a rousing welcome and a testimonial dinner of the type generally reserved for conquering heros. General Howard and Colonel Miles recommended repatriation to Lapwai or even to the Wallowa, recommendations which they would actively press, formally and informally, for the rest of their lives. The Commissioner for Indian Affairs, however, remained unmoved. Joseph and his people were transported to Oklahoma. Many died there of malaria; the remainder were eventually allowed to return to the Northwest, but not to their homeland. They were settled on the Colville Reservation in northeastern Washington. There, on September 21, 1904, Joseph died, far from home. At the time of his death he was still trying to get permission to return to the Wallowa, where a town had already been named in his honor—a town in which he was not allowed to reside. It is little wonder that on his death certificate, signed by the reservation doctor, the cause of death is listed simply and succinctly as "a broken heart."

4
Miners, Murders, and More Steamboats

Less than a year after Joseph's defeat, the short, brutal Bannock War of 1878 rounded up the last scattered remnants of the Shoshone people and drove them onto reservations at Fort Hall and Duck Valley. Just over seventy years after white men had first entered the region, the conquest of the canyon country was complete; so short was the time elapsed that a son fathered by Captain Clark during his expedition's layover on the upper Clearwater in 1806 had lived to fight for his mother's people on their long, bitter retreat and to go into exile with them in Oklahoma.

But the removal of the Indians did not mean that Hells Canyon had become civilized; the great gulf was, in fact, very nearly uncivilizable. The towering black walls, the harsh, unforgiving terrain, and the overpowering heat at the bottom of this raw gash in the earth were more efficient barriers to the onslought of civilization than all the Indian tribes in North America, and though many attempts were made to overcome these obstacles, the success rate was small. The harsh conditions brought out the harshness in men. Here, years after it had disappeared elsewhere, the frontier lingered.

For a long time after the Nez Perce left, the principal inhabitants of the canyon were prospectors and placer miners. Stockmen came, but only in the winter, summering their herds on the much more hospitable plateau high above; homesteaders and ranchers came, but most were soon driven out again, beaten and poverty-stricken, to try again elsewhere in friendlier country. But the miners and prospectors, their hopes buoyed by the bonanza that seemed continuously just beyond their fingertips, stayed. No fortunes were made, no glory holes sunk, but the hope—the tantalizing hope—remained. And in the spring of 1887 that hope, combined with race prejudice, greed, and the bitterest form of envy, became the root cause of one of the bloodiest and most spectacular mass murders in American history.

Six months before, in the fall of 1886, thirty-two Chinese placer miners had moved onto the bar at the mouth of Deep Creek, six miles up the Snake from its confluence with the Imnaha, deep in Hells Canyon. It was an austere and spectacular spot of closed vistas and little vegetation, perched on a tiny shelf beside a deep, narrow side canyon, frowned down upon by the great black layer cake of the Deadhorse Rim a few miles to the west beyond the Imnaha. Rapids thundered past the front door; the nearest town was fifty miles away, over the rim and in another world.

Other than the absence of "No Chinese Employed Here" signs, it is difficult to imagine just what it was that brought these thirty-two men here and what kept them once they had arrived. There was gold there, to be sure, but it was neither abundant nor easily worked. Snake River placer deposits, at Deep Creek and elsewhere, occur as highly localized lenses called "skim bars," each stretching for just a few feet along the leading edge of an alluvial deposit: A bar a quarter of a mile long may contain a net total of less than five hundred feet of workable sand six to eight inches deep. Within the skim bars the gold content averages less than .0015 ounces per cubic yard, so little that nearly seven hundred cubic yards of sand must be sifted to obtain one ounce of glitter—a pile twice as large as the average house for an amount of product that will fit on a thumbnail. To add to the difficulty, the individual particles of gold are so small that they can barely be seen, tiny cup-shaped flakes averaging one ten-millionth of an ounce each, perfectly capable of flowing out over the edge of a gold pan with the water instead of sinking to the bottom where they belong. It is difficult—it is, in fact, next to impossible—to make any more than a marginal living in such circumstances, and the Chinese of Deep Creek were probably not succeeding at it.

Yet rumors persisted that they were. Though there is no hard evidence to suggest that the Chinese who roamed the West during the various gold rushes of the late nineteenth century were any better at placer mining than their white counterparts, it was widely believed that they were, and the stories going around Hells Canyon country that winter of 1886–1887 reflected this belief. The most commonly accepted account credited the Deep Creek Chinese with the possession of "seventeen flasks of gold dust," each worth between $500 and $1,000. One such flask actually turned up at the site of their camp many years later, lending some credence to the tale, but the other sixteen—if they ever existed—have never been found. Whether or not the gold actually existed is not important, anyway; what matters is that others *believed* it existed and that this belief, coupled with the mingled hatred, distrust, and envy that goes by the name of race prejudice, was enough to move certain men to action.

There were eight involved in the original plot, all hired hands employed by a rancher running cattle on the Snake-Salmon Divide, which at that point forms the east rim of Hells Canyon. It is not known who the ringleader was, nor is it important. The eight men had all seen the Chinese camp, the neat sluice boxes, the stone-walled dugouts back by the cliff, and the busy men; they had heard the rumors of great wealth, more than a cowhand could earn in twenty years. Funny little yellow-skinned bastards shouldn't be allowed to have that kind of money, they felt, and by god, they wouldn't, either.

The eight men entered into a solemn pact. They would leave the cattle for a day, ride down to the Chinese camp, shoot all the Chinese, bury the gold, and climb back out of the canyon to their cows. When the inevitable but small furor over the murders died down they could go back to the camp, uncover the gold cache, and be rich.

But during the night, one of the younger men, Carl Hughes, changed his mind and begged to be left out, and so there were seven men in the party when it left the plateau behind and rode down a steep draw into the Snake.

It was early afternoon when they arrived at the Chinese camp. One of the canyon's spring heat spells had struck; the still air, caught between the great black walls, shimmered in waves like the shudderings of a frightened animal. Most of the miners had sought the coolness of their dugouts. The seven murderers rode directly into the camp and opened fire immediately, at close range. Caught completely by surprise, the Chinese had no chance at all to resist. Many were shot as they lay in their dugouts. Others attempted to flee and were caught and killed before they could even begin to get out of range. One man reached the river and attempted to swim to safety; the grinning cowhands took turns firing at his bobbing head. He was hit just before he reached the far bank. His body sank out of sight immediately; soon it appeared again, caught on a rock jutting out from the Idaho shore, bobbing gently with the current.

Silence descended on the carnage that had been a camp. When the bodies and the dugouts had been looted and the gold had been buried on the bar, the murderers, for reasons of their own, decided to tidy up the place a bit. There was a boat tied up to the bar that looked big enough to hold all the bodies. Wouldn't hurt to try, anyway. Slowly, in the heat of the afternoon, the murderers carried the victims down the steep bank to the water. The pile in the boat grew until there were twenty-nine bodies in it. It was testified later that the men "became fatigued" at that point; perhaps that is the reason they stopped there, but it seems more likely that the boat simply would hold no more. Whatever the reason, three of the bodies—two on the Deep Creek bar and one across the river—were left where they were. A hole was knocked in the side of the boat, and it was set adrift to sink in the rapids. The skittish horses were caught and mounted; the seven men rode out of the dead camp, back to the plateau and the cattle and, at least in some cases, the private hells of their guilty consciences.

If the murderers had hoped that throwing the bodies in the river would hide their crime, they were seriously mistaken. Within days, the bodies, liberated from the sinking boat, were floating past Lewiston or washing up on the bar at Dead Man's Eddy, a few miles upstream. The alarmed local authorities sent a party to Deep Creek to investigate. In the silent wreck of the camp the awed and sickened men found the bodies that had been left behind, partially decomposed, each with a neat bullet hole through the head. They found bloodied stones where other bodies had lain as well as drag marks leading down toward the river; and they found tidy little mounds of cartridge shells, each marking a spot where one of the murderers had stood, pumping bullets at the fleeing men as if they had been ducks in a shooting gallery. They took note of all these things, and they rode back up to Enterprise and reported, first to the sheriff and then to the *Mountain Sentinel*.

And now the second miscalculation of the murderers became apparent. They had counted on the strong local prejudice against Chinese to gloss over their crime and make it seem unimportant. It did not. Hating and distrusting the Chinese was one thing; indiscriminate and wholesale murder was quite another. The local newspapers called it the "crime of the century"; abbreviated accounts appeared as far away as the East Coast, where they came to the attention of Chinese ambassador Tsui Yin in Washington, D.C. An international scandal broke out. Ambassador Tsui dispatched a high embassy official, Pung Kwang Yu, to the Snake River country; Pung made a shrewd and thorough investigation, causing a considerable local sensation, and submitted a report that became the basis for an indemnity claim filed by the government of China against the government of the United States of America. The claim was eventually settled for $275,000—at that time a record sum.

The investigation did not smoke out the murderers, but the publicity—so much more than they had expected—did. Worried that all that activity at the Deep Creek bar would uncover their gold cache, they sent one of their number—a man named J. C. Canfield—to dig it up and take it to some remote location to convert it to coin. Canfield never returned. According to some accounts, he was shadowed and murdered by two of his companions; according to others, he simply skipped with the loot. Whatever the cause, his prolonged absence made the already jittery men even more jittery, and in time one of them, Frank Vaughan, broke down and confessed. He was taken into custody along with Carl Hughes, the man who had backed out on the morning of the massacre. The others faded away and were never apprehended. And fifteen years later, in 1902, when the brief, exciting Eureka Boom brought renewed interest in prospecting to Hells Canyon, two young men who had been trying their luck at Deep Creek showed up in Joseph one day bearing a flask of oriental workmanship partially filled with gold dust, worth approximately $700. Was it something that Canfield had overlooked? Or was it the entire sum of the Chinese wealth, the whole cache, and had thirty-two men been murdered for $21.88 apiece?

The answer will never be known.

ii

In the early 1890s there was a brief, renewed flurry of interest in the copper deposits of the Seven Devils, and—the failure of the *Shoshone* notwithstanding—a second attempt was made to promote steamship navigation on the upper Snake. A new sternwheeler, the *Norma,* was built at Huntington, Oregon. She was even less successful than the *Shoshone* had been. The intervening twenty years had brought the railroad to Idaho, and a bridge had been built at Huntington—a substantial, solid bridge, with no drawspan. Penned into the thirty-mile stretch of river between Huntington and the head of the canyon, the *Norma* was next to useless. The railroad line could not be persuaded to install a drawspan in its bridge in order to extend the *Norma's* run. There was only one solution, and that was to do what Bas Miller had done with the *Shoshone* a quarter of a century earlier: bring her down through Hells Canyon.

The man chosen to pilot the boat on the perilous run to Lewiston was William Polk Gray, a dry-humored, soft-spoken fifty-year-old with more than thirty years' experience as a pilot on the lower Snake and Columbia River systems. Widely considered one of the best sternwheeler captains in the United States, Gray was an authority on navigation and the only man ever to successfully run Priest Rapids on the Columbia with a full load of passengers. With a hand-picked crew that included his brother A. W. as mate; veteran engineer Charles H. Jennings; and the former construction foreman for the Oregon Steam Navigation Company, Thomas Wright, as carpenter, Gray arrived at the *Norma's* Huntington berth in mid-May 1895. A quick inspection of the boat assured him that all was in working order, and at two in the afternoon on May 17 he cast off and headed down the river.

Troubles began almost immediately. The Army Corps of Engineers had been doing channel improvements in the thirty-mile stretch between Huntington and the canyon, and Gray, who was unfamiliar with the upper river, was depending on their work and on the navigation chart that they had prepared to guide him down as far as the Oxbow. This, he would soon find out, was a serious mistake. Three miles below Huntington, in the middle of the Bay Horse Rapids, the boat suddenly fetched up against the broken-off end of a two-inch steel drill that the corps had left sticking up in the middle of their "improved" channel. Several large holes were punched in the bottom of the boat; the drill caught in one of them, and the current swung the *Norma* crossways and slammed her stern against a large rock. It took several hours' work with lines and spars to work her free and two days of shore time to repair the extensive damage.

They had hardly got under way after that mishap before they grounded once more. They were following the corps's chart, which A. W. was watching carefully, when Gray saw what looked like riffles ahead. According to the account he wrote in 1920 for the U.S. Geological Survey—and which has since become a minor classic of steamboating literature—the next bit of conversation went something like this:

GRAY: "It don't look good. What does the chart say?"

A.W.: "All clear—there is a black rock marked on the shore."

The chart, of course, was wrong: A. W. had hardly finished speaking when the boat struck heavily, ripping a forty-foot gash out of her starboard side. "I grabbed the chart," Gray wrote, "and flung it out of the window, and we touched no reefs or rocks afterward except at Copper Creek Falls."

Two more days of shore time were required for the new repairs. Gray sensed a considerable amount of discouragement on the part of his crew, and he approached them individually to ask whether they wanted to go forward or return to Huntington. According to his account:

> "Every man wanted to go back. Approaching the engineer I said: "Charlie, this boat is worthless up here, what do you think about going back?" He replied: "We came up to get her.

I say go on or put her where they can't find her." I replied:
"Charlie, you're my man. The boys think I am going to make
a short trip down a few miles to test our new bulkhead, but we
will forget to come back."

Ten miles or so down river, "the boys," as Gray put it, "accepted their fate." But more difficulties were in the offing. The biggest of these was Copper Ledge Falls—the tremendous eighteen-
foot drop in the river that had delayed the *Shoshone* for a year and
then almost wrecked her. Many years later Gray told the story of
his own passage of that barrier in his account for the geological
survey:

For an hour I watched and studied the currents, eddies, and
backlash of the water, and decided that the least damage to the
boat would be done by dropping over the fall on the Idaho side
and let the back-lash hold me from the cliff as much as possible. . . . The underside of the point of this cliff has been worn
away until the overhang extends over the water a good many
feet and a considerable amount of the current passes under the
cliff.

When I returned to the boat I called the carpenter, who had
been foreman on construction for many years with the Oregon
Steam Navigation Company and had asked to go with me for
the excitement, and putting my foot on the starboard guard
about ten feet abaft the stem said: "She will strike about there.
I want you to run in a bulkhead six feet back of that to the
midship keelson, then have the mate back it up with cordwood
in case water should rush in hard enough to tear away your
bulkhead."

He examined the falls and replied: "You ain't intending to
go over that place, are you; you will drown us all." I looked at
him a moment and then asked: "Tom, you never had much
notoriety, did you?" "No, why?" "They have all our names
that are on this boat, and if you should be drowned your name
would be in every paper in the United States and Europe." His
reply: "Oh! Go to Hell" sounded like the decree of fate. I
replied: "Put in the bulkhead, Tom. We'll chance the other
place." An hour later the sounds of hammer ceased and I

heard mumbling. Walking softly to the bulkhead hatch I heard: "Damned old fool; going to be drowned for excitement because a damned fool wants notoriety." But the bulkhead went in good.

The next morning I made the only quarterdeck speech in my life. Calling the crew together, I said, "Boys, you have persuaded yourselves that there is danger to your lives in going over those falls, but there is not a particle of danger to your lives. This boat is built of wood enough to float her machinery and there are forty cords of wood in the hold. We could knock her bow and side in and while the wreck is floating we have boats enough to carry all of us ashore. There are life preservers enough for three apiece if you want them, but don't get excited and jump overboard. Snake River never gives up her dead. Now get ready to go."

When we dropped over the fall we seemed to be facing certain destruction on the cliff below, but I knew my engineer was "all there" and would answer promptly. Backing slowly and within ten feet of rock to starboard her bow passed the mouth of Copper Creek, where an eddy, emptying, gave her a slight swing out and I backed strong with helm hard to starboard— the bow must take its chances now; the stern must not. Almost before one could speak the bow touched the point of the cliff just hard enough to break three guard timbers without touching the hull, and we bounded into the still water below. The carpenter, who had stationed himself on the hurricane deck outside of the pilot house with two life preservers around him, stepped out in front of the pilot house and shouted: "Hurrah, Cap! You start her for Hell and I'll go with you from this on."

There were no further adventures, even in the depths of the canyon where the men reported in awe that they could see stars at midday and where Captain Gray estimated the drop of the river at "over a hundred feet a mile." They tied up for the night at Johnson's Bar and reached Lewiston the next day, May 24, as the second and last steamboat crew to successfully traverse the entire dark, narrow, tortuous length of Hells Canyon.

iii

The voyage of the *Norma* marked the end of the last abortive attempt to establish steamboat service on the Snake River above Hells Canyon. But in the depths of the canyon itself, the steamboat era was by no means over. The big sternwheelers continued to bull their way upriver from Lewiston for well over a decade, and for a brief span of three years, from 1903 to 1906, there was regularly scheduled service to a point nearly a fourth of the way up the mile-deep, rapids-strewn lower gorge—surely the most unusual, difficult, and exciting "milk run" in the history of steamboating!

The upper terminal for this improbable exercise in commercial navigation was the town of Eureka, a mining camp set on a tiny bar backed up against the great west wall of the canyon, just north of the mouth of the Imnaha River. There are a considerable number of mysteries surrounding the story of Eureka and few facts to go with them. Most accounts call the place a gold camp, but there is little evidence to suggest that there was ever any gold there. The records of discovery, in June of 1899, are for a copper strike, but assays by the U.S. Bureau of Mines in 1968 failed to find more than a trace of copper, either. At least one longtime student of the canyon and its history, John Barker of Lewiston, is personally convinced that the whole thing was a monumental con game, set up and carried through in order to fleece a large group of eastern investors. This may be true: There is no question that eastern money was involved and that the bubble burst at a highly convenient time for certain people. But like all the facts about Eureka, the swindle—if one existed—is shrouded by conundrums and enigmas. The Eureka Boom has vanished from history, leaving scarcely a ripple behind; its full story, like others of its kind, will probably never be known.

Here are the facts, as far as they can be reasonably determined:

Early in the year 1900, word of a fantastic new copper discovery near the mouth of the Imnaha River began to leak out of Hells Canyon country. The discovery—so went the tale—had been made by one M. E. Barton and one Bart Hibbs in June 1899. "The ore lies in a vast deposit," reported one promoter, "which shows a value of twenty-five percent of copper from the very surface. A ledge forty feet wide cuts a high cliff and the copper glistens in the sun when the moss is swept away. . . .''

The story of the discovery was a masterpiece, with just the right blend of romance and realism to stir the imagination to the utmost without sounding implausible. It began, according to a contemporary account in the Lewiston *Tribune*, with Indian tales of "gold that glittered in the sun" near the mouth of the Imnaha. Attracted by this legend, prospectors had worked their way into this remote, inaccessible spot only to find that the "gold" was chalcopyrite and to turn away, disappointed.This happened many times. Then, at an evening campfire on a cattle spread near Joseph, someone told the tale in the hearing of a miner who knew the value of chalcopyrite as a copper ore, and subsequently the *Tribune* reported:

> a race for a copper mine followed. Barton and Hibbs, mounted on swift horses, outrode their competitors in a night race over the roughest mountain trails in the northwest and at daylight reached and scaled the walls of the box canyon. When the next in the race looked into the canyon, these men were each sitting upon a ledge of rich ore ready to defend their rights. . . . This is the history of the discovery of what promises to be one of the great copper districts of the west.

Barton and Hibbs bonded their claims to the Idaho Exploration and Copper Company for a sum reputed to be in the neighborhood of $100,000 and retired from the scene. By that time, the cliffs above the Imnaha were becoming riddled with prospect holes and reports were circulating of discoveries which had assayed out as high as $38 per ton. Despite these glowing assessments, however, nothing concrete was forthcoming save a small amount of extremely low-grade ore from a shaft sunk at the site of Barton and Hibbs's original discovery; and by the summer of 1902 the fever appeared to have about run its course.

It was at this remarkably convenient time that the Eureka gold strike was announced. The rock that contained the copper ore, it developed, also held significant amounts of gold! Earlier reports of gold prospectors turning up their noses at those same rocks were disregarded or forgotten; the stampede was on. Within a remarkably short time there were 2,000 men living on the half-mile-long bar at the mouth of the Imnaha River. By August 1903, a post office had been established, a Eureka Mining Company incorporated, and the foundations for a gigantic stamp mill were crawling up the canyon wall. Remote and inaccessible as it was, the town of Eureka, Oregon, was on the map.

Because of the difficulty of travel over the canyon rim from Joseph, all heavy traffic had to come by way of the Snake River. The Eureka Mining Company had its hand in that, too. A wholly owned subsidiary, the Lewiston Southern Company, was put together early in 1903 to run steamboats between Lewiston and Eureka Bar. The first of the big sternwheelers, the *Imnaha*, went into operation on June 30, 1903. There is evidence to suggest that she had been built in a hurry: There were only five bulkheads in her 125-foot length, her hull was made of two-inch timbers instead of the four-inch stock specified for the same company's later *Mountain Gem,* and the enclosures around her eccentrics were conspicuously absent. But she floated and she ran and transport was essential. The company began sending her on regular runs up the river.

The lower half of the *Imnaha*'s run, from Lewiston to the Grande Ronde, was easy enough; but the upper half was a challenge. This part of the river was full of rapids extraordinarily difficult to navigate. There were two particularly hazardous locations. One, Wild Goose Rapids, about halfway between Lewiston and Eureka, was the "very considerable fall" noted in Lewis and Clark's journal. The other, Mountain Sheep Rapids, two miles below Eureka, was a deceptively smooth-looking piece of swiftly moving water whose principal hazard lay in its narrowness; at one point the cliff-to-cliff distance was barely sixty-two feet. The Lewiston Southern Company had prevailed upon the Army Corps of Engineers to do channel-improvement work in the area early in 1903, and the rapids had been tamed somewhat by dynamite, but they were still vicious. A sternwheeler could not hope to ascend these white staircases of angry water under its own power; help was required. It came in the form of a great iron ring set firmly into the canyon wall well above each rapid. A steel cable was attached to each ring; an empty barrel was fastened to the free end of the cable to mark it and keep it afloat. The *Imnaha* carried a powerful winch. Approaching the rapid, she would locate the barrel, fish it out of the water, tie onto the cable, and draw herself up to the calmer water above. There the barrel would be released to float back over the rapid and lie in wait for the next trip.

The stamp mill for the Eureka mines arrived in Lewiston early in November 1903 and was immediately loaded on the *Imnaha*, by this time a seasoned river traveler with thirteen trips under her belt. On Sunday, November 8, with Cap. Harry Baugham at the wheel, she pulled away from the dock to begin trip number fourteen. It was to prove her last voyage. Late that evening or early the next morning—the record is unclear—while negotiating the Mountain Sheep Rapids, she fouled her paddle wheel on that helpful cable-and-barrel arrangement. The wheel jammed; the eccentrics bent. The engine killed. Powerless, the *Imnaha* drifted back into Mountain Sheep Rapids. Halfway down she swung crossways and hung up, caught like a cork in the narrow channel; the water backed up behind her, and the pressure tore her in two. The stamp mill went to the bottom of the river.

It is at this point that we enter the realm of speculation. We know when and where the *Imnaha* sank. We do not know—and shall probably never know—*why*. Some, John Barker among them, suggest darkly that the cause was sabotage and that the boat was sunk on purpose. "All the indications I get," Barker told me in December of 1975,

> are that they got some money up, started the basic mining, and built the foundations for the stamp mill—and had nothing. They continued to sell stock, and everything, got all this money—and then when they had the stamp mill on the *Imnaha*, took it up there, and were at the point where they were going to have to start producing something for the stockholders, the *Imnaha* mysteriously is lost in the rapids and sunk. Obviously bankrupting the company, after somebody had lined their pockets very well.

Whatever the cause of the wreck, it finished the town. Eureka did not die all at once, but it was dying from the moment the *Imnaha* broke up. Within three weeks, men were being laid off at the mines. Cargo runs on the *Imnaha*'s successor, the *Mountain Gem*—built with money raised by subscription from Lewiston businessmen—slowed to a trickle, then ceased altogether. The post office was closed. Today, seventy years later, almost nothing remains. There is the great Incan ruin of the stamp mill foundation, stretching forlornly up the cliff behind the empty bar; there are the iron rings set in the rock above Mountain Sheep and Wild Goose rapids, rusted now but still sturdy enough to haul a steamboat, where once the cables were tied that winched the *Imnaha* and the *Mountain Gem* through the white water. And built into the walls of Elmer Earl's barn at Captain John Creek, thirty miles downstream, there are two great planks, each fourteen inches wide and a good thirty feet long, hand-planed and showing the effects of the passage of much water. They are all that is left of the *Imnaha*, the boat that sank a town one long-ago autumn day.

INTERLUDE: COPPERFIELD

At some point very early in the twentieth century, there occurred a subtle but profound shift in the way men looked at the Snake River.

Earlier, the predominant view of the canyon had always been that of an obstacle to be overcome. It was a nuisance, an impediment, a rocky hell that blocked transport and made the jobs of those that had to deal with it much more difficult and hazardous than should have been necessary. "A convict at Botany Bay is a gentleman at ease compared to my trappers," complained the Hudson's Bay Company's Peter Skene Ogden after one expedition into the canyon country. It was a typical remark. Though there were always a few exceptions—men who shared Benjamin Bonneville's "awe and delight" at the splendid majesty of the vast gorge—the majority opinion was that the canyon could cheerfully be done without; would be, too, if men could have their way. The long history of attempts at channel improvements by the Army Corps of Engineers suggests as much.

But as the world hummed into the twentieth century, this jaundiced view rapidly became passé. Suddenly, the canyon was no longer an obstacle but a resource, a treasure, a thing to be put to work; and the very qualities that had repelled men earlier, the steepness and height of the walls and the power and impetuousness of the big river at their feet, were precisely the things that now gave it the most value. These qualities made the canyon a thing of beauty and a resource for the spirit. They also made it one hell of a splendid place to build a power dam.

Thomas Edison had given the first public demonstration of his most important invention, the incandescent electric light, at his Menlo Park, New Jersey, laboratory in December 1879. Demand for this new wonder of science had spread with a speed that would seem incredible even today, used as we are to the rapid dissemination of new products. Within three months Grand Rapids, Michigan, had opened a commercial hydroelectric plant; within ten years electric plants and Edison lamps were commonplace items coast to coast and had already moved from the category of toy into that of necessity. In that tenth year, 1889, a hydro plant was put into operation at the falls of the Willamette River in western Oregon to serve the city of Portland, thirteen miles away, and long-distance transmission of electric power was proved commercially feasible. The age of electricity had arrived: So pervasive had it become already that, fifteen years later, when the town of Eureka was springing up in the depths of Hells Canyon, about as remote and inaccessible a location as it is possible to imagine, one of the first things planned for was a hydroelectric dam across the Imnaha River.

Electric light had come to Idaho, to the twin towns of Hailey and Ketchum on the Big Wood River, in 1885. That was a sawdust-fired plant, but hydro was not far behind. In 1887, the year of the Chinese massacre, two water-powered generators hummed into operation to provide light for the city of Boise. They provided fifteen kilowatts of power each and were driven by water falling sixty-two feet through a penstock from an irrigation ditch called the Ridenbaugh Canal in the southern part of the city. Harnessing the Snake itself took a little more imagination and a little more daring, but it was accomplished in 1902 at American Falls, near Pocatello. And now men began looking downstream for more sites and greater generating potential.

Among the most promising of the sites investigated during those very early years of the twentieth century was the Oxbow. Here, where ancient Idaho Lake had spilled over Windy Ridge into the drainage of the Salmon, reversing the flow of Pine and Indian creeks and forming the lower Snake River and Hells Canyon, the river curves in a long, lazy bend more than two miles long, doubling back on itself so that at the end of those two miles it is just over half a mile from where it began. The drop is great for a large river—better than ten feet per mile—so that the water on the downstream side of the Oxbow's neck is more than twenty feet lower than that on the upstream side. And those twenty feet, on a river the size of the Snake, represent an energy potential of more than 36,000 horsepower.

Development of the Oxbow began in the autumn of 1906. On November 3 of that year, the clerk at the county courthouse in Baker, Oregon, recorded the filing of rights to 8,000 cubic feet per second (cfs) of Snake River water by a group calling itself the Idaho-Oregon Power Company. Six weeks later, on December 18, the same group was granted a right of power site withdrawal at the Oxbow by the federal government. At about the same time they released the plans for their project, which, they claimed, would "revolutionize eastern Oregon." A small dam would be built across the river, a concrete-lined tunnel 3,000 feet long and 36 feet in diameter would be punched through the neck of the Oxbow, and a 25,000-kilowatt generator would be installed at the downstream end. And cities would blossom in the desert.

It was not long before a city did, indeed, so blossom. Unfortunately, it was not exactly the type of city the promoters of the Oxbow project had painted such a rosy picture of. Its name was Copperfield, and it went on very quickly to become one of the blackest blots ever recorded on the history of Oregon.

ii

The city of Copperfield was built on a small, sagebrush-covered flat near the mouth of Pine Creek, just downstream from the Oxbow. It was said of the town in its heyday that it had grown overnight, in 1909, like a "poisonous toadstool of the badlands"; but this is something of an exaggeration. A community of sorts had existed there as early as 1900, numbering among its citizens homesteaders, prospectors, and miners engaged in developing the nearby copper belt. By 1907 it had a name and enough substance to be chosen as construction headquarters for the branch line that the Oregon Railway and Navigation Company was profoundly hoping would someday connect Huntington to Lewiston by way of Hells Canyon; and when the Idaho-Oregon Power Company began punching its tunnel through the Oxbow the same year—boosting the number of construction workers in the area to over 2,000—it appeared that little Copperfield was headed, hell-bound, for riches and glory.

Such prognoses are always bound to attract speculation, and Copperfield did. Early in 1908, four men from Baker came to Copperfield and quietly bought up a quarter-section of land located strategically between the railroad right-of-way and the proposed power plant site. They then proceeded to subdivide and sell it all back off again, lot by tiny lot. In six months they had cleared the entire piece, made their pile, and retired to Baker, while behind them, on the land they had owned so briefly, the legend of Copperfield was already noisily being born.

There were saloons. There were dance halls, whorehouses, and gambling dens. Sunday closing hours were openly violated; laws against dispensing liquor to minors, habitual drunkards, and inebriated persons were casually ignored. Bitter rivalries developed between the power company construction workers and the railroad crews, and fistfights, brawls, and wholesale riots became commonplace. "One conflict that lasted more than an hour was accompanied by the tinny tunes from the mechanical piano in Barney Goldberg's saloon," reminisced one anonymous writer more than twenty years later. "Rocks and beer bottles, and other missles, as well as fists, were used, but when truce was finally called from sheer exhaustion, enemies drank from the same bottle, bound up each other's wounds, and set the date for the next encounter." There were no jails, no policemen, no law-enforcement apparatus of any kind. There were also—it almost goes without saying—no churches. Copperfield was, as Mark Twain had written earlier of Virginia City in *Roughing It*, "no place for a Presbyterian," and it was proud of the fact.

There were also, scattered here and there, a few ordinary

businesses: a general store or two, some warehouses, a railway depot, a tiny school. The gentlemen who ran these establishments were mortified by their town's rapidly exploding notoriety, but they could do little. The mayor, H. A. Stewart, was the owner of one of the rowdiest of the saloons; and he presided over a city council made up of his business partner, Tony Warner; Bill Wiegand, another saloonkeeper; and Wiegand's bartender, Charlie Kuntz. It was hardly what you could call a reform-minded government. The town stayed wide open, and few voices could be found brave enough to protest it.

That was how things stood in 1913 when the boom began to collapse.

The powerhouse tunnel was now complete, and the Idaho-Oregon Power Company, tottering near bankruptcy, had drastically revised its plans, lowering the proposed output of the plant from 25,000 kilowatts to a token 600; the building of this tiny powerhouse did not employ a significant number of men. The railroad had reached Homestead, cast a jaundiced eye at the 130 miles of deep, tortuous canyon it would have to contend with to extend the line to Lewiston, and announced that for the time being, at least, Homestead would be the end of the line. Trade decreased drastically at the saloons and bawdy houses, and competition stiffened. The saloonkeepers, divided into two rival factions, began quarreling among themselves; arson reared its ugly head, and several taverns burned to the ground. The respectable citizens of Copperfield saw in the growing split an opportunity for action, and toward the end of the year they got up a petition, obtained fifty-five signatures on it, and sent it over to Gov. Oswald West in the statehouse at Salem. The gist of it was that crime was running rampant through their community, and they could get no assistance from county officials, and would Governor West please use the powers of the state of Oregon to come in and clean up their town for them?

It was the opening salvo of what would later be called, in headlines from coast to coast and in most of the major capitols of Europe, "the Copperfield Affair."

Os West was a young man who was energetic, forward looking, shrewdly political, and, in the escalating Prohibition argument, militantly Dry. He reacted to the petition from Copperfield with characteristic swiftness, dispatching a wire to Sheriff Ed Rand of Baker County with a peremptory order: "You are hereby directed to close at once and keep closed until further notice all saloons and other places in said town wherein intoxicating liquors are sold. . . ." The tone was softened somewhat by an offer of "all the aid necessary" to carry out the order, but it was still an order, a meddling in the internal affairs of Baker County by the distant state, and it got Ed Rand's dander up. He refused flatly to carry out West's instructions, adding that he knew of no law under which he could act and that anyway there was nothing going on in Copperfield but "petty squabbles"—hardly worth all the flurry. West's response was immediate. "Well," he told the press, "I will close the saloons there myself, and I will close any other saloons in that county that need closing." He gave Rand till Christmas, less than a week away, to act. Rand pointedly ignored the deadline and issued a statement of his own: The only way, he said, for the governor to get what he wanted would be to "declare martial law at Copperfield and send in the militia." The county wouldn't do it for him.

Christmas came and went. Nothing happened.

On December 30, Os West called the press to his office for an announcement. He reminded the reporters present of his pledge to clean up Copperfield—as if they could have forgotten—and of Sheriff Rand's statement that he would have to send in the militia to do it. He paused. The pencils poised. Then the governor said calmly: "The District Attorney and the Sheriff of the county having reported to me that they cannot do it, I shall send my private secretary, Miss Fern Hobbs, to Copperfield to close the saloons. Judging from her past work, I have not the slightest doubt she will succeed. If those men who are sworn to enforce the law and have the great arm of the law back cf them cannot close the saloons, we shall see what a woman can do."

That was all. No explanation of tactics, no hint as to whether or not the lady would act alone. Miss Hobbs would clean up Copperfield, period. Canny politician that he was, West refused to answer reporters' questions. "You just watch Copperfield" was the only response he would make.

Nor could the frustrated reporters do any better with Fern Hobbs herself. Demure and smiling, she skillfully parried all their requests for information. They knew her to be a young lady of considerable determination; it took that, in those days, for a woman to become an attorney, and it was a matter of record that Miss Hobbs had been admitted to the Oregon State Bar the year before, at the age of twenty-four. But Copperfield was full of big, rowdy men, all armed, all pledged to resist, by any and all means, the governor's orders. Miss Hobbs stood five feet three inches tall with her boots on and weighed in at barely 104 pounds. Just what on earth did she expect to accomplish?

Well, anyhow, it made good copy. The story blinked out over the wires, the eastern editions picked it up, and suddenly the whole world was watching Sweetness and Light go into battle with the Forces of Darkness in Copperfield, Oregon, just inside the upstream end of the deepest gorge on earth.

Over in Baker County, the word was received with something less than equanimity. "Ridiculous!" snorted Sheriff Rand. "The District Attorney," sniffed the district attorney icily, when pressed, "is acting through the courts and not through the newspapers." Copperfield's Mayor Stewart had a slightly longer message. Miss Hobbs, he said, would be given the town's best. The whole population would greet her at the station; the streets would be decorated with bunting and the saloons with pink and blue ribbons; flowers would bedeck the bars. The city officials would listen to her politely. But, the mayor assured reporters, they would "pay no attention" to whatever messages the governor was planning to transmit through her.

On January 1, Fern Hobbs passed through Portland by train on her way east from Salem. The reporters who converged on the depot to interview her were treated to the same evasive answers they had been given in Governor West's office a few days before. The lady appeared to be treating the whole thing lightly, as if it were some sort of lark. "Armed?" she replied to one reporter's question. "Well, yes, I am. I have a dressing bag, a portfolio, and an umbrella. I don't suppose I can do much damage with those. Do I look like Carrie Nation to you?" She insisted that she was alone;

but just before the train pulled out an alert newsman noticed that several cars back, grim, unsmiling, and in civilian clothes, sat Warden B. K. Lawson of the State Penitentiary—who also happened to be a colonel in the National Guard. With him were the chief of the penitentiary guards, one of his men, and five other burly individuals who, it developed, were veteran, picked members of the state militia. Were they escorting Miss Hobbs to Copperfield? The dour Colonel Lawson had no comment. The mystified newsmen wired their colleagues in Salem, who contacted Governor West. He sidestepped the question, commenting instead on the preparations afoot in Copperfield. "All this talk," he said, "about flowers, the decoration of the saloons, etc., is appropriate for the occasion. Flowers usually are in order when last sad rites are to be performed."

The train carrying Miss Hobbs reached Copperfield at two in the afternoon on January 2, 1914. Mayor Stewart stepped out of the crowd of 100 or more citizens huddled on the cold little station platform and greeted her cordially. A light rain was falling; The mayor apologized for the weather and held the lady's umbrella gallantly over her head as he escorted her to the town hall. Lawson and his men, who had abandoned the pretense of separateness when they changed trains in Huntington, strode hard-eyed behind. At the hall—a dance hall converted for the occasion—the colonel and two of his men took up strategic positions at the door while Miss Hobbs was escorted to the rostrum, mounted it, and addressed the crowd. The governor, she said, had sent her to seek the resignations of every city official with any connection to the saloon business. She had letters prepared for them to sign. She passed the letters to Mayor Stewart, who looked at them, passed them back, and announced firmly that no one had any intention of resigning. Fern Hobbs stood silently for a moment, as if listening to some inner voice. Then she slipped the four unsigned letters of resignation back into her portfolio and removed a fifth sheet of paper. "Gentlemen," she said, in what was later reported as a "clear, precise, and unhurried" voice, "you have heard me read the governor's letter and submit his proposition, and you have refused to comply with his request. Therefore martial law will at once supplant your city government."

She called Colonel Lawson, who came forward and read the declaration of martial law. The bars were to be closed and stripped of their fixtures, which were to be shipped, along with all liquor in the town, to warehouses in Baker. The mayor and the city councilmen were under arrest. All other citizens were to disperse in an orderly manner, leaving all weapons at the door.

The citizens, weaponless, filed glumly out into the cold street, leaving behind a pile containing more than 170 revolvers. A carpenter named Sam Grim took the oath of office as the new mayor. Fern Hobbs caught the southbound train. She had been in the town of Copperfield for less than ninety minutes. "No one held an umbrella over me as I wended my way back to the station," she told a reporter for the *New York Times*. "I went alone, but I was not afraid."

The outraged saloon owners threatened to seek a court order enjoining the state against further action. "Enjoin and be damned," thundered the governor, and he wired specific instructions to Colonel Lawson to ignore all legal documents. An injunction was, indeed, issued by wire from Baker; Lawson tore it up and threw it in the face of the deputy who tried to deliver it. Then he asked the governor for fifty more troops. "I don't want Sheriff Rand coming up here with a bunch of deputies and throwing me in the Baker County jail," he explained. The continual flow of messages between the saloon men and their attorney at Baker irritated him, and at one point he threatened to tear out all telephone and telegraph lines, relenting only on the condition that all incoming and outgoing messages were to be personally monitored by him. The reinforcements arrived. Wiegand and Carlson, two of the deposed city officials, tried to escape on a railroad "speeder"—a mechanized handcar—and were caught in the best western style by a couple of the guardsmen.

Meanwhile, Fern Hobbs, safely back in Salem, found herself the center of quite unprecedented attention from the national media. She ignored most of it, but she did grant one or two interviews in which the entire story was revealed. Sending her to Copperfield had been a ploy by Governor West designed to detract attention from Colonel Lawson and his guardsmen. If the militia had simply moved in unilaterally, there would certainly have been armed resistance.This way, with the city officials and the press all concentrating on the governor's female secretary, the militia could come in almost unnoticed, and there would be no time to organize resistance. The whole thing had worked beautifully. Was she frightened? A little, she admitted. "I wouldn't have done it for any other man in the world but Governor West," she told the *New York Times* on January 5, 1914, "and I wouldn't do it again for him."

The whole thing blew over eventually, of course. Copperfield wheezed a few more times and was silent. None of the saloons ever reopened; most were destroyed by a fire—another suspected arson—within a few months of Fern Hobbs's visit. In time, even the legitimate businesses closed up and moved away. There is little left of Copperfield today. In the deep concave bend of the river are a few foundations, a few bricks, a few rotting boards—nothing else. Over them the high, grim walls of the canyon frown down as they always have. Other events would be played out at the Oxbow, with other characters, at other times. They would have no more than the most tenuous of relationships to Copperfield, to Prohibition, or to Miss Fern Hobbs, who in 1914 for a few brief exciting days was the toast of every newspaper reader and every suffragette in the country.

iii

Copperfield was, in a sense, a monument to the failure to plan ahead.

The Oregon Railway & Navigation Company had begun their line through the canyon to Lewiston without properly knowing what they were getting into, and when a survey was belatedly run in 1911, they were left with a dead-end line to nowhere. The Idaho-Oregon Power Company's development at the Oxbow was built mostly because it looked like a good place for a power plant, not because it was a vital part of a comprehensive plan for river development. The results of each of these grandiose shots in the dark were the same: a spurt of furious activity followed by the doldrums. The activity had built Copperfield, and the doldrums had killed it. Fern Hobbs and Col. B. K. Lawson were merely accessories.

This pattern was not lost on boosters and promoters in Idaho and eastern Oregon. Thereafter, little of substance would be done in the canyon without the benefit of comprehensive surveys designed to show just how carefully whatever-it-was fit into a unified plan for the overall benefit of the two-state region. In practice, this meant that little of substance would be done at all for more than thirty years. For Hells Canyon, the period from the demise of Copperfield to the close of World War II might well be called the age of surveys.

The first of these surveys was carried out by the Oregon state engineer's office in 1916. This study, which was termed *preliminary*, identified six major damsites in the 100-mile stretch between the Oxbow and the Oregon border. One of the six—and for a time the only one to receive any serious consideration—was a grandiose, Rube Goldberg type scheme called the Salmon River Diversion Project. A 9-mile tunnel was to be drilled under the Seven Devils from the canyon of the Salmon to the canyon of the Snake, and the waters of the Salmon were to be diverted through it, entering Hells Canyon at a point more than 400 feet up the Idaho wall just south of Pittsburgh Landing. A 500-foot-high dam at Corral Creek on the Snake and a 125-foot-high dam on the Salmon just below the eastern portal of the tunnel, about halfway between Riggins and White Bird, would complete the project. It was estimated that more than 500,000 horsepower could be produced in this manner—a far cry from the paltry 447 the Oxbow plant was currently putting out. No one seemed to care that in doing so it would dry up more than 60 miles of the lower Salmon, ruining what was even then recognized as the richest producer of anadromous fish in the nation.

A 1922 study by an engineer named W. G. Hoyt for the United States Geological Survey also emphasized the Salmon River Diversion scheme; and six years later, in 1928, the whole thing came very close to becoming a reality. A German chemical and metallurgical firm, Farbenindustrie & Anilinfbank, working through an American of German descent named A. G. Liebmann, went so far as to obtain flow and storage permits for the site from the Idaho Department of Reclamation. But the owner of the proposed Snake River portal of the tunnel, a rancher from Stanfield, Oregon, refused to cooperate, and the plan was eventually dropped, eliminating the possibility that Snake River water would power the Third Reich into World War II.

In 1927 the Union Pacific Railway made one final attempt to find a route for rails through the canyon, using the new tool of aerial photography as well as on-the-ground techniques. This survey proved two things: that even hard-boiled World War I combat pilots could turn pale at the difficulties of flying over the deepest gorge on earth, and that the line would cost—this was 1927, remember—$198,000 a mile to build. The idea was permanently abandoned, and more than half of the rails that had already been laid from Huntington to Homestead were pulled up for use elsewhere.

The National Park Service also got into the act. Partly as a result of the publicity generated by men like the adventurer Amos Berg, who took a canoe through the canyon in the mid-1920s, several studies of the scenic and recreational potential of the area were initiated during the twenties and thirties, the last one in 1939. The recommendations of these surveys were uniformly favorable, but they were lukewarm recommendations and nothing was ever done with them. Future U.S. senator Richard Neuberger—beginning what was to be a long love affair with the canyon—laid the blame for this inaction on the German military threat. "Washington is not in a spending mood right now," he wrote in the April 1939 issue of *Harpers* magazine, "unless the spending pertains to national defense; and Hitler can hardly be said to have Freezeout Saddle as his next objective." A park for Hells Canyon, Neuberger correctly deduced, would have to wait.

It was Neuberger also, with a flurry of articles in a number of national magazines, who managed to fix the name "Hells Canyon" firmly in the public vocabulary. He didn't invent the name—it had been around for a while—but it was his use of it that gave it ascendancy over its competitors. Strange as it may seem, until that time no one name had been fixed firmly on the great gorge. Some called it Box Canyon, some Hells Canyon, some Seven Devils Gorge. The Oregon Board of Geographic Names sidestepped the issue with Grand Canyon of the Snake, and fought the use of the term *Hells Canyon* for more than twenty years. It was a losing battle. Though the board could correctly point out that the derivation of the term had nothing to do with Hades, that it was a corruption of the name "Hellers Canyon," and that it officially belonged to a small side gorge entering from the Oregon side at River Mile 246, the fact was that for this dark, narrow crack in the earth a name suggesting the netherworld was singularly appropriate. Neuberger could hardly be blamed for spreading statements to the effect that it was named for its "sinister splendor," nor could the public be blamed for latching onto them. Hells Canyon it was from then on.

In the canyon itself, things were quiet. The tide of civilization had swept in and ebbed back out again. Eureka was only a stone foundation and a memory; Copperfield, so recently notorious, was less than that. The last serious mining venture, the Iron Dyke Copper Mine at Homestead, had closed down in 1922; there were noises and rumors at the Red Ledge and elsewhere but little of substance to go with them. Even ranching and stock-raising had begun to decrease. Press Brewink and Cap MacFarlane, who had inaugurated modern mail service to the lower canyon in 1910 with their gasoline launch, the *Flyer*, and who had continued to make weekly cargo and mail runs up from Lewiston since that time, found their ledger books slipping toward the red ink. They began advertising to attract sight-seeing tourists. A new industry was modestly born.

A few prospectors and stockmen did stay on, of course. One of these was Len Jordan, who later would become governor of Idaho and then a United States senator. Another, Lem Wilson, had a major role to play many years later in what became known as the "Great Snake Land War" of the early 1970s.

The folklore of the canyon was also beginning to be collected and published during this period by Neuberger, Stewart Holbrook, Robert G. Bailey, and others. Lewis A. McArthur's *Oregon Geographic Names*, first printed in 1928 and revised regularly since, was a particularly delightful source of this lore; in it, one could read of the origin of place names such as Temperance Creek (where Ben Johnson ran out of coffee); Joy (the people who lived nearby were finally getting mail service); Hat Creek (Alex Warnock's hat was lodged in a bush there for many years, out of reach, after he had been bucked off a horse); Granny Creek (named for a horse called Granny, not for somebody's grandmother); and many more. One name McArthur fudged on was PO Saddle. He put it down for a shortened form of the words *peep over,* but it is virtually certain that he knew that the real name, as recorded on early maps of the area, is Pissover Saddle.

Such was the canyon in the quiet twenties and thirties, but trouble was brewing.

In 1925 the United States Congress, acting under the authority of a law it had passed in 1902, published a massive compilation of preliminary data on all streams in the United States where comprehensive water development might be possible. This volume, House Document 308 of the Sixty-ninth Congress, First Session, also called for further studies of a number of stream systems— including the Snake-Columbia—by the Army Corps of Engineers. Money for these studies was voted in 1927, and the corps went to work. The result was the "308 Review Report of Columbia River and Tributaries," submitted to Congress in 1932 and published in 1933 and 1934 as HD 103 and HD 190. The title was rather unwieldy, and it soon became shortened in the popular press to "308 Report." Such brevity would prove extremely valuable; unlike many government documents, the 308 Report was headed for a long and contentious life.

PART II:
THE POLITICS
OF POWER

"Government is not complex; but it is complicated! Deep down I have always suspected that this complication exists to keep the public just a bit intimidated."

—Joan Reiss
Sierra Club

5

Hells Canyon Creek:
The Battle Begins

It all began rather quietly.

In September 1943, the Commerce Committee of the United States Senate passed a resolution directing the Corps of Engineers to "review the reports on Columbia River and Tributaries submitted under the provisions of House Document Numbered 308 . . . with a view to determining whether any modification of existing projects or recommended comprehensive plans of improvement should be made at this time." Since the army was rather occupied at the moment fighting World War II, little was done immediately to implement this order; but preliminary field work directed toward just such a review had been completed before war had broken out, and with that base to build on, it took only a short time after the armistice to collect, coordinate, and publish twenty-nine thick volumes of statistics and plans for the Snake and Columbia River systems. The task was completed in early 1947, and several public hearings were set; for Hells Canyon, the key meeting would take place in Lewiston on July 9, 1947. Testimony for and against the army's plans for the canyon was invited at that time.

These plans were rather spectacular. A number of alternative damsites were discussed in detail, with plan drawings, statistics, and most of the preliminary design and test work complete.

Various combinations of these were fitted into a series of comprehensive development plan alternatives, one of which the army hoped it would ultimately be allowed to build. There was no secret about which of these comprehensive plans was preferred, and it was the most grandiose one of the bunch. It called for two Hoover-sized dams to be plopped down in the canyon, each capable of generating more than a million kilowatts of prime power; the reservoir of one would lap against the tailrace of the other. One, called Nez Perce, was to be built near the mouth of Cherry Creek, a little over three miles downstream from the mouth of the Salmon River. It would create a two-pronged reservoir more than 600 feet deep, one sixty-mile-long arm to occupy the lower Salmon River canyon, the other to stretch very nearly all the way through the main Hells Canyon itself, clear to Hells Canyon Creek. Here the second dam would rise, a towering wall of concrete thrust more than 700 feet above bedrock, in a gorge so tight that the reservoir thus created would be scarcely wider than the river it replaced. Copper Ledge Falls, where the *Shoshone* and the *Norma* nearly had wrecked, would go under more than 600 feet of reservoir. Traveling upstream from the dam, a boatman would go ninety miles before hitting running water. The army called this monster, simply, Hells Canyon Dam. They suggested that this be built first in order to give them time to work out what they modestly admitted were some problems with fish passage at the Nez Perce site.

That was the army's preferred plan. It was also, with certain minor modifications, the plan of the federal government's other dam-building agency, the Interior Department's Bureau of Reclamation, as expressed in a study they had made the year before, in 1946. But it was not the *only* plan; and in Hells Canyon, fittingly, all hell was about to break loose.

At the Oxbow, which the army was planning to drown, there still existed the remains of the little 600-kilowatt power plant built by the Idaho-Oregon Power Company in the glory days of Copperfield. The army was planning to drown that, too. As things stood, of course, it wouldn't be much of a loss: The old plant was like Gunga Din's costume, "nothing much before and rather less than 'arf o' that behind." Idaho-Oregon had gone into receivership before the work had been completed; the plant had never amounted to much, and it hadn't operated at all for years. The machinery was rusting and full of cobwebs, the frame building it was housed in was falling apart, and the massive tunnel through the Oxbow's neck was, except for seasonal flooding, dry as a bone. However, two important things remained intact. One was the certificate of damsite withdrawal issued to the company by the federal government; the other was that Oregon water right of 8,000 cubic feet per second. Both were good for fifty years. Only forty years had passed.

Both the site-withdrawal certificate and the Oregon water right were now in the hands of the Idaho Power Company, a large private utility with a service area encompassing all of southern Idaho and parts of eastern Oregon and northern Nevada. Idaho Power had been formed in 1915 out of the ruins of more than fifty small companies, most of which, like Idaho-Oregon, were either dying or already defunct. The economics of size had prevailed; Idaho Power had prospered. It hadn't done anything with the Oxbow site yet, but that didn't mean it wasn't going to.

On June 18, 1947—three weeks to the day before the army's 308 Report hearing was to open in Lewiston—the Idaho Power Company filed an application with the Federal Power Commission for a preliminary permit to develop the Oxbow site, "in order," it read, "that the applicant may secure and maintain priority for a license. . . ." Two days later, on June 20, they wrote to the Corps of Engineers' Portland office "to officially advise that Idaho Power Company is the owner of the Oxbow power site." The glove had been cast down, and the duel was about to begin.

ii

The company's first move was to take over the Baker Chamber of Commerce.

It is not totally clear how much of this was an overt takeover and how much was simply a sympathetic attitude on the part of the Chamber of Commerce's general manager, Robert W. Ball, and a minority of the members who happened to hold a majority on the board of directors. The chamber continued to act independently on matters unrelated to Hells Canyon: It did not, as it was later accused, become simply an arm of Idaho Power's public relations department. But it is true that for most of manager Ball's three years at the helm there existed a cozy, convenient, and suspiciously well-coordinated relationship between the power company and the chamber. And it is also true that these suspicions could hardly have been allayed when, in January 1949, Ball announced that he was leaving his chamber job to do public relations work for Idaho Power. The news met with no surprise in eastern Oregon. Just what else, Baker old-timers wanted to know, had Bob Ball ever done?

The first moves in the chamber–Idaho Power campaign came in May 1947, before the Oxbow filing was officially made. These were reasonable enough: an announcement that the chamber would support the Oxbow Project, followed by a speech to the membership, outlining the project, by power company president C. J. Strike. They were received cordially enough, and Ball was emboldened to go a few cautious steps further. On July 9 he led a delegation to the Corps of Engineers hearings in Lewiston for the specific purpose of denouncing the federal high dam at the Hells Canyon site. The chamber's official position paper for this hearing was prepared by a power company lawyer, A. S. Grant of the California-Pacific Utilities Company. There was nothing overtly wrong about this, of course; it could be argued quite reasonably that Grant was the logical person to prepare testimony because of his intimate knowledge of utility issues and needs. What made it suspicious was that no vote of the membership had yet been taken. That either dam—or *any* dam—was actually preferred by the chamber at large was not yet known.

A month later, in the same unilateral style, Ball and Grant put the chamber on record against the Oregon Highway Commission. The commission had examined Idaho Power's preliminary plans and discovered that the company intended to flood a section of state highway, without bothering to take care of such niggling little details as replacement of the roadbed or even notification of the agency in charge. This, the commission insisted, was highly improper; no permits should be issued until it was taken care of. It seemed a reasonable enough request, but those now speaking for the chamber didn't see it that way. "It is not incumbent upon a state agency," growled Grant, "to go out of its way to stop development of our natural resources." Neither he nor Ball bothered to remind anyone that the "development" they were defending so vehemently was 95 percent smaller than the "development" represented by the government's Hells Canyon Project—and that the government did intend to replace the highways.

Having thus established a policy of misleading half-truths, the federal dam opposition now proceeded to cross the line to outright misinformation and falsehood. Testifying before the Oregon Hydroelectric Board on Idaho Power's application to build Oxbow, for instance, Grant indicated that the government's dam would flood valuable farmland—a highly questionable statement, since the reservoir would be contained within the canyon for almost its entire length—built that into a fear that dams on the Snake would destroy Baker County's productive Powder River Irrigation District, and then proceeded to allay those fears as far as Oxbow was concerned by casually moving the mouth of the Powder downstream some twenty miles. According to Grant, the river entered the Snake below the Oxbow. According to all the geography books, it entered above. Perhaps the geography books were wrong.

While A. S. Grant was verbally remodeling eastern Oregon for the benefit of Idaho Power, other friends of the company were busy elsewhere. An obstacle they thought they had got rid of had cropped up again, and it looked as though they were going to have to try to remove it once more. And this time around it might not be so easy.

The obstacle was section 610 of Oregon revised statute number 543, otherwise known as the Oregon Hydroelectric Act of 1931. As written, ORS 543.610 allowed the state or a public agency within the state the right to assume ownership of private power developments: All that was necessary was two years' notice and payment of "fair value" for the developments as determined by a set of rather lenient provisions written directly into the act. Utility companies operating within the state argued, with some justification, that this measure placed an unfair burden on them; that it was difficult enough to arrange long-term financing for hydroelectric developments, and to justify major capital outlays to their stockholders, without the threat of imminent nationalization hanging over them. Once granted a fifty-year license, the companies felt that they should be reasonably assured of living out the entire fifty years. With that assurance, they could plan for the future; without it, they were floundering in the dark.

Early in the 1947 legislative session, the Oregon state legislature had passed—over Gov. Earl Snell's veto—a bill, SB 99, that amended this troublesome provision of the Hydroelectric Act. It removed the two-years'-notice and fair-value clauses, substituting new language to the effect that the government would be allowed to take over a private power plant only at the close of its fifty-year license period and subject to normal condemnation procedures. It was only after this bill was safely through that Idaho Power had filed its preliminary permit for the Oxbow site with the Federal Power Commission. But as the election of 1948 approached, it became clear that there had been a slight miscalculation. ORS 543.610 was not dead after all; in fact, it was already beginning to raise its ugly head again. The Oregon State Grange had decided that the new law represented a threat to low-cost power and therefore to the agricultural industry, and they had initiated a successful petition drive to refer the whole thing to the people as Ballot Measure #306. So the SB 99 lobbying effort would have to begin all over again, this time with the entire population of the state of Oregon, not just the legislature, as the target.

The last four months before the election were marked by hectic, no-holds-barred campaigning on both sides. The Baker Kiwanis Club was induced to support #306 in a stacked, low-attendance July meeting, angering many Kiwanians. The Baker chamber's board of directors turned manager Bob Ball loose to spend full time campaigning as head of something called the "More Power for Oregon Committee." The occurrence of rumors, innuendos, and straight-out falsehoods increased dramatically. It was said that power from the Hells Canyon high dam would cost $1,730 per installed kilowatt, a figure at least five times too high. Misleading statements confusing the Nez Perce and Hells Canyon damsites gained currency: The Oxbow Project "did not involve the Hells Canyon project on Snake River," the Hells Canyon Dam "is a proposal to build a big dam on the Snake near Lewiston.'' Predictions were tossed about implying that irrigation diversion in the upper Snake basin would reduce power output at the high Hells Canyon Dam by 40 to 45 percent within ten years of the dam's completion. That was some of the propaganda urging a ''yes'' vote. It wasn't very pretty, but in fairness it must be said that the work of the opposition wasn't much prettier. A highlight of the Oregon State Grange campaign to defeat #306, for example, was a series of advertisements in leading Oregon newspapers depicting Idaho Power as a bloated, top-hatted, cigar-chomping capitalist clutching bulging bags of money in each hand; it was captioned ''Vote No on 306—Alias SB 99—Alias Idaho Dam Grab.'' It did not condescend to explain why.

The election came and went. Truman defeated Dewey, and SB 99 went down in flames, 242,000 to 173,000. The Hydroelectric Act reverted to its original form. Bob Ball joined the promotions department at Idaho Power.

iii

If the opponents of Idaho Power thought that the final defeat of SB 99 would kill the company's plans for the Oxbow, however, they were greatly mistaken.

For some time after the election, to be sure, this did seem to be the case. Idaho Power was quiet; the main focus of attention was on the federal Hells Canyon project, which was beginning to make some pretty fair strides toward realization. One potential roadblock, the possibility of interagency rivalry between the Corps of Engineers and the Bureau of Reclamation over who should build the thing, was resolved nicely in April 1949, with an agreement between the two agencies to divide the Snake drainage at the mouth of the Salmon River, the corps taking jurisdiction for projects below that point (including Nez Perce) and the bureau retaining responsibility for everything upstream (including Hells Canyon). That same year, comprehensive legislation authorizing a whole new series of dams on the Columbia and Snake systems, as proposed by the 308 Report, was prepared and submitted to the Eighty-first Congress. Here it received a slight setback. Corps projects are traditionally handled by the Senate's Committee on Public Works; bureau projects, by the Interior Committee. Because of the new agreement between the two agencies, this bill contained projects of both. To which committee did it belong? This dilemma was solved by slicing the bill in two and railroading one part to each committee, a solution that salved the egos of the politicians involved but did little for the legislation. The corps's half of the bill passed handily and was signed into law. The bureau's half bogged down in committee over a section calling for the establishment of a controversial "Columbia Valley Association," similar to the Tennessee Valley Authority, and never reached the floor. However, this seemed little more than a minor setback. The Bureau of Reclamation half of the original bill could be introduced again in the next Congress, cleansed of its CVA provision, and it would most likely go through.

That, at least, was how the high dam's backers felt until December 15, 1950. That was the day that Idaho Power, having decided at last to ignore ORS 543.610, applied to the Federal Power Commission for a final construction permit at the Oxbow site and suggested, without formally applying for them, four other projects it was prepared to build in that reach of the river which, when combined with Oxbow, would utilize the same 600-foot head as the big federal project. The proponents of the high dam were suddenly faced with a valid permit application for a viable alternative project that, though radically different in concept, would develop the same reach of river to the same order of magnitude. And they were, predictably, more than mildly upset.

The push for the high dam was being coordinated in eastern Oregon by a group called the Hells Canyon Development Association, which had been formed in the summer of 1949 by two Baker businessmen, one a newspaper publisher, the other a real estate operator. The publisher, Byron Brinton, was one of the Kiwanians who had been angered by the ramrodding through of the Baker Kiwanis's pro-Idaho Power resolution in the summer of 1948. His paper, the *Record-Courier*, was a strong voice in support of the federal dam and as a consequence was suffering from an economic boycott imposed by some of its former advertisers. The real estate man was a relative newcomer to eastern Oregon. Born in eastern

Montana, brought up on the shores of Washington's Puget Sound, he had worked his way through Whitman College and Columbia University Law School in the years immediately preceding World War II. After the war he had married a Baker girl, settled in her home town, and gone into business with his father-in-law. At the time he helped By Brinton form the HCDA, he was a Republican, rather firmly small-town, and apparently destined to remain in that mold for the rest of his life. But fate—and Hells Canyon—had different things in store. Strongly attracted by the high Hells Canyon Dam and repelled by his party's negative attitude toward it, he became a Democrat in 1950. Four years later, his reputation established by his hard-hitting role as a leader in the Hells Canyon fray, he ran for the House of Representatives in Oregon's Second District against the Republican incumbent, Sam Coon. He didn't make it that time, but two years afterward, on his second try, he did. He has been in Congress ever since; as of 1976, he was, as chairman of the House Ways and Means Committee, one of the two or three most powerful men in the United States. His name: Albert C. Ullman.

Al Ullman is a big, easygoing man with an infectious grin, a great leonine head, and the almost imperceptible trace of a German accent handed down from his immigrant parents. He formed his career in Hells Canyon, and he still likes to talk about the place he refers to as fondly as "the most beautiful area in the world." "I think it was more than twenty-eight years ago that I came up into the canyon," he said not long ago. "I hiked it; I came on motorcycle; I came on horseback; Byron Brinton is here to testify because he was along on many of those trips. We saw . . . one of the greatest of America's resources. And all of these years it has been the intention of most of us to do what is best for America with one of America's greatest resources."

In the early 1950s, what was best seemed to Ullman and Brinton to be the high Hells Canyon Dam, and as chairman and secretary, respectively, of the Hells Canyon Development Association, they set out enthusiastically to prove it. Because of the efficiency factor involved in the use of falling water just once instead of five times for the same head, the big dam would generate more electricity than the five small ones proposed by the power company. The big dam would provide nearly four million acre-feet of flood-control storage; the IPC's five small dams would all be run-of-the-river projects that would provide no storage at all. The big dam would provide ninety miles of unimpeded slackwater navigation amid the awesome Hells Canyon scenery; to cover the same ninety miles under the Idaho Power plan would require lifting a boat out of the water and putting it back four times. Since the power company would have to make a profit, while the government power could be sold at cost, the high dam's electricity would be available at a fraction of the price of that from the five low dams, significantly improving chances for development of southern Idaho's massive phosphate deposits (phosphate extraction is a highly energy-consumptive industry). Finally, it was felt that the local tourist industry would benefit greatly from the presence of what the newspapers were already calling "the world's highest dam in the continent's deepest canyon." With a combination of superlatives like that, how could you avoid packing 'em in?

The Idaho Power Company didn't have answers to all these points, but it did have answers to some of them, and it had a few points of its own to make, too. There was, for example, the matter of cost. If the federal high dam were built, it would be to the tune of 300 million tax dollars; if the IPC projects were constructed instead, they would not only not require tax monies to finance, but they would actually generate a significant amount of new tax revenue. There was also the problem of upstream water rights: In a low-water year there might not be enough flow in the Snake River to satisfy irrigation needs in southern Idaho and still drive the big dam's turbines in an efficient manner, and southern Idaho farmers expressed a fear that if such a situation developed it would be their crops—not the generating capacity of the dam—that would be sacrificed. Idaho's governor, former Hells Canyon sheep rancher Len Jordan, opposed the federal dam on these grounds. Idaho Power's five run-of-the-river plants would provide far greater flexibility for balancing limited water supplies between irrigation and power-generation uses. As far as flood control was concerned, the company argued, Corps of Engineers' figures showed that a high dam at Hells Canyon Creek would lower flood crests at Portland, 1,000 miles downriver, by only a few inches; as to this business of "cheap federal power," well, utilities operate in a heavily regulated industry where even private firms like Idaho Power are considered quasi-public agencies, and the company couldn't charge more than the states of Idaho and Oregon would allow, even if it wanted to.

The first opportunity for the two sides to test each other's strength came in 1952. That was the year that Sen. Wayne Morse from Oregon and Congresswoman Gracie Pfost from Idaho introduced legislation in both houses of the federal legislature specifically authorizing construction of the high Hells Canyon dam. Idaho Power responded by placing a series of provocative ads in national publications, juxtaposing a spectacular photograph of the canyon with the question: "Would you throw 300 million tax dollars into Hells Canyon?" Hearings on Pfost's bill were held in the House Interior Committee in April. Al Ullman led a combined delegation to Washington from eastern Oregon and southwestern Idaho to lobby for the bill, giving the future chairman of the House Ways and Means Committee his first inside look at the workings of the federal legislature. But no action was taken, and the bill died with the Eighty-second Congress.

In November 1952, federal dam proponents received a major setback with the election of Dwight D. Eisenhower as president of the United States. The preceding Truman administration had been a strong supporter of the dam; the Morse/Pfost bill had been drafted by the legal staff of the Interior Department, and both Interior and Agriculture were formal intervenors against the Idaho Power five-dam plan in the Federal Power Commission's Hells Canyon hearings. But Eisenhower's election changed all that. In his very first state-of-the-union message, in January 1953, the new president launched what came to be known as the "partnership policy," advocating less intervention by the government in the operation of private utilities. Less than a month later, the Department of Agriculture's intervention in the FPC proceedings was withdrawn. Interior was in a little deeper, and it took a little longer to pull them out: Formal withdrawal didn't come until May 5. Five days after that, on May 10, the Idaho Power Company filed two more construction applications, one for a low dam at the contested Hells Canyon Creek site itself, the other for a gigantic earth-fill project at the site of the old Brownlee's Ferry. The single Brownlee Dam was designed to take the place of three run-of-the-river projects in the power company's original five-dam plan, and it answered one of the principal objections to that plan—the lack of the flood-control function—by providing a full 1,000,000 acre-feet of flood storage.

Hearings were scheduled for all three Idaho Power applications beginning in July 1953.

Interior's withdrawal left a big hole in the proceedings, which Ullman and Brinton saw as direly in need of filling. To do so, they proposed a new organization, broader in scope and constituency than the strictly local Hells Canyon Development Association had been and thus able to swing more clout with the FPC as an intervenor. For assistance in forming the new group they turned to Gus Norwood of the Northwest Public Power Association in Vancouver, Washington; to the National Rural Electric Cooperative Association; to public utility districts and REA cooperatives throughout the Northwest; to the Grange; and to various labor organizations and citizens' groups. Early in July, this milieu coalesced into something called the National Hells Canyon Association. J. T. Marr of Portland was chosen chairman, and a young journalist from eastern Oregon named Lloyd Tupling was hired as general manager. The new organization immediately filed a petition for intervention with the Federal Power Commission; looking beyond that, Al Ullman—who had long since given up trying to move Congressman Sam Coon into agreement with him—began planning a run for Congress himself. He had stationery printed with a blue letterhead reading "Ullman for Congress" and identifying Tupling as his campaign manager. One of the greatest careers in the history of Oregon electoral politics was alive and on the move.

iv

The marathon hearings before the Federal Power Commission on Idaho Power's three-dam plan began on July 7, 1953, and lasted—including recesses—one year and two days, to July 9, 1954. The hearings' record, a small library in itself, runs to 159 volumes containing nearly 20,000 pages of oral transcript and more than 400 technical exhibits. Presiding with great patience and humor over

the swirl of contention, accusation, and name-calling that formed
the bulk of the daily proceedings, Examiner William J. Costello—
an attorney from Great Falls, Montana, who had served the FPC in
a similar capacity on other occasions—heard Interior Secretary
Douglas McKay, a former Oregon governor, accused of "stacking
the cards against the public" through a policy of "suppressing
reports which show the many shortcomings of the Idaho Power
Company's plan for river development." He heard the Bureau of
Reclamation accused of "subterfuge" and of the development of
"fictitious" benefits in its efforts to justify the high dam. And he
heard the FPC itself accused of "a substantial miscarriage of
justice." He also heard the Oregon Fish and Game Commissions
"vigorously protest" *both* plans for damming the canyon due to
the "irreparable loss" it would inflict on Oregon's fish and wildlife
(but nobody was listening to them yet). Figures flew about like
storks in mating season: According to whom you talked to or
whose side you were on, the high dam would produce anything
from 646,000 to 1,513,000 kilowatts of prime power; the three low
dams, anywhere from 505,000 to 675,000. Cost estimates on the
competing projects ranged from 130 to 400 million dollars. And in
the midst of it all, the Portland *Oregonian* got a letter to the editor
on July 11, 1953, that brought back, for knowledgeable readers,
echoes of an earlier time:

> The only mistake I made, while governor, was when I sent my
> secretary, Miss Fern Hobbs, to settle the Whiskey dispute at
> Copperfield, on the Snake—where the Idaho Power Company
> was then undertaking construction of the Oxbow project—
> that I did not give her further instructions to settle the Hells
> Canyon-Idaho Power matter while on the ground. Thus she
> could have saved the U.S. Government, the several states and
> the politicians much worry and expense. All my fault!
>
> Oswald West

While all this brouhaha was going on in the Federal Power Commission, the supporters of a high Hells Canyon Dam in Congress
continued to have difficulty moving legislation.

As early as April 16, 1953—four months before the official

beginning of the FPC proceedings—Sen. Wayne Morse and Rep. Gracie Pfost had reintroduced their bills to build the Hells Canyon Dam. Like their predecessors, these bills failed to go anywhere. Their principal usefulness was the function they served as rallying points for the senatorial race in the fall of 1954, in which veteran Sen. Guy Condon of Oregon was defeated by a political newcomer named Richard Neuberger—the same Richard Neuberger whose articles in national magazines in the early 1940s had established the name "Hells Canyon" in the public vocabulary. The pleased Morse began planning yet another introduction of the bill, with Neuberger's help, in 1955.

When the new bill was dropped in the hopper in March, it carried twenty-nine cosponsors—a full 30 percent of the Senate. It was an impressive show of support, and it enabled the legislation to move quickly, for a change, through the Senate's procedural maze. Hearings began in the Interior Committee on April 4, less than a month after introduction; the committee reported the bill out, favorably, on June 8. Things moved a little more slowly on the House side, but they did move, and on July 27, following the lead of the upper chamber, the House Interior Committee also reported the dam bill favorably. By that time, however, it was a little late. Congress was already into its last week, moving toward an August 2 adjournment. In those hectic final days, there was little time for Hells Canyon. Neither body scheduled floor action; the fate of both bills was left up in the air. They didn't exactly die: It would be the second session of the same Congress that would convene in January, and all unfinished business would simply be carried over. But even their strongest proponents agreed that neither bill looked very lively.

Still, no one was quite prepared for the speed of the next development.

The FPC's examiner, William J. Costello, had emerged from the mountains of testimony and exhibits that had been placed before him as a result of the 1953–1954 hearings and issued his formal opinion on May 6, 1955. In doing so, he had attempted to strike a sort of middle ground between the two competing plans. The federal dam proponents, he ruled, had not proved their case sufficiently—but neither had Idaho Power. He was not satisfied that the electrical load growth of the Idaho utility justified the building of such a large combined project. His formal recommendation, therefore, was to issue a license to the company for Brownlee *only,* with the fate of the Hells Canyon site itself left temporarily open. The five-man FPC had taken this opinion, as well as the 20,000 pages of oral testimony and the result of further oral arguments before the full board on July 6 and had retired to consider a verdict. On August 4, two days after the close of the 1955 session of Congress, that verdict was announced. Examiner Costello's recommendation was overturned; Idaho Power got everything it asked for. Brownlee, Oxbow, and the low Hells Canyon Dams would be built. Two major stipulations were attached: The company was to complete Brownlee by 1958, Oxbow by 1961, and Hells Canyon by 1964; and they were to negotiate with the fish and game commissions of Idaho and Oregon on proper fishway design and fair-share payment of construction, operation, and design costs of passage facilities for migrant fish. Other than that, they were essentially free to do with the river what they wanted.

When it leaked out that the commission had actually made its decision on July 27—the same day the House committee had cleared the Hells Canyon bill—but had withheld announcement until Congress had adjourned, congressional leaders were furious. Richard Neuberger fumed to the newspapers about "private power favoritism on the part of the Republican Party." Wayne Morse noted acidly that "a majority of the Federal Power Commissioners were hand-picked by the Eisenhower Administration to do this job, and they have done it in hot and unseemly haste." In Oregon, the National Hells Canyon Association announced it would "undoubtably" begin court action to overturn the license. The FPC itself was officially mum. There would be plenty of time for infighting when the case actually got to court. Besides, it had other things to do—things that would soon be generating even more controversy within the jagged black confines of the gorge.

6

Pleasant Valley:
The Plot Thickens

A little over thirty miles downstream from the Hells Canyon dam-site lies Pittsburg Bar. Here, where little Kurry Creek comes tumbling down from the Idaho rim, the towering walls pull back briefly to make room for the canyon's largest alluvial bench—a sun-baked Shangri-La two miles long and nearly a mile wide sunk in a sheer-walled hole five thousand feet deep and threaded by the indolent green river. On this bench sits the canyon's last remaining cattle ranch, the Circle C. A road of sorts snakes its way down from Idaho; at its end, accessible under normal conditions only by four-wheel-drive vehicles, is Pittsburg Landing, the single spot within the canyon on the Idaho side where boats may be launched. It is either just below or just above here—the exact spot is uncertain—that the *Colonel Wright* was forced to turn back on her first-ever steamboat run up Hells Canyon.

Pittsburg Bar is an anomaly in the canyon's geography, and it does not last. Below it the walls close in again, squeezing the river between castellated banks that leap upward in great towers and bat-tlements, almost, it seems, to the end of sight. The stone is black and hard. It is a lovely, terrible spot, and its presence has given Pittsburg Bar a second name. After the cramped gloominess of the narrows, the airy bar seems so open and peaceful and hospitable that people have long referred to it as Pleasant Valley.

Early in 1955, less than a week after New Year's Day and a full eight months before the Federal Power Commission decision granting the Hells Canyon damsite to Idaho Power had come down, the peace of Pleasant Valley began to shatter. First came men with theodolites and transits, shouting to each other as they scrambled over the rocks at the downstream gates of the valley like ants on a rooftile. Shortly afterward came machines—chattering compressors and thumping drills, the angry-bumblebee whine of high-powered outboard motors, and the curious, bone-rattling *pocketa-whrrrr* of helicopters. The men carrying the theodolites and those running the machines carried with them sets of preliminary plan drawings based on the army's 308 Report, and what those drawings showed was rather spectacular. At the head of that narrow gorge would rise the world's third highest concrete-arch dam. Below the dam, in a squat, sturdy powerhouse, the world's five largest generators would spin out a quiet, steady, awesome 170,000 kilowatts each. Nor was this all: Downstream a little over twenty miles, a short mile above the mouth of the Imnaha River, a second dam would crouch, a low-head, gravity-type structure whose primary function would be to reregulate the flow of the river and smooth out the wide fluctuations in water level caused by the operation of the gigantic powerhouse upstream, but which would incidentally be capable of turning out over 300,000 kilowatts of power on its own. Pleasant Valley, the only wide spot in Hells Canyon, would become the only wide spot in a ribbon of reservoir that would stretch from the Imnaha to Hells Canyon Creek—or, counting the three separate Idaho Power projects, from the Imnaha to the Weiser. And the brand-new Pacific Northwest Power Company, then less than a year old, would have filled in the bottom of the deepest gorge on earth with the largest private power development on earth.

What was this upstart, the Pacific Northwest Power Company? Where did it come from, and why did it choose Pleasant Valley as its first building site?

"I'll give you a bit of background," says Hugh Smith, leaning back in his chair. Smith is a large, ruddy, jovial man in his mid-fifties who looks, aside from his thatch of silvering hair, as though he had just come from a practice scrimmage with the Los Angeles Rams. From the windows of his cluttered corner office on the fourteenth floor of Portland's Public Service Building can be seen much of downtown Portland, including the Multnomah County Courthouse, the big department stores lining Sixth Avenue, and, beyond the tall square spire of the new First National Bank building, a small section of the city's waterfront on the Willamette River.

"The federal government preempted hydroelectric construction during the thirties. Now, you can't find a law that says, 'We Hereby Preempt,' but as a matter of practical politics they did. They were building projects, they were building them well ahead of need. They were marketing the output of the projects at costs that none of the private firms could come close to matching. They were also using that power as a means of promoting the formation of public agencies, with the intent of taking over the private utility sector of the market, bit by bit and piece by piece. Under those circumstances, the companies had to keep their rates as low as possible. However much they might have wanted to build hydro then, and have their own generation, it wasn't prudent to do so."

This policy was overdue for a change, and it came in 1950, as the nation plunged into the darkness and uncertainty of the Korean War. That year there was a meeting in Seattle of all utilities, public and private, in the Northwest, called by the federal Office of Emergency Management. "They said," recalls Smith, "that the national emergency was such, particularly for the production of aluminum in the plants of the Northwest, that they were no longer going to preempt hydro; they would take extraordinary measures to help local utilities get projects under way and on the line as quickly as possible." The companies came away from that meeting invigorated and a bit bedazzled by the new realm that had suddenly been opened up to them. Projects like Washington Water Power's Cabinet Gorge Dam, Portland General Electric's Pelton and Round Butte developments, and Pacific Power & Light's Yale plant, came off the shelves and were dusted off and updated for rapid construction. Idaho Power raised its sites from the Oxbow alone to the entire stretch of the Snake from Hells Canyon Creek to Weiser. The Federal Power Commission quickly became swamped.

These were all relatively small projects, but there were bigger things in the air. For some time now, the large private utilities had been watching—with a certain amount of frustration, because the economic climate prevented them from getting involved—the growth of the technology that had made possible truly enormous dams like Hoover and Grand Coulee. The government's new policy seemed to release them to tackle such sites. None of them separately had the financial resources to construct anything that overwhelmingly huge, but together they might manage something.

Six companies—Pacific Power & Light, Portland General Electric, Mountain States Power & Light, Montana Power & Light, Washington Water Power, and the Idaho Power Company—hired a firm called Ebasco Services, Inc., to do a study that might determine just where in the Northwest there remained large undeveloped damsites that the companies might, by pooling their resources, put into production.

By the time the Ebasco Report came down, Mountain States had merged with Pacific, and Idaho Power had opted out altogether to pursue its own battle in Hells Canyon, so the joint group was down to four companies. The report, based largely on the Corps of Engineers' 308 Report, listed five principal sites. One, Bruces Eddy, was on the Clearwater River in central Idaho. The other four were in Hells Canyon: Reading upstream, these were Nez Perce (just below the mouth of the Salmon); High Mountain Sheep (just above the Salmon); Appaloosa (six miles above the mouth of the Imnaha); and Pleasant Valley.

With the Ebasco Report in hand and a concrete set of projects to look at, the four companies began seriously discussing how best to join their operations so that they could actually begin construction. They would have to proceed carefully. They could not simply set up a giant superutility in which each company would own equal shares of stock: Sec. 203(a) of the Federal Power Act clearly prohibited that. Nor could they sell outside shares and control the operation through a subsidiary board of directors on which executives from each company would serve: *That* would run afoul of Sec. 305(b), which outlaws interlocking directorates among public utilities. But suppose they were to incorporate not as a utility at all but as an operating company, to build and maintain the project but not to market its power? Was there a loophole there through which they could squeeze? The directors of the four companies turned the problem over to the law firm of Rives, Bonyhadi, Hall & Epstein (now Rives, Bonyhadi & Drummond), general counsel for Pacific Power & Light, who in turn passed the matter on to one of their new young lawyers, who as yet had little to do but who would now build his entire career around the job of chief counsel for this infant combine now being called the Pacific Northwest Power Company. He was Hugh Smith, Esquire.

ii

"A great deal of this," says Smith now, recalling those years, "is the accident of availability. This law firm became the general counsel for PNPC, because at the time it was set up we had available time and none of the other companies' counsel were in that position. That's how I got into it. I was new in the office, and they were looking for somebody who wasn't already weighted down with . . . other jobs. . . . I spent—oh, off and on, it changed a great deal, but there were some years in which I spent literally all my time on PNPC matters."

Smith's first job was to draw up the incorporation papers for the new company. This was completed early in 1954; and on April 13 of that year, at a small gathering of company brass in Portland, the Pacific Northwest Power Company was officially incorporated under the laws of the state of Oregon. Kinsey Robinson of Washington Water Power in Spokane was made chairman of the board; John Burke of Montana Power & Light was named president. Water Power's Clem Stearns would handle publicity. The working management would remain in Portland, with Hugh Smith.

Now the principal decision to be made was which of the projects in the Ebasco Report the new company should pursue. For a time, the Bruces Eddy project on the Clearwater seemed the best choice. A Federal Power Commission preliminary permit was obtained for this site, and investigation began late in the spring. But no one's heart was fully in it. The supreme challenge of Hells Canyon was drawing the company like a magnet; almost from the beginning, it was not a question of "whether" but of "which site." By late October, the decision had been made: The company yielded up its permit on Bruces Eddy, and on November 9, 1954, it filed a new application with the Federal Power Commission, for a new preliminary permit—this time, on the Pleasant Valley site.

The reaction of public power groups was immediate and vehement. A dam at Pleasant Valley, they saw clearly, would be to the Nez Perce project what the Oxbow Dam was to the High Hells Canyon project—a usurper of reservoir space, a destroyer of opportunity. The Pleasant Valley reservoir would occupy most of the Snake River arm of the proposed Nez Perce reservoir, and Nez Perce would therefore become impossible to build. Public power backers, already smelling defeat in their Hells Canyon Creek battle, were enraged to find the other major damsite of the 308 Report slipping away from them as well, and they were not about to let it go without a fight. The Northwest Public Power Association led the charge, letting loose a broadside blast opposing "the building of dams in the bottom of Nez Perce Reservoir," and coupling that attack with a call for a moratorium on dam building in the middle Snake "pending a more complete study of the multiple purpose development of this stretch of the river." There was never any doubt in anybody's mind that "multiple purpose development," in this context, meant "Nez Perce Dam."

The Pacific Northwest Power Company could have staved off much of this sort of thing from the beginning, of course, by filing on the Nez Perce site themselves. They did not, and their reasons for choosing not to do so bear some scrutiny. Part of the reason was purely economic: Pleasant Valley, at something around two million kilowatts of prime power, was all the dam they needed, and it would be wasteful to go to more. But this was not the only, or even necessarily the most important, reason. The Pacific Northwest Power Company was acutely aware of the principal drawback of Nez Perce: that it was below the mouth of the Salmon, and that its construction would block off the spawning grounds of at least 30 percent of the anadromous fish population of the Snake-Columbia system. Smith recalls that the discussion of the merits of Pleasant Valley as opposed to Nez Perce among members of the board of directors was all political and that the decision was made on political grounds. "It was the judgment of the board that wisdom should prevail and that we should not antagonize the fishery interests." The company pulled all the way back, not only above the

Salmon but also above the smaller runs of the Imnaha. It was a shrewd move. Because of it, PNPC could legitimately label itself the conservationist alternative, gaining in the process a considerable amount of support before the Federal Power Commission that it would not otherwise have been able to call upon.

The Federal Power Commission granted Pacific Northwest Power Company its preliminary permit on April 8, 1955. The permit was good for three years—until March 31, 1958—and it gave the company the right to explore alternative projects in what was called the "Middle Snake" (Hells Canyon) and to file for a license to construct one, provided that this filing came within the three-year life of the permit. It was mostly a formality: The company already knew what it wanted. Fieldwork at Pleasant Valley had begun three months before. A month after that—still two months before the granting of the FPC permit—the state of Idaho had granted water use and diversion rights for the project. Now PNPC was waiting primarily on the Oregon Hydroelectric Commission, and when their preliminary permit from that body came down on August 18, they were ready to move. On September 7, barely five months into the life of their thirty-six-month preliminary permit, they filed license applications with both the Federal Power Commission and the Oregon Hydroelectric Commission to build a 534-foot arch-type dam at Pleasant Valley and a so-called reregulating structure twenty miles downstream at the Low Mountain Sheep site, just above the mouth of the Imnaha River.

The Northwest Public Power Association and the National Hells Canyon Association lost little time in counterattacking. Toward the end of July, NPPA chairman Gus Norwood had written to the Federal Power Commission asking to be notified if and when Pacific Northwest Power filed its application for the Pleasant Valley-Mountain Sheep complex. After receiving this notification in early September, Norwood wrote to Evelyn Cooper—the lawyer who was handling the Hells Canyon controversy—in Washington and asked her to look into intervention in the Pleasant Valley proceedings. Cooper agreed to seek such intervention, noting that this was one sure way of guaranteeing extensive hearings. "We can be certain," she wrote confidently, "that it wouldn't be another Hells

Canyon ordeal." It was a statement she would later have plenty of time to regret.

The petition for intervention was filed on September 28, 1955. On October 4, Pacific Northwest Power filed an answering brief: "The petition," it charged, "is scurrilous and contemptuous and is filed to delay and hinder the work of the commission and not to protect any interest of the petitioners." Norwood shot off a quick note to Cooper: "This one may get rough." Just how accurate that statement was, no one could possibly have predicted.

7

The Congress
and the Courts

Meanwhile, what of Hells Canyon Dam?

Within a few days of the announcement of the FPC decision authorizing the Idaho Power development, in August 1955, machinery had been set in motion to appeal that decision through the federal courts. One requirement for a court appeal of an administrative decision of this nature is that all conceivable administrative remedies must be exhausted first; so a *pro forma* request for a review of the decision was prepared and submitted to the FPC itself on September 1. This, as its backers had expected, was denied four weeks later. Now there was just one formality for the National Hells Canyon Association and its sympathizers to wait for: final FPC approval of Idaho Power's detailed plans, which had been submitted on September 13. This approval was handed down on November 10. Eighteen days later the Hells Canyon Association's suit was filed with the United States Court of Appeals in Washington, D.C. The language of the initial brief was not exactly temperate: It accused the FPC of "an act of administrative lawlessness" and "violence to the federal comprehensive plans for the Columbia River basin."

Idaho Power, of course, had also been waiting eagerly for the commission's final approval of the Brownlee-Oxbow-Hells Canyon scheme. In mid-October they had signed a contract with the Morrison-Knudsen Company, a heavy construction firm based in Boise (later to gain a certain amount of notoriety as the contractor on the Bureau of Reclamation's ill-fated Teton Dam, which collapsed in the summer of 1976). So they were primed and ready to go when the approval came down. Within twenty-four hours of the announcement on November 10, Morrison-Knudsen's big crawling tractors and giant Euclid earth-moving machines were tearing away at the Snake's banks at the Brownlee site. Great banks of lights were set up so that the equipment could operate up to twenty hours a day. This activity was in full swing by the time the NHCA's appeal was filed, and the court action failed to slow it by even the tiniest amount. Idaho Power's president Tom Roach announced that the building of the dams would proceed ''as rapidly as possible,'' adding that the suit was ''in keeping with the objectives of the Hells Canyon and other public power associations who want federal power or nothing, and are attempting to obstruct and blockade every nonfederal effort for development of new power supplies for the Pacific Northwest.''

Construction of the coffer dams and the half-mile-long diversion tunnel that would carry the Snake around the Brownlee site during the actual construction phase began in mid-January 1956. At the same time the power company applied, a bit belatedly, for a license from the Oregon Hydroelectric Board. It was evident that this application was considered merely a formal nuisance: There were by that time nearly 500 men employed at the site, and no attempt was made to slow them down while the Hydroelectric Board proceedings went forward. The company also applied to the Corps of Engineers for permission to build a bridge at Brownlee, and then, when the permission failed to materialize quickly, went ahead and built the bridge anyway. It was quite evident that they weren't out to win popularity contests. The Hydroelectric Board, faced with this clear defiance of its regulations, acted bravely, forthrightly, and decisively. They passed the buck. Action on the Idaho Power Company's application was deferred pending the appeals court decision. And maybe if the appeals court didn't save them, Congress would authorize a high Hells Canyon Dam by then and they could squeak out of a confrontation *that* way.

For Congress—at last—did show signs of moving on the issue. Prodded by Morse and Neuberger, and still smarting over the Federal Power Commission's timing of its announcement of the granting of Idaho Power's license the previous August, the Senate Interior Committee began markup sessions on the Hells Canyon Dam bill in the late spring of 1956. The bill was cleared for floor action on June 19, with debate scheduled to begin on July 18. At the same time, Gracie Pfost managed to get consideration of her companion bill in the House Interior Committee. Action was thwarted at first by a massive Republican walkout that left the committee without an operating quorum, but a week later, on June 27, the issue was forced to a vote and sent through to the Rules Committee—the final step before floor action—by a tight 15 to 13 margin. The division was almost completely along party lines. One of two Democrats to oppose the bill, James A. Haley of Florida, had been persuaded to stay away in the interest of party unity; one Republican, George Chenoweth of Colorado, had logrolled his vote in return for support from the western Democrats for the Fryingpan-Arkansas Project in his district. But for those two rather dubious "deals," the legislation would have died right there.

As it turned out, though, the bill didn't have long to live anyway. The House Rules Committee opened hearings on it July 13, then abruptly adjourned with six scheduled witnesses yet to be heard. The action was never resumed. Before it could be taken up again, the Senate had voted, defeating the Hells Canyon legislation by a narrow 51 to 41 vote on July 19. Reaction was, predictably, mixed. Tom Roach of Idaho Power called it a victory; Al Ullman, stumping hard for the second time against Sam Coon for Oregon's Second District congressional seat, called it a disaster. Wayne Morse vowed that he would continue the fight. In the canyon itself the river flowed on as it always had, loud at Copper Ledge Falls and Granite Creek and Wild Goose, quiet at Joseph's Crossing and Pittsburg Landing, rushing past the Chinese numerals and the bloodstains at Deep Creek, chuckling over the wreckage of the *Imnaha* at Mountain Sheep. It paid no attention to the half-mile-long tunnel that was being prepared to receive it at Brownlee or to the fact that men were virtually at each other's throats over its destiny in Washington, D.C., across the continent and three thousand miles away.

ii

With the failure of their legislation in the Senate and with their appeal of the Federal Power Commission license to Idaho Power still pending in the courts, the proponents of a high federal dam at the Hells Canyon site began to get a bit anxious.

When they had filed their appeal, back at the end of November, they had purposely not sought an injunction to halt Idaho Power's work at the Brownlee site. Because of the bond requirements of the injunction process, it can be an extremely expensive procedure, and the National Hells Canyon Association was not feeling overly flush at the moment. Besides, they had argued, an injunction shouldn't be needed. With court action pending against it, IPC in all probability would not be able to arrange financing for its three dams, and construction would be effectively brought to a halt anyway.

It was a nice, plausible theory, and it should have worked. The only trouble was that the Idaho Power Company refused to play along. Far from sputtering lamely to a halt, the company had actually increased its production schedule; work was now going on at Brownlee around the clock. The diversion works were essentially complete, and crews of Morrison-Knudsen workers, sweating in the hundred-degree heat of a Hells Canyon summer, were preparing to lay the foundation for the dam's clay core. Alarmed, the NHCA appealed to Supreme Court Associate Justice Hugo Black to order a halt to construction pending the outcome of the appeal. Black refused. This was undoubtably highly pleasing to the power company, but they had little time to gloat, for less than a week later they found themselves embroiled in an entirely new court action. A Baker County grand jury had voted to indict them for failure to observe the licensing requirements of the 1931 Oregon Hydroelectric Act. A state judge quashed the indictment almost immediately on the grounds that the Federal Power Act removed the issue from the state's jurisdiction, but his decision was rapidly appealed to the state supreme court, which agreed to put the case on its 1957 docket. A few weeks later, while the new state case hung fire, the federal case moved to a new plane with a unanimous ruling by the three-judge court of appeals in favor of the Federal Power Commission and the Idaho Power Company. The National Hells Canyon Association announced, to no one's surprise, that it would carry the appeal to the United States Supreme Court. This gave the Idaho Power Company and Hells Canyon the dubious distinction of facing simultaneous court actions in both the highest tribunal in the state of Oregon and the highest tribunal in the nation. The whole thing was rapidly becoming a lawyer's nightmare. But the building went on.

And now the political climate, never what could be called very favorable to the company, began to turn even further against it. In the 1956 elections, while Dwight Eisenhower was trouncing Adlai Stevenson for the second time in a row, Idaho voters bucked the Republican tide to throw out Sen. Herman Welker, a staunch and outspoken opponent of the federal Hells Canyon Dam. He was replaced with a young Democrat named Frank Church who just happened to support the high dam. And across the canyon in Oregon, things were even worse. Not only did Oregon voters return Idaho Power's nemesis, Wayne Morse, to the Senate, reelecting him by a substantial majority over Douglas McKay, who had quit his Interior post specifically to try to boot the old Tiger out; but they compounded things in the Second Congressional District by tossing out Sam Coon at last and replacing him with the National Hells Canyon Association's Al Ullman. Frank Church could and did say in later years that the Hells Canyon Dam issue was not a factor in his election that year, but there could be no such question about Al Ullman's victory. Exultantly, the young Republican-turned-Democrat vowed to make Hells Canyon Dam authorization the number one priority of his first term in office.

The authorizing legislation was introduced on January 14, 1957, almost immediately after the beginning of the new session of Congress. In the Senate, Wayne Morse had lined up twenty-eight cosponsors, including Frank Church; in the House, where the rules forbade cosponsorship, separate but identical bills were introduced simultaneously by Al Ullman and Gracie Pfost. In the canyon, Brownlee continued to rise. There was a temporary setback in late February when a flood wiped out the cofferdams and sent the Snake surging back into its old channel, inundating the construction site, but it was rapidly corrected; there seemed little doubt that the Power Commission's requirement of completion in 1958 would be met.

The National Hells Canyon Association filed its petition for review with the Supreme Court on Valentine's Day, 1957. The high court listened, took briefs from the opposing sides on March 15, and seventeen days later, on April 1, voted 8 to 1 to deny a review of the appeals court decision. The lone dissenting vote belonged to Associate Justice William O. Douglas, a circumstance that had more import than was realized at the moment. Idaho Power was jubilant. President Tom Roach called the decision "more of a triumph for the orderly process of government than for the Idaho Power Company," adding with a grin: "Needless to say, we are very gratified." But the Oregon court action was still hanging over them.

Five weeks later, on May 8, the Oregon Supreme Court met in Pendleton to hear arguments pro and con in the case of the State of Oregon versus Idaho Power Company; and six weeks later, on June 19, the court brought down a verdict in favor of Idaho Power. By then, however, the news was overshadowed by the impending Senate floor debate on Wayne Morse's Hells Canyon Dam bill. Capitol-watchers this time gave the bill a good chance of going through. That, of course, would mean that what the Oregon Supreme Court did or did not do to Idaho Power was irrelevant. If the bill passed and was signed into law by the president, Hells Canyon Dam would be built and the half-constructed Brownlee project would go under nearly 500 feet of water. The power company realized that it would take something far more dramatic than a victory in the Oregon Supreme Court to head off the passage of the bill. It would take a grandstand maneuver. And that is exactly what the company proceeded to effect.

Several months before, Idaho Power had applied for and received sixty-five million dollars' worth of rapid tax write-off certificates from the federal government. Administered through the Office of Defense Mobilization, these certificates were designed to encourage capital expansion in what were thought of as "essential" industries, such as electric generation. They allowed the company the option of amortizing construction costs on their three dams over a period of five years instead of twenty, dramatically lowering taxes for those five years and therefore amounting, critics charged, to substantial interest-free loans from the government. If this were so, then the government would be footing part of the bill for these private dams, and the argument that had been so heavily emphasized in the FPC hearings—that the dams would be built "at no cost to the federal government"—would no longer hold. Thus it came as no surprise to anyone when a fair-sized thunderstorm arose over the granting of these certificates. The company had won its point and retained its rapid write-off, but the wounds still showed. And now, with the Senate vote on the Hells Canyon Dam bill quickly approaching, these raw and throbbing scars provided a perfect opportunity for dramatic self-sacrifice.

On June 20, the day after their victory in the Oregon Supreme Court and with the vote in the Senate less than twenty-four hours away, the Idaho Power Company announced that it was returning its rapid tax write-off certificates to the government, "to eliminate," it said, "the further beclouding of real issues." It was a nice move, and under normal circumstances it probably would have been effective; but these were not normal circumstances. Through one of those strange quirks which make the study of history so interesting, the issue of civil rights for the American Negro was about to interject itself into the destiny of Hells Canyon.

The Eisenhower-backed Civil Rights Act of 1957, barring interference with voting on the basis of color and creating the Civil Rights Section of the Justice Department, had been maneuvered past strident southern opposition and brought to a floor vote on June 20, the same day that Idaho Power had renounced the special privilege of the rapid tax write-off. Passage of the rights bill had come by an overwhelming 60 to 15 majority, the 15 all being southern Democrats. In the past, this bloc of southerners had always voted against the Hells Canyon Dam. Now, however, smarting over their civil rights defeat, they were eager to vote against the Eisenhower administration on just about anything they could get their hands on—and, as luck would have it, the Hells Canyon Dam bill, which the administration opposed, was the next major piece of legislation in the hopper. The dam bill came up for a vote the next day, June 21, the southern bloc abandoned its traditional opposition, and it sailed through to passage, 45 to 38. A standing-room-only crowd in the Senate gallery, which included Oregon's governor, Robert D. Holmes, broke into a spontaneous demonstration of handclapping and huzzahing and had to be quelled by the gallery guards.

But there was still the House to deal with, where Gracie Pfost's bill remained bottled up in the Interior Committee's Subcommittee on Irrigation. Ullman and Pfost thought that they could pass legislation if it could be brought to the floor—the operative word in that sentence being *if*. The subcommittee, it developed, was going to be a rocky road to travel, the biggest rock being a Pennsylvania Republican named John Phillips Saylor.

John Saylor is an interesting and important figure in the legislative history of Hells Canyon, and it may be worthwhile to examine his biography here. Born and brought up in Conemaugh, a small town in south central Pennsylvania, he went through the public schools, left briefly to attend college and law school, and came back to hang out his attorney's shingle in Johnstown, within shouting distance of his birthplace, in 1934. He joined the navy in World War II, serving in the Pacific, where he participated in the battles of Iwo Jima and Okinawa and was present for the signing of the armistice in Tokyo Bay. Afterwards, he returned to the practice of law in Johnstown. In 1949, in a special election called to fill the seat of freshman congressman Robert L. Coffey—killed in a plane crash in New Mexico less than four months into his first term—Saylor was elected to the United States House of Representatives. He was to remain in that body for the rest of his life.

In the House, Saylor quickly developed a reputation for hard work, attention to his constituents, and strong, tough-minded ideological conservatism. Like others of this breed, he favored business, built up the military, and otherwise kept a tight fist on the public's purse strings. But he had one quirk that tended to set him aside from the general run of his conservative brethren: He was a staunch and outspoken advocate of wild places and the natural environment, and the greatest achievement of his long and productive career would be not a typically conservative piece of legislation but the Wilderness Act of 1964.

When the Hells Canyon Dam bill came before the House Irrigation Subcommittee in the summer of 1958, the Wilderness Act was still six years in the future. But Saylor was already feeling its pull, and it gave him two excellent reasons to oppose the dam legislation. The first reason was his support, as a conservative Republican, of private enterprise over governmental intervention and therefore Idaho Power over the Corps of Engineers and the Bureau of

Reclamation; the second reason, no less important, was his recognition that the power company's low-head Hells Canyon Dam would do far less damage to the natural wonder that was Hells Canyon than would the Hoover-sized monstrosity proposed by the Ullman and Pfost bills. Either reason would have been important; together, they were compelling. Saylor vowed to stop the bill.

It would not be easy. Memories of the year before, when George Chenoweth had logrolled his vote and James A. Haley had been persuaded to stay away, remained clear, and there was every indication that the same thing would happen again if a vote were scheduled on a straight up-and-down motion to send the bill to the full Interior Committee. A surprise attack would have to be made when Chenoweth and Haley were both present and could vote their consciences. The ideal time to do this would be during the so-called markup session, when amendments to the bill were being considered. A motion to kill the bill outright would be out of order at that time, but there is more than one way to skin a cat.

On July 2, 1957, while the subcommittee was in the midst of a routine consideration of amendments to bring Gracie Pfost's bill into conformation with the measure already passed by the Senate, Saylor proposed an amendment of his own. He moved to strike everything in the bill following the enacting clause. It was a precedence motion, requiring an immediate vote, and there was no time for logrolling or arm-twisting. The Saylor amendment passed, 15 to 12. "Certain things," remarked the Pennsylvanian with satisfaction, "are dead in this country, extinct like the dodo bird— and Hells Canyon is one of them." He was right. The Pfost bill would never raise its head again. To the press, Al Ullman expressed considerable anger: "I don't think history is going to condone this type of gross underdevelopment." But the high dam was dead.

iii

In the meantime, behind the smoke screen created by the final acts of the Hells Canyon drama, the FPC proceedings concerning Pleasant Valley were going quietly forward. Hearings were held on PNPC's application during the last half of 1956. At those hearings, most of the testimony, predictably enough, centered around Nez

Perce. To cite two typical comments, culled from better than 7,300 pages of transcript: U. S. Fish & Wildlife's Samuel J. Hutchison, assistant regional director in the Portland office, testifying on September 28 that his agency is unalterably opposed to Nez Perce "due to the terrific impact it would have on Columbia River fish. . . . These fish are of such value that their very existence should not be jeopardized by placing reliance upon undesigned and untried fish facilities." And Gus Norwood, pleading on November 9 that "we cannot afford to lose the Nez Perce site. It is conceded by Army and Reclamation Bureau engineers to be the finest storage site in the Columbia River basin." Other testimony centered on Washington Water Power's role in a recent Public Utility District election in the state of Washington. Water Power's Kinsey Robinson lost his temper during intense cross-examination on this point; the newspapers reported gleefully that he had pounded the arm of his chair and shouted at Evelyn Cooper as he demanded an apology from her for accusations that he was being "careless with the truth."

And at a few points along the line, some people even remembered to slip in a few comments about the Pleasant Valley and Mountain Sheep dams.

The hearings ended a week before Christmas, and the adversaries retired to their corners to lick their wounds and await the examiner's verdict. The commission's technical staff prepared a report on the issue, recommending denial of the permit in favor of Nez Perce, which had somehow grown in the popular press to a height of 800 feet. There was a wait of more than seven months. Finally, on July 23, three weeks after John Saylor had dealt the death blow to the high Hells Canyon Dam, Examiner Edward B. Marsh filed his recommendations with the full commission concerning Pleasant Valley. Pacific Northwest Power, he said, should be granted its license for Pleasant Valley-Mountain Sheep. Despite the conclusions of the staff report and the protestations of the Northwest Public Power Association, Nez Perce was not a necessary project: A study of the hearings record failed to show "quite the urgency or the seriousness of the need" for that much upstream storage.

Oral hearings were held before the full Federal Power Commission beginning on November 26, 1957. They were very brief, and nothing new was presented, although a six-man delegation of Democratic congressmen did come down from the Hill to ask for a delay pending joint study by the Bureau of Reclamation and the Corps of Engineers. The assumption was that the examiner would be upheld, and those seeking federal development of the river thought that they were fighting a desperate rearguard action, in which time would be a crucial factor. The delay was not granted, but, as it turned out, it didn't matter. The full commission handed down its final opinion on January 20, 1958. Examiner Marsh's recommendation was overturned; the Pacific Northwest Power Company was denied its license. "Any combination of projects which includes Nez Perce," the commission ruled, "is consistently superior to any combination of projects which does not include Nez Perce." It downplayed the hazards to the anadromous fish popula-tion of the Salmon River: The fishery problem, said the ruling, "is generally similar to that at other high dams. . . . We are of the view that this engineering problem is no greater than many others that must be solved in connection with any project the size of Nez Perce." Public power had won a stunning victory, and the future course for the deepest gorge on earth seemed clearly spelled out.

It would become the deepest reservoir on earth.

iv

The FPC's decision drew a great deal of commentary, most of it adverse.

The Portland *Oregonian*, for example, which had earlier editorialized in favor of the Pleasant Valley site, printed a cartoon showing Nez Perce Dam as a sacrificial altar with the FPC blessing a dead salmon on its crest. Senator Richard L. Neuberger, a friend of public power who had campaigned vigorously in favor of the high Hells Canyon Dam, was considerably less friendly to Nez Perce: "The whole area of the middle Snake River," he told the Oregon Izaac Walton League, "should be reserved until more is known about the [fish] problem. . . . We can win conservation battles in Congress, but have conservationists ever won a battle before the Federal Power Commission? The Federal Power Commission is just an agency to license concrete pouring." Even Senator Wayne Morse—that tireless advocate of public power and of big federal dams in Hells Canyon—announced that he could not "at this time" support the construction of a dam at the Nez Perce site, while former Hells Canyon Development Association Chairman Al Ullman topped that by coming out in favor of a freeze on further development in Hells Canyon until a plan of comprehensive development could be worked out that would protect the fisheries resource. The FPC had its defenders, too, of course—the Northwest Public Power Association, for example—but just at this point they seemed few and far between.

Nearly everyone in Oregon was incensed by the timing of the FPC announcement, which came precisely one day before the State Water Resources Board was scheduled to begin hearings on the Nez Perce–Pleasant Valley controversy. These hearings had been announced well in advance, the commission had been formally requested to refrain from a decision until the Water Board could take a position, and the commissioners' studied disregard of these facts could only be interpreted as a deliberate slap in the face for the state agency and the interests of the state in general. This was undoubtably a principal cause of the anger Water Board Chairman L. C. Binford displayed a week later as he pounded the podium in the Portland City Club and demanded that the dam builders "forget the old fight between public and private power and get the job done. . . . If you want to make yourself a hell of a little man get in and make a hell of a noise for a high Hells Canyon Dam or some other dam combination, opposing all other dams in the dam system for the Snake. Let's end the dam nonsense and get the dam job done!"

That was the kind of rhetoric that was being flung about in the wake of the FPC's January 20 announcement, and it was to continue for a while. But the biggest bombshell had yet to be dropped, and it wasn't rhetorical. Everyone seemed to have forgotten two significant facts: that the Pacific Northwest Power Company's preliminary permit for the middle Snake covered the whole Hells Canyon reach of the river, not just the Pleasant Valley site, and that this permit still had a useful life of two months and ten days before it was due to expire.

Hugh Smith remembers those seventy days as a period of intense activity. The Nez Perce site was considered and rejected once more: It still seemed too much of a risk to the fish. The company settled on the Mountain Sheep site, below the Imnaha but still a half mile above the mouth of the Salmon. A 670-foot-high dam could be built there, providing nearly three million acre-feet of storage, without interfering at all with the Idaho Power Company's plans for Hells Canyon Creek. Together with the nearly complete Brownlee, this High Mountain Sheep dam could provide the full four million acre-feet of storage that the Corps's 308 Report had said was necessary on that part of the Snake. The directors of the Pacific Northwest Power company smiled at each other. Let's see them use the lack-of-storage argument against *that*!

On March 31, only hours before the preliminary permit was due to expire, PNPC filed a formal license application for the High Mountain Sheep site. Because of the press of time, certain important figures in the application were estimates rather than design measurements. It would take later amendments to the application to fix the exact height and river location of the proposed dam.

Many rapids break the Snake River into white water through the deep canyon north of Homestead, Oregon. These rapids are located at the first tunnel along the Red Ledge mine road along the Idaho side of the Snake. The abrupt rocky walls of the Oregon side of the river are shown in the background. (*Oregon State Highway Photo #Y4826*)

The steamer *Imnaha* headed downstream at the confluence of the Snake and Salmon rivers in 1903. (*Courtesy Idaho Historical Society*)

Snowstorm at Freezeout Saddle, head of Saddle Creek, Oregon rim (*Courtesy U.S. Forest Service, Department of Agriculture*)

Balanced Rock at the Oregon rim near Black Mountain (*Courtesy U.S. Forest Service, Department of Agriculture*)

Trail on Oregon side of Hells Canyon, near Saddle Creek (*Courtesy U.S. Forest Service, Department of Agriculture*)

Wild Sheep Rapid (*Courtesy U.S. Forest Service, Department of Agriculture*)

Prickly pear in bloom. At the bottom of Hells Canyon the botanist may find at least twenty-four species of plants that can be found nowhere else in the world. (*Photograph by William Ashworth*)

Ancient Indian petroglyphs found on the walls of the canyon (*Photograph by William Ashworth*)

Brownlee Dam (*Photograph by Bob Brown; courtesy Idaho Power Company*)

Hells Canyon Dam (*Photograph by Bob Brown; courtesy Idaho Power Company*)

The Idaho Power Company's Hells Canyon Park, viewed here from high on the Oregon side of man-made Hells Canyon Lake. (*Photograph by Bob Brown; courtesy Idaho Power Company*)

Oxbow Dam. The city of Copperfield was located on the bar in the extreme lower left. (*Photograph by Bob Brown, courtesy Idaho Power Company*)

South from the head of Battle Creek, Oregon rim (*Photograph courtesy U.S. Forest Service, Department of Agriculture*)

8

The Oxbow Incident

In order to understand the next development in the history of Hells Canyon, we must digress a little from a direct chronological account.

Historically, one of the greatest attributes of the Snake River and its tributaries above the city of Lewiston has always been its role as a major producer of anadromous fish—Chinook salmon and Pacific steelhead. These fish, which are close cousins, are basically saltwater species, spending most of their lives in the vast green depths of the Pacific Ocean, where they range from the Tropic of Cancer to the Arctic Circle and as far as several hundred miles offshore from the North American continent. When the time comes to spawn, however, they leave the ocean behind, entering the rivers and streams of western North America and swimming upstream for long distances—in some cases, more than 1,000 miles—to lay their eggs in the headwaters tributaries, high in the western mountains. "Runs" of Chinook, great masses of fish migrating together, appear in the spring and fall; runs of steelhead, in the summer and the winter. Several months after the spawning runs, the young salmonids emerge from the streambed gravels. They remain in the vicinity of their birth for periods ranging from two months to two years; then, following an ancient impulse that science has yet to explain, they flock together into schools numbering up to several million juvenile fish (known as "smolts," or, from their size at this point in their lives, "fingerlings") and begin the long migration back to the sea.

The Snake River system is the world's second largest producer of Chinook and steelhead, exceeded only by Canada's Fraser River. More than half of the adult salmon entering the mouth of the Columbia eventually find their way into the Snake system, in numbers ranging up to more than 200,000 three- to four-foot-long fish per year. This, of course, counts only those that escape from the multi-million-dollar salmon fishing industry headquartered at the mouth of the Columbia. At the time of the Hells Canyon controversy, more than 70 percent of these fish—up to 165,000— spawned in the Salmon River. Another 5 percent utilized the Imnaha. The remaining fish—fully one-fourth of the Snake River run—went on up the main stem, through the canyon, past the Oxbow, and as far upstream as Swan Falls. In actual numbers, this ranged, in the late 1950s, from 40,000 to 55,000 adult salmon annually. It was a resource of major economic significance and one to be treated with a considerable amount of care.

The Federal Power Commission, contrary to numerous nasty rumors at the time, was aware of this resource and its value and did its best within what it considered its limits to make sure that the salmon runs would be protected during the construction and operation of the Idaho Power Company's three dams. Articles 34-36 of the company's license were specifically devoted to this problem. They provided that Idaho Power should spend a minimum of $250,000 on studies of the fisheries problem before and during construction; that the company would have to build any "reasonable" fish passage and handling facilities that might be suggested by state and federal fish agencies; and that the company would have to bear a fair proportion of the cost of maintaining and operating these facilities, the exact percentage being left up to negotiations between the company and the agencies. These precautions seemed adequate, and they might have been so if the problem they were designed to solve had been of normal proportions. It was not. It was, in fact, so huge as to be overwhelming, and tackling it with articles 34 through 36 proved about as effective as going after an elephant with a peashooter.

A dam creates a barrier in a river. If it is under about ten feet in height, it is possible—though very difficult—for an adult salmon to leap over it. If it is too high to leap, the adults must be passed around it in some manner. There are two principal means of doing this. One is to lure the fish into a trap, capture them, and truck them around the dam; the second is to build a "ladder"—a series of stairstepped pools up which the salmon may leap from pool to pool, slowly gaining altitude until they reach the level of the reservoir. Neither method is perfect, but both will work after a fashion, and there is no real theoretical limit on the number of upstream migrants that may be passed over a dam or on the height of the structure that they may be passed over.

Unfortunately, the same cannot be said of the juvenile migrants that are headed downstream. Here the same two methods of trucking and direct passage are employed, but the problems associated with each are far more formidable than those faced by the upstream-swimming adults. Young salmon prefer to migrate tail-first, drifting with the current. But there is no current in a reservoir; the fish must turn about and propel itself, sapping its energy and experiencing—especially in large, deep reservoirs—a considerable amount of confusion over which direction it is to travel. At the dam itself, the young fish is either swept pell-mell over the spillway or passed down the penstock and through the turbines. The latter method can lead to injuries and death; the former, to an insidious condition known as nitrogen narcosis, or, in divers' parlance, "the bends." It is caused by improper aeration of the splash pool at the base of the spillway, and it is very often fatal.

Trucking can avoid the hazards of the turbines and the bends, but it has problems of its own. It is far more difficult to catch the smolt than adult salmon without harming them. And those that are successfully caught and released downstream often exhibit strange behavior patterns on their return to spawn, milling about in a confused mass at the point of release as if waiting for the truck to come back and pick them up.

Those are the problems that fishway designers face everywhere in connection with dams. At Brownlee-Oxbow-Hells Canyon, they were complicated by two further factors. The first was the vast size of the structures involved, two and three times the height over which fish had successfully been passed previously. The second was the attitude of the Idaho Power Company, which was never more than grudgingly cooperative with the fisheries agencies and often openly antagonistic to them. "They have acted from the beginning," says one Oregon Fish and Wildlife Agency man, "as if they wanted out of the fish business." "Since Brownlee Dam construction began in 1955," reads a recent Idaho Power brochure, *Fun Country*, "Idaho Power has pursued a program unmatched for size and complexity to conserve migrant-fish resources in the Hells Canyon reach. Its goal: to transplant Hells Canyon's spring Chinook salmon and steelhead runs to the Salmon River watershed." Very well. That program, just now, happens to be working commendably. But the *original* goal, as seen by the FPC and by the fisheries agencies, was to pass the fish around the dams to their natural spawning areas—not to transfer the runs off the Snake completely. And the failure of that original goal was due in no small part to Idaho Power's apparently total lack of commitment to its success.

This problem was evident from the very beginning, as the fish agencies tried to work with the company to design passage facilities for downstream migrants. It was agreed by both parties that capturing the fingerlings at Brownlee and trucking them to Hells Canyon Creek was the most practical way to attack the problem. But agreement could not be reached on the design of the traps. Ideally, these should have been installed flush with the upstream face of the dam, set so a small "attraction current" could constantly flow through them, and with the penstocks leading to the turbines sunk at least 120 feet below minimum pool level so that the young fish would not confuse them with the traps. But to sink the penstocks that low would require a major change in the design of the dam, from rockfill to concrete, and this the company refused to do. The agencies suggested the placement of a "curtain wall" of concrete in front of the penstocks that would reach down to the 120-foot depth, allowing the penstocks themselves to be at any height the company's engineers wished. This was also turned down. Instead, the company proposed a plan of its own: a gigantic net of plastic mesh strung across the reservoir a mile upriver from the dam to keep the fish from coming any closer, with traps in the form of floating barges stationed along it. The fishery agencies were dubious about the success of this "skimmer," as it was called, but by this time it was early 1958 and Brownlee was nearly complete. Something had to be done. Reluctantly, the agencies approved the company's design.

Deployment of the skimmer began in mid-August of that same year. There were difficulties with it from the start. The great net, more than seven acres of small-mesh plastic, proved extraordinarily difficult to handle. It hung improperly from its floating boom; it clung to itself; it developed numerous small holes and tears. Teams of scuba divers sent down to make repairs reported difficulty working at the required depths, 100 feet and more beneath the surface. Work was suspended briefly on August 27 for a small ceremony marking the first output of power from the new project. "In spite of all the roadblocks put in our way by public-power-or-nothing advocates, we have reached our first goal," said Idaho Power president Tom Roach. "The company promised to put Brownlee's first power on the line by September, and here it goes." He closed a switch. Ninety thousand kilowatts crackled out over the transmission lines. The workmen went back to the tangled net.

Despite its troubles with the skimmer, Idaho Power continued to insist that it would eventually work and that they were handling the migrant-fish problem successfully. But even as the switch was closed on the first Brownlee generator, a new problem was developing at the Oxbow, a problem that would rapidly blossom into a major crisis that would be remembered among fisheries people for years to come as "that infamous Oxbow Incident."

ii

In late May, 1958, a fish trap for upstream-migrating salmon had been put into operation at the mouth of the old Idaho-Oregon Power Company tunnel through the Oxbow, now being used as a diversion tunnel in conjunction with the cofferdam that had been built to dry up the construction site for Oxbow Dam. This trap consisted of a short, dead-end ladder topped by a finger weir and a slatted hopper.

In early July, after barely a month of operation, the trap began to malfunction; water conditions were poor in the ladder, and turbulence was developing in the river below the trap's entrance. By the end of the first week in August the turbulence was quite pronounced, and the fisheries personnel monitoring the site were getting worried. There was, however, little they could do; Idaho Power had cut off its financial support of the monitoring program at the end of June, claiming that the $250,000 stipulated for it in the FPC license had become exhausted—a fact that the fisheries agencies disputed. Despite the failure of funding, some monitoring continued, primarily because the agencies were concerned that something was wrong.

On August 20, three U.S. Bureau of Commercial Fisheries personnel—including the coordinator for the middle Snake monitoring team, L. E. Perry—visited the Oxbow trap in the company of an independent fisheries engineering consultant named Milo Bell. The turbulence in front of the trap was quite pronounced, interfering drastically with its operation. Worse than that, though, was the large crack that Bell and one of the government men, Charles H. Wagner, noticed in the retaining wall behind the trap. Alarmed, they investigated more closely and discovered, to their consternation, that the outwash from the diversion tunnel had washed the rock and soil from under the foundations of the fish trap. The whole trap was about to drop into the river. The four men immediately sought out Idaho Power's on-site superintendent and told him what they had discovered. A number of consultations were held, and the company agreed to repair the trap, holding up work on the dam itself, if necessary, to accomplish the repairs.

The repairs began on August 26 at ten in the evening, with the closure of the gates at Brownlee and the consequent reduction of the Snake River's flow from its natural 14,000 cubic feet per second to about 2,000. There was a certain amount of controversy about that reduction. The resident fish in the river, and the salmon already migrating upstream as the fall Chinook run began, could conceivably be damaged by such low flow levels. Nevertheless, the company insisted, the reduction was necessary. They had already tried driving emergency pilings of corrugated sheet steel three-eighths of an inch thick and found that they could not be handled in the full flow of the river. So they had asked the Corps of Engineers for permission to lower the flow level. No formal permission had been granted, but the need had been "understood." The drop was made.

All the next day, while the dedication ceremonies went on at Brownlee, workers labored desperately in the reduced flow of the Snake at Oxbow, trying to get the pilings driven. By Saturday, August 30, the pilings were in after a fashion, and the entire flow of the river was sent back through the tunnel. But the steel pilings washed out as if they had been so much plasterboard.

The brand-new generators at Brownlee were shut down while a temporary cofferdam was thrown up across the mouth of the diversion tunnel. This dried up the flow of the river entirely, for all practical purposes, for the next seven hours, while the pilings were driven once more. At the end of that time the cofferdam was removed and Brownlee was reopened. But the renewed surge of water through the tunnel took out the pilings once more, twisting them so grotesquely that one reporter described them as looking "like cookie dough."

By now it was apparent that emergency measures were simply not going to do the job and that something much more permanent and large scale was going to have to be done. Idaho Power officials reluctantly gave the order, and Morrison-Knudsen engineers blew a hole in the main Oxbow cofferdam. The hydroelectric construction site went sixty feet underwater. A new, semipermanent cofferdam was thrown across the diversion tunnel, and workmen began a complete rebuild, top to bottom and inside to outside, of the damaged fish trap. It was a race against time: The first of the fall Chinook had arrived. The main run had not yet been sighted in the Columbia, but they could not be too far out at sea.

On September 9, with work proceeding frantically on the trap, 20,000 Chinook were counted crossing Bonneville Dam.

On September 12, the whole thing blew up in the papers. There had been reports before, but they had been minor and incomplete; now the whole issue was bannered across the front pages of northwestern newspapers like campaign bunting. Charges and countercharges were thrown about with a great deal of élan. Oregon's governor Robert D. Holmes accused the power company of totally drying up the river "for fifty miles from Oxbow damsite to the mouth of the Imnaha, causing the death of thousands of fish, including migratory species." IPC's Tom Roach responded that "absolutely no migrating fish were destroyed," that there were two creeks entering the Snake just below the damsite so the riverbed could not have gone completely dry, and that anyway, the agencies had been informed of the reduced flow before it happened. The Corps of Engineers agreed that it had been informed but insisted that it had not approved: "In no instance did we imply an agreement to drop the river to zero. We did not even approve the drop to 2,000 feet." The director of the Oregon Fish Commission, Albert Day, accused Idaho Power of building the trap on the old powerhouse foundation from the days of Copperfield, "presumably to save money," adding emphatically, "I'm convinced that if IPC had not tried to save the foundations there would have been no washout." The company denied this allegation altogether. The old foundations had been blasted away before the trap was set, and anyway, the trap itself—foundation and all—was intact. It was the hillside below that had caved away. Governor Holmes accused the "metropolitan press" of a cover-up. The metropolitan press in question accused Holmes in turn of "playing politics" with the disaster. And all the time the small voice of the original monitoring team could be heard, almost lost in the fray, crying frantically for more help for the fish.

For the fish had arrived. By September 15 there were several hundred big, silver-gray Chinook leaping about in the large splash pool below the breach in the main cofferdam, where turbulence caused by the pour of water through the narrow opening had created an impassable rapid. Within forty-eight hours, that estimate had to be revised upward to over a thousand. The Chinook breeding cycle operates within very narrow temporal limits, and if these fish were delayed too long here at the Oxbow, they would not be able to spawn. It was obvious that passage facilities to get them beyond Brownlee would have to be arranged immediately if the run were to be saved.

And now began one of the saddest tragedies in the history of Hells Canyon, in which a bad situation managed to become compounded by human error into a major disaster. The Idaho Power Company must bear the brunt of the responsibility for what happened—a little less cost-cutting and a little more foresight would have prevented it all—but the fisheries agencies are not entirely blameless. The actions of agency personnel over the next few days, the confusing and often contradictory recommendations they made to the power company, and the constant, compulsive tinkering they engaged in as they attempted to improve the rescue operation are strikingly reminiscent of the general in the old tale who mounted his horse and rode off in all directions. When it was over, a major resource lay dying, and no amount of wishful thinking, name-calling, or research money could ever bring it back.

The problem boiled down to finding an alternative to the decommissioned trap to capture the fish for transfer to the trucks that were standing by to lift them above Brownlee. The power company proposed that this be done by a combination of seining and dip-netting. The biologists disagreed. They wanted a temporary trap constructed near the breach in the cofferdam, complete with stub ladder, finger weir, and trapping hopper. They suggested that the ladder pools should be made eight feet square. The next day, with excavating equipment already on hand, they revised the design to include one pool twelve feet square. Still later, a gate six feet wide was added to one side of the twelve-foot pool. Three days after the trap was originally suggested, construction on it finally began, and four days after that—and a week after the emergency had arisen—the stub ladder was completed. The trap had yet to be installed at the top of it, and the pipe for introducing water into it was not yet laid. The pipe was there, and there were pipefitters to work with it, but they were standing around twiddling their thumbs. No one had thought to provide them with a crane.

While this temporary trap was getting not-built, a stopgap dip-netting operation was under way. It was a disaster. Because of water conditions, the dipnetting could only be successful at one point on the Idaho shore. All the facilities for transporting the fish to Brownlee were on the Oregon shore. So they couldn't just be dumped into the hopper trucks; they had to be transferred across the river first. In the beginning, this was done by tying individual fish into plastic bags, floating them several hundred yards downstream to a boat landing, and rowing them across with the bags tied to the side of a boat and immersed in the river. Later, a high-line was rigged up, with a waterproof hopper that could be moved back and forth across the river. That was better, but it was still too much handling for the nervous systems of the fish to tolerate, and many of them died before they could be released into the reservoir above Brownlee. The stink of dead salmon began to hang over the canyon like a pall.

Repairs to the permanent trap were completed by October 1, and preparations began to redivert the river through the Oxbow tunnel. The temporary trap had been in operation for a week by this time, and that and the dipnetting had managed to pass an estimated 3,500 fish around Brownlee, but even that large number seemed like a mere drop in the bucket. Thousands remained in the river, most of them congregated in the large pool below the cofferdam breach. And there were ugly rumors floating around that half the fish that had been "saved" had been dumped on the shores of Brownlee Reservoir dead and had been quickly trucked off and buried, "so," as one unidentified Morrison-Knudsen worker put it, "as not to be conspicuous." Cornered by reporters, power company president Roach was testy about that rumor. "I'm sure it isn't true," he snapped, adding pointedly that "the procedures we are using for handling fish have been and are under the direction of representatives of the fishery agencies." He continued to insist that the runs would not be "materially damaged." The fisheries people disagreed: They were privately predicting losses of up to ten thousand fish. And the worst was yet to come.

Rediversion of the river began late at night on October 6, with the dismantling of the cofferdam across the mouth of the upstream tunnel. This was in accord with the plan worked out by the fisheries personnel. The theory was that the salmon withdrew from the dam area at night anyway and that a rapid drying up of the river at that time should drive them even further downstream, where they could be picked up by the newly repaired permanent trap. Unfortunately, no one told the salmon about this, and they failed to cooperate. By midday on October 7 it was evident that a major disaster was brewing. The flow of water over the breach in the cofferdam had slowed to a trickle, the outflow from the big splash pool below it had dried up, and the fish in the pool—thousands of them, virtually the entire run—were stranded.

Salmon are big fish, and they use oxygen rapidly. Without an inflow of fresh, aerated water into the pool, it was evident that the dissolved oxygen would quickly be used up and the fish would die. The urgency of the situation was not lost on the fisheries observers, and they sent out a frantic request for pumps. These were located and brought in, but the effort was too little and too late. On August 4, 1959, one of the fisheries personnel, Robert T. Gunsolus, wrote a succinct account of the next few hours for the Fish Commission of Oregon:

> Shortly after 1:00 P.M. the water supply to the stranded fish failed and at 2:15 P.M. the first fish was observed to rise to the surface, turn belly up, and sink slowly from sight. This act together with frantic dashes across the surface was evidence of the impending catastrophe. The request for pumped water was constantly pressed, but the rapidly receding water on the gradually sloping upstream side of the breach made it necessary for the pipe fitters to continually re-rig the pump intake. Ten c.f.s. of pumped water was finally obtained at 3:07 P.M. At 3:15 P.M. the water supply failed when the intake was once again stranded. Shortly thereafter compressed air was introduced into the pool and within minutes the fish remaining alive responded to the increased oxygen. It was estimated that at least half the fish in the pool were lost. When the success of the compressed air was obvious, attempts at pumping water ceased.

The compressed air came from a drill compressor that happened to be standing nearby. Gunsolus did not say—possibly because he was too embarrassed to do so—that the suggestion to use it had to be made by one of the Morrison-Knudsen construction engineers. None of the seven fishery agency people present seems to have been able to think of anything but pumps and fresh water.

When the living fish had been captured and removed and the pool drained, more than four thousand dead salmon were recovered from the bottom of it. Most had died in a single dark hour on that sunny October afternoon. The market value alone of those decaying carcasses would have been in excess of $24,000; the monetary loss from their failure to spawn was literally incalculable. It was one of the greatest anadromous fish disasters in history.

iii

Deplorable as it was, the Oxbow incident had two positive, re-deeming features: It focused public attention on the problem of fish versus dams on the Snake River; and it demonstrated—with a conclusiveness no rhetoric could possibly match—just how far those problems still were from solution. It had been a widespread article of faith that technology was making great strides forward in its ability to pass migrant fish around high dams. There were peo-ple who still believed in it after the Oxbow disaster, but their num-bers had shrunk drastically. In the government fish agencies, jokes began making the rounds to the effect that the dam builders, like Hitler with the Jews, had found a "Final Solution" to the salmon problem.

The immediate practical effect of this loss of faith was to give a strong boost to efforts toward establishing a moratorium on fur-ther dam building in the middle Snake until it could be proved that the fish runs would not suffer any more damage. Such a proposal had been put forward by Idaho's Sen. Frank Church nearly a year earlier, but it had received little attention; now, suddenly, everyone wanted to hop aboard. Secretary of the Interior Fred Seaton wrote to Secretary of the Army Wilber Brucker—releasing a copy to the press—suggesting that the two government dam-building agencies, Army's Corp of Engineers and Interior's Bureau of Reclamation, should support such a moratorium. The Oregon State Water Re-sources Board began a round of hearings on an order withdrawing the Nez Perce-Mountain Sheep area from development pending solution of the fisheries problem. And even the prodam National Hells Canyon Association approved a resolution urging Congress to authorize a thorough study of fisheries problems in the middle Snake (reserving the area for federal development when the studies were completed). In the House of Representatives, as the Eighty-sixth Congress opened, Al Ullman thumped hard for "conditional authorization" of Nez Perce. "I am not saying," he emphasized to his colleagues, "that the Nez Perce Dam be constructed while the fish problem remains unsolved. But I am strongly urging that this stretch of the Snake River be reserved for optimum development at a later date when there *is* a solution to the fish problem." Across the Hill in the Senate, Richard Neuberger was tackling the problem head on, seeking authorization and funding for a five-year crash research program "realistically solving the apparent impasse between fish and high dams." Neither bill would get anywhere, but both were symbolic of the times, which were, as Bob Dylan was to write a few years later, "a-changin'."

In March 1959, the Corps of Engineers opened a set of hearings on a new revision of the old 308 Report and found that attitudes had altered considerably since the last go-around. At each meeting the emphasis seemed to be on the fish problem. In Portland, the corps heard Oregon's new young governor, Mark O. Hatfield, urge adoption of the fisheries moratorium. In Washington, D.C., the corps heard the National Wildlife Federation call for a reevaluation of the Pleasant Valley site to avoid blocking the Imnaha, while the AFL-CIO called for the building of Nez Perce, but only after a "full-scale fish passage research program." But it was at the Lewiston hearing that the most significant development occurred. Here, while the Pacific Northwest Power Company and the National Hells Canyon Association traded body blows, a group of eastern Oregon Izaac Walton League chapters repudiated their national organization's official stand in support of High Mountain Sheep and issued a strong condemnation of *both* projects. It was the first major surfacing of preservationist sentiment for Hells Canyon, the first recognition that perhaps the best dam for the big canyon was no dam at all. This was not recognized by either party to the dispute: Both the Nez Perce advocates and the Pacific Northwest Power Company chose to brush the idea aside and ignore it. That was a mistake. It was a small spark, to be sure, this militant stand by a few dissident radicals in the IWL; but it had a great latent fire behind it.

In September there came, almost quietly, the last act of the Oxbow Incident, as the fisheries subcommittee of the Columbia Basin Interagency Commission met in Spokane, Washington, to hear Oregon Fish Commission Director Albert M. Day tell about the Brownlee skimmer. He had one word for it: "murderous." The young Chinook seemed to be passing through it or under it at will, and instead of being skimmed off to be trucked downstream they were being swept over Brownlee Dam. Great flocks of gulls had gathered to feed on the dead and dying fingerlings in the dam's tail-

race. "On August 6," reported Day, "the research barge traps below Brownlee had picked up 97 young Chinook salmon, of which
80 were dead. On August 7, the traps caught 149 Chinook, with 143
of them dead. . . . From our best estimates, at least 1,000,000
fingerlings should have passed downstream, but no more than
one-fourth that number can be accounted for." He told how headwaters studies had shown that only about half of the adult fish that
had survived the tragedy at the Oxbow had managed to spawn.
"Now we are watching the offspring of that ill-fated run in their attempt to return to the Pacific Ocean," he said, and added succinctly: "They are in trouble."

Day was right: The fish were in trouble. The skimmer never did
work properly. In the beginning it was plagued by small holes and
tears that managed to pass whole schools of follow-the-leader
fingerlings, one at a time. Later, it was discovered that the plastic
the net was made of softened in the water to a point where the fish
could swim right through it as if it weren't there. During the winter
of 1959 one of the trapping barges sank, taking out nearly an acre
of net on the Oregon shore. Four years later, the experiment would
be given up, the net would be withdrawn from the water, and all attempts to pass migratory fish at the Oxbow-Brownlee-Hells Canyon project would cease. The upper Snake runs, the great masses of
big, silver-gray fish leaping upstream through the rapids of Hells
Canyon, would be only a memory.

In January 1960, the Oregon State Water Resources Board, after
a week of intensive hearings on the subject, gave the Pacific
Northwest Power Company's High Mountain Sheep project its re-
luctant approval. Shortly afterward, the Federal Power Commission announced that hearings had finally been scheduled on the
project: They would open on March 21 in Washington, D.C. It
appeared that a third replay of the public power/private power
controversy, as lately performed at Hells Canyon Creek and at
Pleasant Valley, was in the offing; the people of the Northwest, sti-
fling yawns, prepared to go through the whole thing again. But it
was not to be. On March 15, six days before the hearings were to
begin, a new player strode suddenly upon the stage, and the com-
plexion of the drama rapidly assumed a whole new—and strikingly
vivid—color.

9

High Mountain Sheep:
The Second Nez Perce War

What happened, basically, on that fateful 1960 Ides of March, was
that the promoters of public power grew tired of always being on
the defensive in the middle Snake River and decided that it was time
for them to take over the ball for a while. The new tack: for a public agency to file a directly competing application with the FPC for
a license to develop the Nez Perce site.

The body chosen by public power groups to make the Nez Perce
application was the Washington Public Power Supply System
(WPPSS, pronounced "whoops"), a group of sixteen public utility
districts from the state of Washington that had banded together in
1957 to form a joint operating company. The reasons behind this
particular choice have always been a matter of some dispute.
"Contrary to the belief of some people," says Owen Hurd, general
manager of WPPSS from its founding till his retirement in 1971,
"the action taken in making this filing was not a calculated move to
prevent the Northwest Power Company from obtaining a license. It
was an effort to insure maximum comprehensive development and
making available power at the lowest possible cost to the Supply
System and its members and others in the Northwest." Hugh Smith
takes a different and somewhat more cynical view of the WPPSS
license application. He does not deny that WPPSS, once commit-

ted, became genuinely enthusiastic about building the project; but he continues to maintain that the original filing was made primarily to keep the private utilities out of the middle Snake River. "They looked around for somebody who might move over there," he chuckles, "and the Supply System was sitting there with nothing to do, and running up a rather substantial bill paying Owen Hurd's salary—it was a convenient chosen instrument, and they dropped it in."

A close examination of the record tends to support Smith's view more closely than Hurd's. Internal memoranda from the files of the Northwest Public Power Association (now in the library of the University of Washington in Seattle) indicate strongly the political nature of the Nez Perce filing. "It is understood," reads one typical memo, "that the Washington PUD operating group may soon file for a preliminary permit to study the site. This group would have preferred status over any subsequent move by PNPC to get into the river again. This would constitute a good holding action until the momentum for a federal development at Nez Perce could be made to roll. . . ." Subsequent letters, memos, and meeting minutes trace quite clearly the course to the final choice of WPPSS and indicate that it was, indeed, designed as a delaying move. Filing on the High Mountain Sheep site itself was considered and rejected because it was felt that it wouldn't be credible in the light of public power's oft-stated preference for the Nez Perce site. A considerable amount of time, paper, and postage was spent deciding precisely who should intervene and figuring out how they could get around the problem of using all that power once they got hold of it. When the Supply System was finally chosen, there was a scramble to get the papers ready in time to file the application before the hearings on PNPC's license request could begin. With the filing came requests to consolidate the hearings with those for PNPC and to delay the whole proceedings in order to give WPPSS time to prepare its case. The task was done, and the voluminous paper work completed, with six days to spare. WPPSS and the Northwest Public Power Association sat smugly back to await the results.

ii

Pacific Northwest Power Company lawyers filed a bristling protest brief on May 6, 1960, with the Federal Power Commission, couched in terms that seem remarkably intemperate for a legal paper. The Supply System, it said, ". . . has not qualified and cannot in the future qualify under the Federal Power Act as an applicant for a license. . . . The application for Nez Perce is not filed in good faith, but to delay and prevent PNP from providing an economic power supply for its customers. The public power group is not financially capable of accepting a license, constructing the project if a license were granted, or owning and operating the project if constructed." WPPSS took few steps to lay these accusations to rest. On the contrary, in a curious reversal of roles, the public power body seemed bent on acting with an arrogance and a unilateral disregard for regulations and for public opinion that were strikingly reminiscent of the Idaho Power Company's role in the earlier Hells Canyon controversy. Thus, while PNPC was applying for—and receiving—the relevant permits from the Idaho Department of Reclamation and the Oregon Hydroelectric Board, WPPSS (citing IPC's precedent) refused to submit itself to the state licensing process. In response to a joint statement by the Oregon, Idaho, and Washington fisheries commissions that they were "unequivocally opposed to the construction of the Nez Perce Dam" because "we have absolutely no faith in the bald assurance of engineers that facilities will be provided and that they will be adequate to pass fish and support the fish runs," WPPSS would only reply—ignoring the total failure at Brownlee—that they were "confident" that the problem was being solved and that they were prepared to go ahead with construction as soon as a license could be granted to them. The Supply System did bring suit in U.S. District Court in Portland to test the legal question of whether or not they had the authority to build outside their home state—and then, when Judge John F. Kilkenny ruled against them, supported a motion by the Washington State Department of Conservation asking the FPC to disregard the judge's ruling. It was a performance that did little to bolster anyone's faith in the righteousness of the public power cause, and little by little that faith, and the support it had generated, began to slip away. Wayne Morse and Al Ullman were uncharacteristically silent; Washington senator Warren G. Magnusun, a Democrat from WPPSS's own state who had heretofore strongly supported public power, told the press he was "not sympathetic" to the Supply System's application. Lloyd Tupling, the former general manager of the National Hells Canyon Association and campaign manager for Al Ullman, who had since served as an aide to Sen. Richard L. Neuberger until the senator's death from a stroke six days before the WPPSS filing on Nez Perce was announced, began edging toward support of a no-dams-at-all policy that would eventually lead him onto the national staff of the nation's most powerful environmental lobbying organization, the Sierra Club.

The WPPSS application had brought about an abrupt cancellation of the March 21 hearing date for PNPC, and a rescheduling of the consolidated hearings for June 16. Subsequent motions for delay by WPPSS attorneys resulted in two additional postponements, first to October 17 and then to November 4. By this time, an important new set of interveners had entered the proceedings. Up to this point, all parties to any FPC action in the Hells Canyon stretch of the Snake River had been lined up on one side or the other of the public/private power controversy. Now, however, a group of eleven fisheries interests—two sportsmen's groups, five commercial fishermen's organizations, and four Indian tribes—horrified by the specter of Nez Perce and, one suspects, moved into action by the Oxbow incident and the failure of the skimmer at Brownlee, intervened officially in the proceedings in opposition to *both* applications. The principal spokesman for this group, James H. Cellars of the Columbia River Salmon & Tuna Packers' Association (CRS&TPA), told the press that if any further high dams were built in Hells Canyon his organization was prepared to demand a share of the revenue from sale of power as a compensation for loss of fish runs. Nez Perce was the worse of the two, but even High Mountain Sheep would do substantial damage to the industry. Cellars moved successfully to get the fisheries phase of the hearings transferred from Washington, D.C., to Portland, where more local witnesses could appear and where the publicity, not incidentally, would be greater. He also managed to void, almost single-handedly, a resolution by the Pacific Marine Fisheries Commission in favor of High Mountain Sheep as a means of blocking Nez Perce; the resolution was actually passed but was rescinded the next day after pressure on several key delegates caused them to switch their votes. It was a striking example of power politics and a clear indication that the utility companies, both public and private, were going to find this new set of intervenors a tough bunch to deal with.

The technical phase of the hearings dragged on through the winter and into the new year, finally drawing to a close on February 17; the fisheries phase was set to open a month later in Portland. The Pacific Northwest Power Company pronounced itself highly pleased with things so far: The Supply System, said PNPC president John Burke, had "experienced a serious breakdown of its case" in the Washington phase of the hearings, where "searching cross-examination again and again revealed the inadequacy of engineering and geological study, and the unpreparedness of the Nez Perce group to go forward." His own company, on the other hand, could start building "within sixty days" of reception of a license and was prepared to foot a payroll that he predicted would ultimately exceed seventy million dollars.

WPPSS, at least as far as the newspapers were concerned, remained mum.

iii

Portland's old Federal Courthouse Building is a squat, seven-story structure of pink sandstone that sits on the crest of a small rise one block west and one block south of Hugh Smith's law office in the Public Service Building. It was here, in the wood-paneled top-floor courtroom of the U.S. District Court of Appeals, that the Federal Power Commission met on March 13, 1961, to begin what the *Oregonian* called the "precedent-shattering" fisheries stage of the combined hearings on the Nez Perce and High Mountain Sheep dam license applications. The ground rules were simple. There would be no direct testimony permitted, no new witnesses called. Counsel for the opposing sides would be limited to cross-examination only, on the basis of the 1,500 pages of written testi-

mony already submitted by the selected witnesses. However, while
this cross-examination was the only thing permitted, it was also
mandatory, and any witness who failed to appear for questioning
would have his testimony stricken from the record.

Intervenors would be allowed equal footing in the cross-
examination with counsel for the principals, Pacific Northwest
Power and the Washington Public Power Supply System.

On Saturday, March 11, with the hearing date two days off,
PNPC and WPPSS held press conferences in Portland to unveil
their separate plans for the handling of anadromous fish at the two
rival projects. Neither was what could be called a particularly
modest scheme. At High Mountain Sheep, PNPC proposed a dual
upstream-passage facility, one section to handle the Imnaha run,
the other to handle the remnant upper Snake main stem run that
the fisheries agencies still hoped might be salvaged from Brownlee.
Snake River fish would climb a fifty-foot ladder into a hopper that
was part of an automated tramway arrangement designed to lift
them the remaining six hundred feet over the dam and drop them
into the reservoir; downstream migrants could be caught above
Brownlee, if they could ever get the skimmer to work, and trucked
to below Mountain Sheep. The Imnaha runs would be handled a little differently. Separated from the fish bound for the upper Snake
by the introduction of pure Imnaha River water into a parallel ladder, the Imnaha fish would also be lifted by tramway—but instead
of being dumped into the reservoir, they would be deposited in the
north end of a seventeen-mile-long canal that would hug the edge
of the reservoir all the way to the head of the Imnaha River arm,
where they would enter a small separate impoundment behind a
twenty-foot-high diversion dam from which they could swim upstream at will. Downstream migrants would be headed off from the
reservoir by the same diversion dam, would swim down the same
canal, be placed in a separate tramcar from the adults, and lowered
into the river below the tailrace. In order to closely approximate the
original riverine conditions the fish were used to, the canal would
be made as much like a natural streambed as possible, with gravel
riffles and resting ponds and, wherever possible, natural building
materials instead of concrete.

WPPSS's plans were considerably different, and a lot less sophisticated. They made no effort to separate the three distinct runs—the Salmon, the Imnaha, and the upper Snake—at the dam but left that task to the fish themselves in the reservoir. Upstream migrants would be led into a mile-long fish ladder with a 270-foot rise that would be partly in a lighted tunnel through the Oregon abutment and partly across the face of the dam itself. At the head of this ladder they would be introduced into a "fish lock" leading to a slanting tunnel through the dam that would enter the reservoir 200 feet below the full-pool level (WPPSS engineers agreed that there might be some harm to the fish caused by the great pressures at this depth but argued that it was necessary because of the structure's tremendous seasonal drawdown). Fingerlings entering the Salmon and Imnaha arms of the reservoir from above would be captured by diversion facilities similar to those proposed by PNPC for the Imnaha, transported by barge to the forebay of the dam, and dumped into a helical chute which would spiral down through the dam to the level of the head of the fish ladder, straighten out, and shoot down through the same tunnel holding the ladder to deposit the young fish in the tailrace near the point where their parents had left it a few months before. On the basis of these plans, WPPSS was ready to paint itself as "the only applicant ready to accept the responsibility of preserving the fishery resource of the middle Snake." PNPC, for some reason, disagreed. So did the vast majority of agency personnel and independent intervenors.

The first few days of the hearing were devoted to the PNPC plans and to the testimony of Dr. J. A. R. Hamilton, a fisheries biologist who had been employed by the company to help create those plans. The cross-examination was handled by Evelyn Cooper, the District of Columbia lawyer who had handled the interventions and court appeals in the Hells Canyon and Pleasant Valley battles for the National Hells Canyon Association. Under intense questioning, Hamilton admitted that the design of the High Mountain Sheep fishways was largely experimental: Though it was made up of ideas that had all worked elsewhere, they had never been tried together as a single package before, or on such a grand scale. He also stated unequivocably that *all* dams cause damage to the fisheries resource. This was not helping his company any, but it was not the worst blow they would suffer in those first few hearings days. A far more important loss was the withdrawal from testimony of two key government witnesses, L. Edward Perry and Richard T. Pressey of the United States Bureau of Commercial Fisheries. The new Kennedy administration, acting through Secretary of the Interior Stewart Udall, had written to the FPC seeking a four-year moratorium on middle Snake dams until "proven methods are found to protect the downstream migrants" on the Snake and Salmon rivers. Because of this proposed construction freeze, Udall had directed Perry and Pressey not to present themselves for cross-examination. Under the rules, this would mean that their testimony would be excluded from the record. It was testimony that was highly damaging to WPPSS, and Hugh Smith badly wanted it to remain.

On March 17, four days into the hearings, the spotlight shifted from PNPC to WPPSS and the Nez Perce fish facilities. The plans for these facilities had been drawn up by a highway engineer, William R. Martin, with the assistance of fisheries biological consultant Harlan B. Holmes; both men were present to submit to cross-examination, Martin going first. Smith and Cellars worked him over pretty badly, eliciting for the record the fact that it would take the average salmon more than eleven hours to climb a 270-foot ladder and that the effects of pressure and low oxygen content in deep water and the ability of upstream migrants to find their way through long, deep reservoirs were both areas where more research was desperately needed. Attorney Joseph T. Mijich, acting for the Washington State Sportsman's Council, brought out the results of tests at Brownlee that had shown oxygen content of the reservoir water at 150 feet to be only 3.2 parts per million, well below the 5 ppm needed to support fish life. Salmon would be introduced into the Nez Perce reservoir at 200 feet. On the witness stand, Martin squirmed. "If there is a problem here," he said finally, "I'm sure we can design around it." He turned the witness chair over to Holmes, who said that "intensive experiments with fingerling salmon" in the thirty-five years he had been with the Fish and Wildlife Service had shown no effects at all from high pressure, and that recent experiments by the International Pacific Salmon Fisheries Commission showed the same thing. He also pointed out, rightly, that what was true for Brownlee would not necessarily be true for

Nez Perce. It was a good beginning; but unfortunately for WPPSS, things would not continue to go so nicely.

The turning point, and the most damaging single moment so far for the Supply System's case, came midway through the ninth day of testimony. Under close questioning by Smith, Holmes admitted that he "did not know" whether the Nez Perce Dam would cause substantial harm to fish and stated that he would not approve of its construction if there were any doubt remaining. Smith then attempted to get him to answer yes or no to whether or not he agreed with WPPSS's Owen Hurd, who had stated that the fish problems at Nez Perce "have been solved." Cooper shot to her feet with a vigorous objection, which was sustained by Examiner William Levy. Smith, nodding, rephrased the question: Did Holmes think that the facilities, as now designed, would solve the fish passage problem? And Holmes, caught in the trap and under oath, responded with four quiet words: "Not in my opinion."

WPPSS's own consulting biologist had been forced to admit that the Nez Perce fish facilities would not work.

The rest was anticlimactic, and it went rather quickly. A parade of witnesses from the various government fisheries agencies entered the witness stand to comment on the two plans. They made it quite clear that they would prefer no dam at all, but that if one had to be built, High Mountain Sheep was vastly superior from a fisheries standpoint. Forrest Hauck of the Idaho Fish and Game Commission estimated that Nez Perce would reduce the present Snake fishery to one-twelfth of its present size. Bill Pitney for the Oregon Game Commission said that the louver trap system planned for Nez Perce had not worked satisfactorily in tests at Oregon's Gold Ray Dam on the Rogue River and that he would not recommend its installation elsewhere. Edward M. Mains for the Washington State Department of Fisheries was the most emphatic of all. Nez Perce, he said, would negate the entire efforts of the fishery development program of the state of Washington. Aside from the passage problem itself, there would be a serious loss of spawning beds by inundation, and no replacement of these would be possible. Fifty-five percent of the fish passing the Nez Perce site were spring Chinook, which cannot be successfully raised in hatcheries. WPPSS's plans, in short, would be a disaster.

Perry and Pressey did not appear, but part of their testimony made its way into the newspapers. Pressey's testimony was in direct contradiction to Holmes's on the effects of pressure on salmon: He said that tests had shown it brought about "reduced sensitivity," which caused the fish to become lethargic. He also called the helical chute idea untried, and pointed out that similar *straight* chutes caused young salmon to lose their sense of equilibrium and become easy prey for bigger fish and for predatory animals and birds. Perry summed up his own opinion in a single devastating sentence: "In view of the numerous experimental features applied to the proposed facilities at Nez Perce, which has resulted in a pyramiding of risks . . . it is my opinion that there is a near certainty of the rapid decline of the Salmon River run if the project is built."

The Portland hearings concluded on March 28. Two weeks later, on April 10—concurrent with the reopening of the hearings in Washington, D.C.—the Army Corps of Engineers released its update of the 308 Report, calling for the building of High Mountain Sheep instead of Nez Perce because of the fisheries problem. And two weeks after *that,* on April 24, WPPSS submitted an amendment to its application before the FPC suggesting that if the commission found that High Mountain Sheep was actually a better project than Nez Perce, the Supply System would like to formally request to be allowed to build the thing in place of the Pacific Northwest Power Company, under the public-preference clause of the Federal Power Act. A certain amount of purpling of faces took place at this announcement, not all of it at PNPC.

In July 1961 there was news from up-canyon: The first power from the new Oxbow plant was going on-line. Acting out of a keen sense of publicity, Idaho Power had searched out two still-living members of the construction crew that had worked on the original Oxbow plant in the days of Copperfield, H. L. Senger and C. O. Crane, and had them on the stand to flip the transmission switches that would send the first 55,000 kilowatts surging out to the load centers in southwestern Idaho. The remaining 165,000, they assured everyone, would be ready by fall. Three weeks later, still in July, work was begun on the road to the Hells Canyon site. Idaho Power appeared to be rolling forward on schedule. Little was said of the fisheries problems, of the total failure of the skimmer or of the fact that the attorneys general for the states of Idaho, Washington, and Oregon had publicly announced that they were considering a three-state suit against the power company to seek damages for the loss of the salmon and steelhead runs.

The hearings record in the PNPC/WPSS battle was closed permanently on September 12, and by April 1962 the proceedings were entirely in the hands of Examiner William Levy. The principal question remaining was what conclusions Levy would come up with from his examination of the truckload of materials involved in the case since PNPC's original license application four years previously, and how those conclusions would affect the final ruling by the Federal Power Commission. That, at least, was how things seemed until June 28, 1962—the day that Stewart Udall abandoned his long-stated support for a moratorium on dam construction in Hells Canyon and announced that he was putting the Interior Department on record in favor of a federal dam at the High Mountain Sheep site. Suddenly, there were *three* separate proposals for a dam in the lower end of Hells Canyon—one private, one municipal, and one federal. And the only thing clear about the situation was that nothing was going to be clear for a long time.

iv

"The reason that Interior got in is one of these oddities," Hugh Smith says today. "The public power people brought considerable pressure on Udall to support them. And there actually was a letter on Udall's desk addressed to the Federal Power Commission in which the Department of the Interior was to endorse Nez Perce, to be built by WPPSS. We got word of the existence of the letter . . . and thereupon passed this information on to certain rather influential people in the fish and wildlife operation, and at four that afternoon one of the influential people was in Udall's office telling Udall that he'd disappear from the face of the earth as far as political future was concerned if he ever signed that letter. As a consequence, the letter was not signed. This, however, left Interior in the awkward position of having no position at all. So somebody in Interior figured out that what WPPSS was really interested in was keeping the project out of our hands, and they'd be just as happy if the project were built by the federal government." He chuckles. "They misunderstood what WPPSS's position was at that point. WPPSS *wanted to build the project*. And they were as furious at the intervention as we were."

"Furious" is hardly the word for it. "Mad as a wet hen" might come a little closer. Both the Supply System and the Pacific Northwest Power Company were utterly, completely, and wholeheartedly irate. And they lost no time, and little kindness, in speaking out on the subject. "Pacific Northwest Power designed the project," said a tight-lipped Kinsey Robinson, "and is committed to operate it in full coordination with the Northwest Power Pool. . . . The Secretary's action today is a contradiction of the Administration's claims" of support for cooperation between private power firms and the government. WPPSS's Owen Hurd issued a statement from Kennewick, Washington, calling Udall's action "irresponsible": The letter from the Secretary, he said, "smacks of political interference with the Federal Power Commission." Within ten days, both applicants had filed formal briefs with the commission opposing Udall's stand. They were supported by the FPC staff, by virtually every one of the independent intervenors, and even by federal dam advocate Sen. Wayne Morse, who wrote to the FPC to express his opinion that Udall should be held to his original advocacy of a moratorium at least long enough for fisheries studies to be completed. Examiner Levy added these papers to the stack already in front of him, dived back in, and promptly disappeared from the sight of man. Wags among the dam-watchers began laying odds as to when—if ever—he would return.

As it turned out, the wait was not as long as some people had feared. On October 8, 1962, exactly three months from the filing of the PNPC and WPPSS briefs denouncing Udall's federal-dam stand, Levy emerged from the maze with a tersely written formal opinion that found for the private Pacific Northwest Power Company on all counts. "The High Mountain Sheep plan," he wrote, "emerges from this record as the comprehensive plan of development for the common reach which provides for prompt and optimum multi-purpose development of the water resource under the standards of the Federal Power Act." He rejected WPPSS's claim to priority under the public-power preference clause of the act on the basis that PNPC had a substantial chronological priority, dating back to its preliminary permit application in 1955. WPPSS should not be permitted "to skim the cream off milk produced by PNPC's efforts. . . . If a municipal loser could be licensed merely by offering to build its rival's successful plan, it would be foolhardy for private utilities to enter such a loaded proceeding . . . their investigation of prospective sites, as envisaged by the Federal Power Act, would cease." In such a case, "the public interest would be the ultimate loser."

Federal construction, as proposed by Udall, was rejected on the same grounds.

WPPSS called Levy's opinion "superficial, misleading, thoroughly arbitrary, and rife with error." Udall, who had heretofore issued only letters of opinion in the case, moved Interior into the position of formal intervenor. The full five-member commission—by now, all Kennedy appointees—noted these things, heard oral arguments in a series of stormy sessions ending on May 20, 1963, and took the case "under advisement." Eight months later, on February 5, 1964, the verdict finally came down. It upheld Levy's recommendations on all important points. PNPC would be given a fifty-year license to build and operate the project: WPPSS's amended application and the intervention by the Interior Department were both found to be without merit.

Kinsey Robinson called it "a welcome decision in the ten-year struggle of PNPC . . . to build a great civil works project that will provide power for expansion of this area." The *Oregonian*, editorializing emphatically on the issue, called it the "right Snake Dam." But the split nature of the decision—a 3 to 2 vote, with the minority favoring WPPSS's application to build High Mountain Sheep including the commission's new chairman, Joseph C. Swindler of Tennessee—made it virtually certain to be appealed through the courts. There was no comment from the fisheries interests, but one was not really needed. At Brownlee, the dismally failing skimmer had been abandoned completely, withdrawn from the forebay of the dam to lie in tattered disarray on the shore before being hauled off to as inconspicuous a disposal as possible. The upper Snake runs were dead, and with them any real hope of ever attaining fish passage over high dams. The commission and the courts had been following this development with considerable interest. In fact, the commission had been forced to rewrite Idaho Power's license because of it, and there was no need to dramatize it to them. Even WPPSS would soon have to admit it: The Nez Perce plans were doomed. It would be Mountain Sheep or nothing.

v

On March 6, 1964, thirty days after the Federal Power Commission's ruling on High Mountain Sheep had come down, the Washington Public Power Supply System—as it had been expected to do—filed a petition for rehearing and stay of the Pacific Northwest Power Company's license. As with the National Hells Canyon Association's appeal of the Idaho Power Company Hells Canyon license ten years before, this step was looked on mostly as a formality, a means of proving that all procedural avenues had been exhausted before turning to the courts. Like the earlier case, too, there was a good chance that the whole thing would become moot before it was settled. Hugh Smith had already given his opinion that the FPC action "confers a valid license and . . . will not be impaired by an appeal to the courts, unless and until a filing is made." He made it quite clear that PNPC would go ahead with construction, as Idaho Power had done. The company formally accepted the license on March 9 and rapidly began fulfilling the pre-construction conditions the commission had ordered, putting together study teams in geology and recreation and preparing the recommended modifications of its plans for the project. This work was interrupted temporarily in April by a surprise announcement from the FPC that it was granting a rehearing; but this turned out to be not a decision on the merits of the rehearing petitions but only a ploy to give the commission more time to rule on those merits. If nothing had been done within thirty days of the filing of the petitions for rehearing, the petitions would have become legally dead. The commission, as it turned out, needed closer to sixty days. At the end of that period, on April 30, the final ruling came down. The original decision was upheld, subject to certain very minor modifications, and the request for a stay pending a court appeal was turned down. The vote was the same 3 to 2 split that had been evident in the original February ruling. Pressed for comment on behalf of WPPSS, Evelyn Cooper would only say: "We expect to appeal." PNPC went back to the river.

WPPSS filed its appeal on July 26, 1964, in the U.S. District Court of Appeals for Washington, D.C.—the same three-judge court that had heard the appeal of the Hells Canyon case a decade earlier. The Washington State Department of Conservation filed concurrently with WPPSS; Udall and the Department of Interior filed separately three days later. Neither the WPPSS petition nor that filed by the Department of the Interior made PNPC a party to the proceedings, but this was not unexpected, and the utility was ready with a petition for intervention, which it presented to the court within twenty-four hours of Udall's filing, stating that PNPC had a "direct, vital, and substantial interest, and is the real party in interest in the proceedings and in the outcome thereof." A long period of silence ensued. On the river, PNPC pressed forward with its final geological reconnaissance. In the dark narrows where the *Imnaha* had gone down, drills chattered into the river bottom and the cliff faces, spewing up what would ultimately amount to almost two-thirds of a mile of core samples. A blue-ribbon panel of independent consultants was put together to evaluate the results. The court may have been standing still; the company was not. Daily, the time for the building of cofferdams and the pouring of concrete came closer and closer.

On April 15, 1965, the court of appeals—crippled by the absence of one of its members, Judge George T. Washington, who was seriously ill—heard oral presentations in the cases of WPPSS versus FPC and Udall versus FPC.

On September 22 the court ordered rearguments in both cases. There was no official word as to why this had been done, but speculation attributed it to Judge Washington's illness.

On November 16 the rehearing took place. Judge Washington was still absent; in fact, he had retired six days before. In his place was a new judge, a man whose name was unfamiliar to the American public at that time but who would, with his next promotion three years later, become something of a household word. The man: Warren E. Burger, fifteenth chief justice of the United States Supreme Court.

On March 24, 1966, more than two full years after the granting of the license and twenty-one months from the initiation of the appeal, the appeals court ruling finally came down. The decision was unanimous, 3 to 0 in favor of the Federal Power Commission and the Pacific Northwest Power Company. "It would," said the court, "be manifestly unfair to one who has expended large sums of money over a long period of time in the necessary investigation if, upon completion and subsequent application for a license, a state or municipality could step in and reap the fruit of his labors by obtaining a license for the site so laboriously determined upon, merely because of the preference granted by the Federal Power Act." That took care of WPPSS. The federal case was rejected just as strenuously. Udall's intervention, the court held, had been too little and too late; there was no concrete evidence that federal construction had ever seriously been considered. An elated Kinsey Robinson called the decision "a great boost for continuing economic progress of the Pacific Northwest," and warned that "a last-ditch appeal to the Supreme Court would be a costly disservice to the entire region." Nevertheless, both Owen Hurd of WPPSS and Stewart Udall of the Interior Department announced that the appeal would be taken up. PNPC bowed to the inevitable; rather than risk more money on a project it might shortly have to abandon, the company submitted a motion to the FPC requesting an extension of the license period to permit construction to be held off until July of 1968. The motion was granted. Work on the river ground to a halt.

The importance of what happened next cannot possibly be overstated.

The Supreme Court is, of course, the highest arbiter in the American judicial system. It does not make law—that is solely the prerogative of Congress—but it is the final authority on what laws, once written, mean, and its decision is binding. There can be no further appeal. This means that what the Court says and what it does are terribly important. It does not accept trivial cases, and its standards for judging what is trivial and what is not are of necessity very high. The Court takes only those cases in which there is a clear difference of opinion over the meaning of a point of law, and where the outcome will be of national importance. It chooses its case load with extraordinary care. The earlier Hells Canyon case, the argument over the Idaho Power Company dams, had not measured up to those rigid standards. This time around, however, WPPSS felt that it had a case that the Court would hear. The same basic point of law was involved—the precise meaning of the public-preference clause of the Federal Power Act—but this time, instead of a concrete private proposal versus an abstract public proposal, the decision was to be made between two concrete proposals. Furthermore, the Department of the Interior, which had held itself aloof from the earlier case, was very much a party to the current proceedings. That alone made it a national issue. It was time for the argument to be settled, and WPPSS thought that they had the case to settle it.

The petition for review was filed on August 29, 1966, by Evelyn Cooper for WPPSS and by attorneys from the Department of Justice for Interior. It accused the court of appeals of a "revolutionary interpretation of the Federal Power Act" which "reverses the policy of Congress which gives preference to public development of power resources . . . puts all competitive planning of river basin development by both public and private entities into 'deep freeze' for the benefit of a sponsor of an admittedly inferior scheme, and injects insupportable confusion into the administration of public lands and navigable streams under other Federal statutes as well as the Federal Power Act." This was not exactly temperate language, but then, temperance was not its purpose. Its purpose was to achieve a hearing before the Supreme Court, and it succeeded admirably. The word came down on November 7: The Court would put the case on its 1967 docket. WPPSS and its supporters held a small party. A glum Hugh Smith went back to his law library.

The oral arguments that brought Hells Canyon into the august presence of the most powerful court on earth took place on April 11, 1967, before the Doric columns and red velvet draperies of the large courtroom that forms the heart of the Court's white marble building just east of the Capitol in Washington. They were held, as tradition dictates, within a most limited framework, a one-hour presentation from each side, with no cross-examination save by the justices themselves. The scene was quiet, subdued, and almost seductively tranquil ("We are very quiet there," Justice Oliver Wendell Holmes once wrote, "but it is the quiet of a storm center"), and when the red lights flashed on at the benches of the opposing counsel, signaling the end of the formal hearing, it was impossible to tell what was going to happen or how long it would take before anyone knew. Both sides suggested to their backers, and to the press, that they had won. But this was sheer speculation. From behind the great bronze doors that shut the press and the public off from the working half of the Supreme Court building—the half housing the justices' private offices, law library, and conference rooms—came no word, only silence.

The key question to be decided, or so everyone thought, was the meaning of the public-preference clause in the Federal Power Act. Would the Court rule, as the appeals court had, that this clause was not strong enough to overrule a priority claim based on time of filing? If so, then PNPC would win, and they would build the dam. Or would the justices decide that Congress had meant the public-preference clause to be supreme? In that case, there seemed to be two possibilities. The public-preference clause could be held to include municipal corporations such as WPPSS, in which case the FPC would have to grant the Washington firm a license, either for Nez Perce or for High Mountain Sheep; or the claims of the federal government on an interstate waterway such as the Snake could be held to take priority, in which case the FPC would have to order the Interior Department to seek congressional approval of a High Mountain Sheep Dam to be built by the Bureau of Reclamation. There were thus three possible courses that the Court might take in its decision.

No one foresaw that the justices themselves might discover a fourth route—a route that would drastically alter the future policies of the Federal Power Commission and would change the course of history in Hells Canyon for all time.

On May 31, Kinsey Robinson told the annual stockholders' meeting of Pacific Northwest Power that he was "confident" that the Court would rule in the company's favor, and that the ruling could probably be expected in early July. He was wrong on both counts. Just five days later, at the Monday hour reserved for announcements of the Court's decisions, Justice William O. Douglas was called upon to read, in his soft western drawl, the opinion that he had written for the majority in the cases of Udall versus FPC and WPPSS versus FPC. It was, to put it mildly, a bombshell. The Court had found for *none* of the parties to the dispute—not PNPC, not WPPSS, not the Department of the Interior. Instead, the Court had remanded the case to the Federal Power Commission with instructions to rehear the entire proceedings on the basis that not enough consideration had been given—by the commission, by its examiner, or by its staff—to the possibility that the best dam for Hells Canyon might be *no dam at all*. The test, wrote Douglas, is not

> solely whether the region will be able to use the electric power. The test is whether the project will be in the public interest. And that determination can be made only after an exploration of all issues relevant to the "public interest," including future power demand and supply, alternate sources of power, the public interest in preserving reaches of wild rivers and wilderness areas, the preservation of anadromous fish for commercial and recreational purposes, and the protection of wildlife.

The commission, the power companies, and even the public watching the debate had forgotten the fact that what was at stake was more than just public power versus private power, or fish versus dams; what was at stake was the battleground itself, an extraordinary wilderness canyon, the deepest gorge on earth. The commission had tossed this little irrelevancy aside. The Court, in one powerful paragraph, had brought it back.

Part III:
The Politics
of Preservation

The great weakness of government is that those who sit in the decision-making chairs are surrounded by layers of reasons not to do something.

—Walter J. Hickel,
former Secretary of the Interior

10

Back to the Drawing Boards

For Hells Canyon, the 1967 Supreme Court decision was a dramatic turning point.

Until then, the questions had always been which dam would be built, where, and by whom. There had been certain voices of dissent—the Columbia River Salmon & Tuna Packers' Association, the eastern Oregon Izaak Walton Leagues—but they had been subdued voices, unfocused and powerless, and little attention had been paid to them. The Supreme Court changed all that. Suddenly there was a point of attack, an avenue, a legitimization of the no-dam alternative. Suddenly, the prime question had become not *where* to dam, but *whether*. And the battle for the canyon would never be the same.

The power companies, understandably, were considerably vexed by the whole thing. "What the hell," Hugh Smith exploded to me not long ago. "WPPSS had fought an issue of *primary* importance to the public power people all the way to the Supreme Court of the United States. It was more important for them to establish that issue than it was to get the project. And, hell, they didn't even get the time of *day*. Nor did we. We were confident that we were right, and we wanted it decided by them. We wanted an affirmation from the Supreme Court. Now, what we've got is something worse than if they'd denied the petition for writ. We've got this little statement that says, in effect, 'We don't have to decide this!' " The court had not decided the issue brought before it; instead, it had used the case to promulgate an entirely new—some said, revolutionary—interpretation of a completely different part of the Federal Power Act. So the companies not only had additional hearings to go through; they would have to go through those hearings still in the dark about how the commission would interpret the public-power clause. There is little wonder that they were furious.

But if the power companies were bitter about Justice Douglas's *obiter dictum*, there were others who were elated. To a middle-aged Lewiston businessman named Floyd Harvey, in particular, the decision was like the opening of a door. He'd been pounding on the outside of that door for years, now. Maybe—just maybe—someone would finally start listening to him.

ii

Floyd Harvey is a short, slight, balding, deceptively mild-mannered individual who sells insurance in Lewiston. For many years, selling insurance was all he did. But then, in 1960, something happened. Casually, almost by accident, acting largely out of a sense of sheer boredom, Harvey became a commercial jet boat operator. And in very short order the river began to get hold of him.

"I started into the business of running a boat, starting for pleasure," he remembers. "And in order to help another fellow out, why, I invested a little money into his business. I had the idea I could use the excursion business as a method of entertaining some of my customers and friends, with the potential of perhaps making some profit off of it. And after—oh, I suppose, the first year—the fellow that I had started into business with got out of it, and I took over completely. Well, at that time, of course, I didn't have any knowledge of the river at all, and—then I became a little more intrigued with it." Far up the deep, narrow canyon, at a place called Willow Bar, Floyd Harvey leased a small piece of land from the Forest Service and put up a tent camp. The bar was tiny; behind it, so close that it seemed ready to crowd the tents right off into the foaming river, the great Idaho wall of the canyon thrust skyward for nearly 7,000 feet, vibrant with the reds and yellows of mineral clays and dotted here and there with ponderosa pine. The vast, close cliffs of Oregon, a stone's throw away, loomed nearly as high. The insurance business faltered and lagged: Harvey began spending nearly all his time on the river.

Like most residents of Lewiston, Floyd Harvey had been vaguely aware of the arguments raging back and forth about the big dam to be built somewhere up-canyon from the city. Before 1960 he had felt little concern one way or the other. But now, as he ran the river, as he became more and more familiar with the canyon's moods, its intimacies, and its awesome and overwhelming size, the conviction began to grow in him that the dams were wrong. Not because they would hurt the fish; not because they would hurt his jet boat business; but because they would hurt the canyon. And the canyon was far too valuable to risk damaging like that. It should be left alone, to be its own extraordinary self.

He looked for others who held this point of view. Few were forthcoming. "PNP had more or less brainwashed the conservationists," he explains. "They felt that, if there was any upset at that time, getting away from PNP's application to build High Mountain Sheep, then the Nez Perce Dam might be built, and that would be even worse than the High Mountain Sheep, so they didn't want anything to do with it." Unsupported but undaunted, Harvey began speaking out himself—quietly at first, then more and more forcefully. Would no one listen? He would simply speak louder. And if one man deserves the credit, finally, for keeping dams out of Hells Canyon, Floyd Harvey is undoubtably that man.

He remembers well those early days and those early discouragements. "I just—oh, I remember, I got so mad at some of the conservationists here in town for not helping me to try and put down the power company, and the power company had them so snowed that they were going right along with the power company! I belonged to the chamber at that time. And I would have to sit by myself at the Chamber of Commerce meetings, because people said—that *idiot*, you know. And I remember walking across the *street*, because one guy, with the Clearwater Power Company, told me how selfish I was and how I was upsetting all of this work that they had done. Even the people that thought the canyon should be saved weren't saying anything about it. There wasn't anybody who would say anything, I mean, it was always—well, we'd rather *have*."

When he could get no hearing locally, Floyd Harvey began reaching out—first to the nearby university towns of Moscow and Pullman, then to the city of Spokane, and finally, in 1965, to the distant city of Seattle, where he contacted the northwest office of the Sierra Club. This got him little further than he had managed to get at home; even at the Sierra Club, his reception was chilly. Northwest representative Mike McCloskey told him bluntly that he was wasting his time, that the club could not afford to get involved in a case it was going to lose. Harvey was disappointed, but he refused to give up. If no one would help, he would simply have to do more by himself. He expanded his activities, speaking everywhere he could get even the hope of a hearing, writing letters, starting a newsletter to press for preservation among his customers, and taking people up the river—lots of people, everybody, anybody he could think of that might be persuaded to help him save the canyon. It was beginning to seem terribly futile, but he persevered. And it was fortunate that he did so, because, although he did not know it yet, he was no longer quite so alone.

Far to the southeast of Hells Canyon, in the lower right-hand corner of Idaho, quite close to Capt. Benjamin Bonneville's 1834 winter camp at the mouth of the Portneuf River, lies the city of Pocatello. Within Pocatello is Idaho State College; and within Idaho State College, in the sociology department, is a professor named Russ Mager, an Idaho native and a lover of the outdoors who had, in the early 1960s, made several trips through Hells Canyon with a 35mm camera.

Up the Snake River about fifty miles from Pocatello, near the mouth of the Henry's Fork, is the city of Idaho Falls; and near Idaho Falls, on the desertlike Snake River Plain, sits the National Reactor Testing Station (NRTS) of the old Atomic Energy Commission. The presence of NRTS (pronounced "nerts") brought many young physicists into Idaho Falls in the early 1960s. They came from Boston and Rhode Island and Philadelphia and Illinois—from the cramped East and the flat Midwest—and the wide-open, sky-topping scenery of Idaho made a profound impression on them. Together with Russ Mager and others from Pocatello and Idaho Falls, they founded the Idaho Alpine Club, associated this organization with the Seattle-based Federation of Western Outdoor Clubs, and began exploring the possibility of setting up a local Sierra Club group in southern Idaho. This put them in contact with the club's northwest office, with Mike McCloskey, and, when McCloskey moved on to a job with the club's national office in San Francisco in early 1967, with the new Northwest representative, a young Seattle lawyer named Brock Evans.

That was how things stood early in 1967 when Russ Mager brought his Hells Canyon slides to an Alpine Club meeting and elicited the strongest of strong reactions from the NRTS physicists from the East and the Midwest. "Several of us were very, very impressed," says one who was there. "It was mind-boggling to think that this area was going to be flooded by a dam." Mager, who was doing the principal contact work for the developing Sierra Club group, was emboldened to begin mentioning the canyon specifically in his letters to Brock Evans in the northwest office.

On this fertile ground—Floyd Harvey to the north of the canyon, the Idaho Alpine Club to the south, and new leadership in the Sierra Club's Seattle office—the June 5, 1967, Supreme Court decision fell like welcome rain, bringing forth new green shoots of great vigor and strength. Within days, Floyd Harvey was back in Seattle, where a sympathetic Brock Evans arranged a meeting of local conservation leaders to hear him present his case. The most enthusiastic convert at that meeting was Evans himself. Soon he was writing to Mager: "It is my intention to take a trip over that way this summer to look at the area and to sound out local sentiment, and to see if there is anything we can do to stop this project. . . . Could you please advise me of your assessment of the local situation and what steps you think I might take in order to get further information." The next day, eight members of the Idaho Alpine Club got together in Mager's living room, picked a name for themselves—the Hells Canyon Preservation Council—and elected a slate of officers. The last battle for the deepest gorge on earth was off to a flying start.

Beginning a new environmental organization is a difficult task:

There are few guidebooks for doing so, and in those days there were virtually none. In its first few months of existence under president Jack Barry, the HCPC floundered. No one blames Barry for this. "We were all new at this sort of thing," says Jerry Jayne, another of the original founders. "We were feeling our way and trying to get organized and set up formally to become a national organization, and we had to wait a long time for our bylaws to be approved, and so on, so that we could be incorporated." No further meetings materialized. A considerable amount of energy in Idaho Falls and Pocatello got siphoned off into the developing Sierra Club group. The whole effort appeared wobbly, shaky, unsure of itself, and ready to go down the drain at any moment.

Throughout this difficult period, it was the unflagging energy of Brock Evans that kept things going. He mailed off a steady barrage of letters, to Mager and Barry and Jayne in the South, to Floyd Harvey in the North. There were words of encouragement, questions about the canyon, helpful bits of advice. And there was, finally, a concrete plan for a major send-off for the Hells Canyon effort: a meeting in the canyon itself, at Floyd Harvey's Willow Bar camp, the weekend of September 9–10. Harvey would provide the transportation and serve as host. And in addition to the Preservation Council members themselves, invitations would be extended to a number of individuals of importance in the conservation movement: people like Dave Brower of the Sierra Club, the Wilderness Society's Cliff Merritt, and Justice Douglas himself. The invitations went out. Brower and Douglas declined, which put a temporary damper on the proceedings; but Merrit accepted, and from that point forth everything went splendidly. The canyon wore its summer's-end clothes, all browns and golds under the turquoise sky. The river was green. Birds sang in the lingering canyon twilight; dusk rose from the river, climbed the towering walls, and settled into night, the sky a thin ribbon of stars overhead between the hulking black shoulders of the two rims. Wandering upriver from camp the next morning, with a breeze freshening and backlight sparkling from the water, Evans and Merritt had a deep, broad-ranging discussion about preservation alternatives. Merely stopping the dams, it was now clear, would not be enough. Somehow the canyon walls, the side canyons, and the vast, encompassing wilderness beyond the rims would have to be protected. A national park would be ideal, but a national park was unrealistic. It would preclude hunting, which would invite opposition from sportsmen's groups. Sportsmen's groups would oppose the dams if they were given half a chance, and there was no sense alienating them from the beginning. What was needed was a national park by another name, one in which hunting could be allowed. Evans and Merritt came up with one. They called it the Hells Canyon-Snake National River. It was an exciting new concept, simple enough and exciting enough to fire the imagination of a large cross section of the American public, and for the next five years that idea, generated along the Snake River early on a Hells Canyon September morning, would be the principal focus of environmental concern.

iii

If the Supreme Court decision had stirred up a hornet's nest among the environmentalists, it had stirred the power companies almost as deeply. There was a movement, a shifting of forces and energies, within the two huge combines—the private PNPC and the public WPPSS: a jockeying for position, a reassessment of priorities. In the offing was a major realignment of a nature that could not have been believed as recently as the end of May. When rumors surfaced about it at the end of August, it still seemed unbelievable—and there were even those who refused to believe it when it was officially announced, minutes before the first prehearing conference for the remanded FPC proceedings on September 28, 1967. Those old archenemies, public and private power, had put aside their differences, locked arms, and come out smiling to announce that they were merging their applications into one and henceforth would seek a *joint* project on the Middle Snake River!

How in the world did this surprising marriage of opposing forces come about? Whose idea was it, and what on earth led anyone to think that it could possibly be successful? Owen Hurd of WPPSS gives the credit to "the adverse consequences of further delays and the growing strength of the opposition to any development in the Snake River." Clem Stearns of PNP says it was to "save some money and time, in the interest of the area and our customers," and he adds, "We may have lost some friends somewhere along the line, but I think it was a good move." But of all the participants, it is Hugh Smith who told the story to me best, one cold February day nine years later in the work-cluttered Portland office where a good part of the agreement itself was born.

"Mike Healy [counsel for WPPSS] called me one day," Smith recalls, "and said, 'Are you free for lunch?' And I met him at the University Club. And Mike's position was very simple. He'd gone all the way to the Supreme Court and hadn't gotten an answer—neither had we—and we were going to get stout opposition out of Interior. We didn't realize how stout at the time. And Mike's proposition was that neither one of us was going to build anything unless we got together.

"We agreed, on what turned out to be the erroneous feeling that Mike's people could have enough influence with Udall to get affirmative support from Interior."

Considering the radical nature of this agreement, and the vitriolic contempt that the two sides had heaped upon each other for so long, the negotiations were extraordinarily low-key. "Mike and I pretty well got most of it done on that first day at lunch," says Smith. "He had told the Supply System bluntly that they weren't going to win. That they had only two options. One was to give up and go away, the other was to make a deal with us." The details of this "deal" were relatively straightforward. Pacific Northwest Power would build and operate the dam, thus making an end run around provisions of Oregon and Idaho law that made WPPSS's construction legally questionable. WPPSS would pay 50 percent of the project's costs and in turn would receive 50 percent of the output of power; it would stipulate its abandonment of its preference claim under the public-preference clause of the Federal Power Act, and abandon all litigation against PNPC.

The first few months of the agreement were shaky ones. The benefits of this merger of interests proved harder to sell to the membership of WPPSS than it had been to the management, and for a time it looked as though there would be open revolt. By the end of October, four of the sixteen PUDs that made up the Supply System had voted to oppose the agreement and withhold those portions of their dues that would go to pay for carrying it out. PNPC, for its part, was exceedingly disappointed by WPPSS's failure to tone down the opposition from the Interior Department, which, far from shrinking away, seemed to be growing. "We want them to withdraw their applications and support federal development," said Undersecretary of the Interior David S. Black, a former FPC member from the Northwest, shortly after the agreement was announced. "We feel that this is an ideal site for federal development." And he added that if the two utility combines went ahead with their application, Interior would "have no alternative but to vigorously and fully press our case in the FPC proceedings." By the end of the year, however, these controversies—though they remained unresolved—had faded into the background; and on January 4, 1968, the two companies filed their official joint application. It proposed a project that was 30 percent larger than the original PNPC High Mountain Sheep application, primarily because of advances in generator and turbine technology: The dam was still to be 670 feet high, but the ultimate installed generating capacity had ballooned upward to nearly 3.5 million kilowatts. Plans for handling the Imnaha fish run remained the same; those for the Snake main stem run had been scrapped due to the final and complete failure of the Brownlee skimmer. The application included a detailed recreation plan for the reservoir as well as a clause that was meant to function as an escape hatch in case the fisheries forces complained too much about blocking the Imnaha. If another site in the canyon was found better suited to a big dam, the document stated, this application "should be deemed an application for license for such alternative."

Rep. Al Ullman was pleased. "I see this," he told reporter A. Robert Smith, "as the only practical way we can get the river developed." But he added a cautionary note: Construction would have to begin within two years, or skyrocketing costs would be likely (in his judgment) to render the whole thing uneconomical. It was a significant moment: the first concrete indication from the former chairman of the Hells Canyon Development Association that he might someday oppose further development of Hells Canyon. But without several years' foreknowledge it was impossible to read, and the press let it slide. They were more interested in the concrete defection of the Idaho Wildlife Federation, which—on

January 7, three days after the joint PNPC/WPPSS filing—voted to withdraw its support of High Mountain Sheep and come out in opposition to all further dams between Lewiston and the Idaho Power Company's development. IWF president Art Manley explained that the Supreme Court decision the previous June appeared to have removed forever the threat of Nez Perce, and the federation therefore felt safe in taking a more hard-line position. He did not explain, though he probably should have, that they had been induced to make the change by some fairly intense lobbying on the part of the Hells Canyon Preservation Council. It was the infant organization's first major conquest of another conservation group. The gate was down, and the horses were beginning to run.

Toward the end of April 1968, the Interior Department completed and published a new series of studies on dams in the middle Snake, including—for the first time—a serious examination of the no-dam alternative. And on May 6, an earlier chapter in Hells Canyon history finally came to a close with the dedication, in the canyon, of Idaho Power's Brownlee/Oxbow/Hells Canyon complex. Idaho governor Don Samuelson and Oregon secretary of state Clay Myers each gave a short address. Idaho Power president Tom Roach and board of directors representative P. G. Butt each expressed satisfaction with the success of the project. Power went on-line from the last set of generators at Hells Canyon Dam. No salmon attended; none, in that stretch of the river, were left to attend. At Brownlee, the forebay net had long since been disposed of: The remnants of the Snake run were being artificially propagated at the Rapid River fish hatchery on the upper Salmon, east of the Seven Devils. That meant that the Salmon was serving as an avenue not only for its own historic run but for the old Snake River run as well, and this made it doubly important to keep it free of dams. Nez Perce was already dead. Now it was erased from the maps.

iv

We will skip lightly over the 1968 FPC hearings, which were much like those that had gone before. William C. Levy was again in the examiner's chair, and the bulk of the testimony centered around High Mountain Sheep. Nez Perce was no longer an issue, and the old archantagonists, PNPC and WPPSS, had joined hands behind a single application: The antagonist with an alternate dam-site to push, this time around, was Interior, which had decided from evidence amassed during its recent survey that High Mountain Sheep itself posed a threat to the anadromous fish runs in the Salmon because it was so close to the confluence of the two rivers that its outwash would be likely to confuse the upstream migrants. Interior was therefore seeking federal construction of Appaloosa, halfway between High Mountain Sheep and Pleasant Valley. On November 9, 1968, the Lewiston *Tribune*, which had been wavering in its support of further dams anyway, came out with a scathing editorial denouncing this latest proposal: "It is appropriate that the proposed Appaloosa dam be named for a horse. It would be doubly appropriate if the downstream re-regulating facility were named Buggy Dam. What could be more fitting than to give a horse and buggy concept a horse and buggy name?" From this time forward, the *Tribune* would come down more and more on the side of preservation.

All these developments would have been more critical if the FPC proceeding had been the principal focus of attention during this period, but it was not. As long as the questions had been which dam to build and who would build it, the FPC had been the arena in which the action was taking place. Now that the question had become whether to dam at all, the action shifted elsewhere. No one pretended that the Supreme Court decision had automatically made the Federal Power Commission over into something different from Richard Neuberger's "agency to license concrete-pouring." There was, in fact, only one body that had the power to positively pro-hibit further damming of Hells Canyon, and it was in that body that the principal battles would now be fought. After an absence of ten years, the gorge was returning to the United States Congress.

It was, in a sense, a horse race, a preservation bill in Congress pitted against a license to build from the Federal Power Commis-sion, and it began virtually as a dead heat. The FPC hearings opened on September 10, 1968; the first bill to prohibit dams, the Church-Jordan Moratorium Bill, was introduced into the Senate on September 12. To dispel any lingering doubts about the interrelatedness of these two events, Sen. Len Jordan, the former Hells Canyon sheep rancher and Idaho governor, specifically threw down the gauntlet in his introductory speech on the Senate floor. "Inasmuch as hearings have just been held on the High Mountain Sheep and Appaloosa sites," he told his colleagues, "it is imperative that all interested parties be put on notice now." The challenge was clear. Congress had recognized the Supreme Court decision as a mandate for a new way of looking at things, and it had no intention of allowing the FPC to proceed with business as usual.

It is perhaps stretching things a bit to refer to the moratorium as a preservation bill. It did not prohibit dams in Hells Canyon forever but only for a period of ten years, and its sponsors were sharply divided among themselves over what would happen at the end of those ten years. Church, no stranger to moratorium legislation (he had introduced a similar bill in 1959 that had gone nowhere) was convinced that the ten years the bill would buy were necessary to build a proper base for permanent prohibition of dams. Jordan, who had lived in the canyon and was as fond of it as anyone, was equally convinced that a dam would ultimately prove necessary, and his main quarrel with the FPC was that it seemed hell-bent on licensing the wrong project for the wrong reasons. Those ten years, he argued, would prove the case for Nez Perce—but as a reclamation dam, not a power dam, with the excess water not going to power generators but to be pumped back, reservoir by reservoir, through Hells Canyon, Oxbow, and Brownlee, to the irrigation canals of southern Idaho.

Preservationists in general tended to agree with Jordan that the bill would eventually lead to the building of Nez Perce, and for this reason they viewed it, with a few exceptions, warily and from a distance. "The moratorium bill," says Brock Evans flatly, "was simply a move to stop *us* rather than the dam builders." Oddly enough, however, the dam builders in question also opposed the bill, though for entirely different reasons. They were not afraid, at that time, that dams would be prohibited: What worried them was that others might lay claim to the water and that the dams would thereby become irrelevant. "We didn't make a lot of noise about this," says PNPC's Clem Stearns, "we just felt that it wasn't right. If the water wasn't being used in Idaho, it would be another lever for the people in the Southwest, the people in California—which has more votes than the people in the Northwest—to say, 'Well, you're not using your water now, why can't we?' " The Southwest—southern California and Arizona, in particular—had been hungering for Snake-Columbia River System water for a long time. PNPC felt that the moratorium bill would simply provide time for planning this expropriation. If that happened, everyone in the Northwest—power companies *and* reclamationists *and* preservationists—would also lose. There simply wouldn't be anything left to argue about.

This led the dam builders, in a roundabout way, to press for a bill of their own. They began negotiating to see if the Department of the Interior could be brought into the PNPC/WPPSS partnership. The rationale behind this rather unusual arrangement was simple: If Interior could gain authorization from Congress for a federal dam, the time-consuming FPC procedures could be effectively bypassed. The power companies could thumb their noses at the Supreme Court and build their dams on schedule.

Discussions leading to this triple partnership were delicate and slow-moving, but they were given a certain impetus by the opening of the FPC hearings and the almost simultaneous announcement of the Church-Jordan bill in September of 1968, and six weeks later the agreement was completed. PNPC/WPPSS would provide part of the construction money through prepayment for fifty years' output of power from the project; they would, in turn, be granted exclusive rights to that power for that fifty-year period. The new triple partnership requested and obtained a six-month delay in the FPC proceedings to allow the secretary of the interior to approach Congress with the authorization request. This announcement sent a certain wave of despair through the ranks of the preservationists. The uniting of all potential dam builders behind a single proposed project might well make that project a reality.

The preservationists needn't have worried: The triple partnership was shaky from the start, and the first thing it proceeded to do was to begin falling apart. Three days before the announcement of the three-way agreement, on November 5, 1968, Richard M. Nixon had been elected president of the United States. That meant that the PNPC/WPPSS agreement had been reached with a lame-duck Interior Department. Stewart Udall was on his way out; Gov. Walter

Hickel of Alaska was on his way in. And the new Interior administration made it quite clear that it did not intend to be bound unquestioningly to the policies of its Democratic predecessor. One of the first things Hickel did was to recall the three-way partnership idea for further study. The original six-month delay in the FPC proceedings grew to eight months, then nine, with the scheduled resumption ultimately set for August 12, 1969. And on August 11, with just one day to go, the triple partnership dissolved completely. Hickel called a press conference to announce that Interior would henceforth "at any time" oppose the building of High Mountain Sheep and suggested that the Federal Power Commission should give serious consideration to a recommendation that the middle Snake as it passed through the canyon be brought under the provisions of the year-old National Wild and Scenic River System. Interior's position was, in short, one of increasing skepticism toward any further development *at all* in the big gorge—and since, by virtue of its still-in-force 1949 agreement with the Corps of Engineers, Interior was the agency responsible for coordinating water resource planning on the Snake from the mouth of the Salmon upstream, that skepticism was significant. The winds were beginning to blow against development, and the power companies were running out of time.

The opening of the FPC hearing the next day was, needless to say, left pretty much in shambles. A desperate-sounding Hugh Smith lambasted Interior's position as "all but frivolous. . . . It would be a horror, shame, and disgrace if the federal government could not now make an intelligent decision in a reasonable time." Noting that Interior had been studying Hells Canyon for at least ten years, he called any further studies "obstruction and delay." All of this was quite possibly true but changed nothing. The hearings were recessed for another five months. And any chance there might have been for a federal law specifically authorizing another dam in the canyon was dead. The best that the power companies could now hope for was that Congress would do nothing—a possibility that seemed increasingly remote, not only because the Church-Jordan Moratorium Bill was gaining momentum but because it was quite clear that the preservationists were about to introduce a bill of their own.

11
A National River?

The Hells Canyon Preservation Council had changed considerably in the two years since Floyd Harvey had transported the tiny, young organization to his camp at Willow Creek and watched the power of the canyon wash the tentativeness and uncertainty from it and give it scope and direction and purpose. That trip "really put the group together," says Pete Henault, council president from 1970 through 1972. "They got all those mailing lists from the Sierra Club and the Federation of Western Outdoor Clubs for a wide area, and over a few weeks they put together a mailing—a newsletter—announcing that the group had been formed and what the purpose was, and stapled and folded those things in Jerry Jayne's living room, and that's how it got going." Ten thousand original newsletters went out to places all over the country. A slide show was circulated throughout the Northwest. The group began branching out: Chapters sprang up in Enterprise and in Lewiston. Ultimately, the membership would grow to more than 2,000 spread through nearly every state in the Union.

But while the group concentrated on growing during those early years, it did not neglect its principal purpose as embodied in its name: Hells Canyon preservation. Over in Seattle, Brock Evans began putting together a National River bill along the lines that he and Cliff Merritt had discussed that autumn morning at Willow Creek. Since Evans was, in a sense, breaking new ground—though a similar bill providing for a Potomac National River was being drafted elsewhere at roughly the same time—the process was slow and, in the beginning, rather tentative. The first draft, in ink on lined paper, never left the northwest office. There followed several typewritten draft versions that were circulated for comment at various stages among the leadership of the Hells Canyon Preservation Council—Russ Mager and Boyd Norton in particular—and to Cliff Merritt and others in established national conservation groups. Eventually, in its final form, it called for the protection of an area of approximately 714,000 acres encompassing parts of three states. Better than 90 percent of that area—664,000 acres— would lie in a single broad block athwart the river from Homestead, Oregon, to below the mouth of the Salmon, covering both faces of the canyon and extending back from the rims on either side to encompass the Seven Devils mountain chain in Idaho and the Imnaha River drainage in Oregon. The remaining 50,000 acres took the form of a quarter-mile-wide strip on either side of the river extending downstream to Asotin, Washington, with extensions reaching forty miles up the Grande Ronde to the town of Troy and one hundred miles up the Salmon to the mouth of Elkhorn Creek, twenty miles above Riggins. Within these boundaries, dams and other large developments would be prohibited. The area would be managed primarily for recreation and natural succession, with much of it remaining in wilderness, although current activities such as ranching and jet boating would be allowed to continue. Improvements were sought to the primitive roads to Dug Bar, near the mouth of the Imnaha; to Pittsburg Landing in Pleasant Valley; and to Hat Point, on the Oregon rim. That would allow for access along established corridors without crisscrossing the area with new developments.

Now the problem became one of finding a sponsor.

Of the four senators and two local congressmen directly concerned with Hells Canyon in the states of Oregon and Idaho, only Frank Church had expressed any interest in preserving the big gorge, and so it was to Frank Church that the Hells Canyon Preservation Council turned first with the National River bill. They got a cool reception. "Church said," recalls Pete Henault, bitterly, " 'No, the time isn't right.' " His commitment to Len Jordan on the moratorium bill would not allow him to sponsor out-and-out preservationist legislation. "Senator Jordan and Senator Church," explains Church's long-time administrative assistant, Mike Wetherell, "had succeeded in forming a working relationship based upon a mutual respect for one another's views. Accordingly, the senator felt honor bound to support the moratorium approach as long as Senator Jordan remained in the Senate." The Hells Canyon Preservation Council understood this reasoning, but they failed to appreciate it. It left them holding a worthless piece of paper—a bill without a sponsor. It would be years before Frank Church would be entirely forgiven.

Rebuffed by Church, and knowing better than to expect anything from Len Jordan, the council next turned its attention to Oregon, where longtime high dam advocate Wayne Morse had just lost a closely contested reelection bid to a Republican state representative from Portland named Bob Packwood. A fourth-generation Oregonian—his great-grandfather had helped draft the state constitution back in 1857—Packwood was a lawyer by profession, a graduate of New York University School of Law, where he had served as student body president. He was tall, athletic, strikingly handsome, widely regarded as one of the best public speakers in Oregon, and just thirty-seven years old. His stand on Hells Canyon was unknown, but he was thought to be sympathetic to environmental causes. It was worth a try.

The HCPC was basically an Idaho group; Bob Packwood was an Oregon senator. That didn't mean he wouldn't listen to them, of course; still, there was no use taking chances. It would be better if he were approached by a bona fide Oregon organization. The leadership of the Preservation Council approached the newly formed Oregon Environmental Council, less than a year old and still operating out of a tiny donated office in Portland's warehouse district, where pesticides and other chemicals were stored. The staff kept incense burning just to ward off the stench. Serving as the OEC's executive director was a young advertising executive named Larry Williams, whose great-great-grandfather, James "Peg Leg" Shields, had helped Packwood's great-grandfather draft the Oregon constitution. Williams had never been in the canyon, but like most Oregonians he was familiar with its reputation, and it didn't take long for the HCPC to convert him. He agreed to throw the weight of the OEC fully behind the preservation effort.

And thus it was that a few weeks later Williams and HCPC board member Boyd Norton got off an airplane in Washington, D.C., carrying a copy of Brock Evans's National River bill to protect Hells Canyon, bound for Bob Packwood's office and what they hoped would be the first step toward legislative protection for the deepest gorge on earth.

If Williams and Norton were worried, they needn't have been. This time, the preservationists had picked the right man. Bob Packwood was, in his own words, "very receptive" to the idea of preserving Hells Canyon. "I was raised all my life in Oregon," he explained recently, "and I had no experience with the East till I went back to the Senate. And as I began to live there, began to travel up and down the East Coast, see what had happened to it—I saw that no matter how much money we would spend now, no matter how much we would want it, there is no way that the damage that has been done to the East Coast can ever be reclaimed. The waters can be cleaned, the air cleaned; the land, that scarred, scraped land, will never, never be reclaimed. And every month that I lived more in the East I made a little pledge to myself that what had happened to the East would not happen to Oregon."

Hells Canyon was his first opportunity to act on that pledge, and he leaped at the chance. "I became convinced that beyond anything I had seen in this country, let alone in the state of Oregon, this was a place to save. All of them put together don't hold a candle to the *jewel* that is Hells Canyon." Such was Packwood's enthusiasm, in fact, that he moved quickly beyond mere sponsorship of the bill to become a genuine leader in the preservation battle, suggesting strategy and tactics, making speeches, and goading the Preservation Council into action, when it faltered, through letters, phone calls, and personal contacts, until in time he became accepted by the HCPC leadership not merely as an instrument for getting the bill through Congress but as one of their own. Next to Floyd Harvey, Bob Packwood is probably the single most important individual in the history of Hells Canyon preservation.

Packwood is, however—despite his enthusiasm—a cautious and careful man. Before introducing the bill, he submitted it to the Senate's Office of Legislative Counsel for redrafting. Ultimately, there were very few changes made—Brock Evans had written a good bill—but the process took time, and in that time the first session of the Ninety-first Congress came to a halt. It was not until after the first of the new sessions that the bill was ready to be introduced, and in the meantime the HCPC had managed to find sponsorship for the legislation in the House. Ideally, this sponsorship should have been local, but neither Al Ullman nor Idaho's James A. McClure would touch it: McClure, Boyd Norton reports, was even "openly antagonistic and abusive to constituents who favored preserving the canyon." So the Preservation Council looked elsewhere, eventually settling on Pennsylvania's John Saylor—the father of the Wilderness Act and the man who had amended the High Hells Canyon Dam bill out of existence in the Irrigation Subcommittee in 1957. Saylor agreed readily to sponsorship. "He cared about Hells Canyon," says one preservation leader who knew him well, "and he was eager to go with the National River bill." Saylor was so eager to go, in fact, that he jumped the gun on Bob Packwood. The National River bill went into the hopper in the House on January 19, 1970—a full five days before Packwood was ready with the Senate version. Packwood, fortunately, had the good grace to refrain from dwelling on this point. Despite the initial failure of coordination, the bill seemed to be off to a good start.

ii

While the Hells Canyon Preservation Council was drafting the National River bill and getting it introduced, Floyd Harvey was pursuing his own course of action up in Lewiston. He did not remain aloof from HCPC matters: He was instrumental in forming the Lewiston chapter of the council, and was one of a delegation of five HCPC leaders sent to Washington in February, 1970, to testify at subcommittee hearings on the Church-Jordan moratorium bill. But along with this he continued to pursue, entirely on his own volition, a program he had begun long before the Preservation Council was even a gleam in Russ Mager's eye: a program of taking influential people—writers, conservationists, entertainers, politicians, anyone who might be able to swing someone's opinion toward preservation—up-canyon on his jet boat for free.

There was, Harvey acknowledges, some danger in this. "It made the canyon more popular," he says. "I wasn't necessarily for *that*—but sometimes you have to do something like that. You end up destroying a resource with too many people rather than let the power companies gobble it up with a piece of concrete in the middle of it." The canyon was not going to be saved, Harvey saw, until enough people knew what was at stake up there, enough to stand up and shout a resounding *no!* to the dam builders. So he kept at it, kept extending invitations, kept arranging trips, until in the summer of 1969 he hit the jackpot.

He got Arthur Godfrey to come out from New York and take a look at the canyon.

Godfrey flew in to Lewiston, rode up the river, spent the night at Willow Creek, and came back dazzled. "I have been to paradise and back," he told reporters who met him at the dock on his return. In New York again, he wrote a long letter to Secretary of the Interior Walter Hickel, urging him to throw the weight of the Interior Department behind the preservation movement. "This," wrote Godfrey fervently, "is the heart of Paradise, believe me."

> I would willingly attempt to swim the entire 96 or 7 miles up that cold river from Lewiston just to see it again. . . . Mr. Secretary, I implore you, I beg of you: make that trip out there as soon as you possibly can and see this place for yourself. . . . Better still, permit me to arrange a trip for you such as I took. I will personally fly you out there and introduce you to the warm, wonderful people who laid on the trip for me. I beg you to see it personally because I believe no one who has ever beheld its priceless, irreplaceable beauty would dream of building another dam there.

Now, as it might be imagined, it was one thing for Floyd Harvey to invite the secretary of the interior to go up Hells Canyon with him; it was quite another thing when the invitation came from someone of the national stature of Arthur Godfrey. Within a short time, Godrey was able to write joyfully to Harvey that Hickel had accepted his invitation. Hells Canyon was about to receive a jolt of publicity several times greater than anything that had ever come before. Not even Fern Hobbs and Copperfield could begin to match it.

The trip took place on the fourth weekend of May in 1970. It was an extravaganza. "There were thirty-five people there," grins Harvey, shaking his head in mild disbelief six years later. "See, in addition to Hickel and his staff, Godfrey brought in two friends of his from Hawaii, specialists in marine biology—and then Hickel invited Burl Ives. Well, I'm certainly not going to turn down *Burl Ives*! And Ives brought Lyle Moraine, a friend of his. Then I got down to *my* invitation list." Among those that Harvey invited personally were state officials from Idaho and several professors, specialists in anthropology, zoology, and botany, from nearby universities in Washington, Idaho, and Montana. Nearly everyone accepted. "And then, of course, we had the press," he adds. "We had the Associated Press, and the United Press, and CBS—and, of course, the headline stuff was terrific." Things had come a long way forward for the "idiot" who had been ostracized at the Lewiston Chamber of Commerce meetings not so many years before for daring to suggest that the dams should not be built.

There was also a list of people who *didn't* get invited. Harvey tells that part of the tale with undisguised relish. "Governor Samuelson wanted to go up the river with us," he chuckles, "and I wouldn't let him." Samuelson was an ardent supporter of dams and development. "We had a party the night before. And I had a call from a Mrs. Pearl Engle, from over by Enterprise, and Judge Farris over there, and they got on the phone, they wanted to present *their* side of the High Mountain Sheep Dam issue to Secretary of the Interior Walter Hickel. And I said, 'This is *my* party, and *I'm* sending out the invitations.' And she says, 'Well, we *demand* to be heard.' And I said, 'Lady, I'm just not going to send you an invitation.' And I had the chief of police waiting down at the door in case they tried to crash the party. But they didn't, they just wrote nasty editorials in the paper over at Wallowa County about it."

The trip itself was a roaring success, which Hickel was to remember later as one of the high points of his tenure as secretary.
"It was a lively trip," he recalls in his book *Who Owns America*,
"with Ives and Godfrey swapping yarns and trading Burl's guitar
back and forth as they outdid each other with humerous back-
country ballads." He speaks with awe of the impression this "fantastically scenic stretch of the Snake River" made on him, and he
remembers wondering aloud if "maybe we should even study which
of the dams already built should be dismantled."

"Oh, he was thrilled with it," agrees Harvey, "he brought along
his mariner's hat. . . . He'd never been involved in anything like
this, even though he was quite a boater himself. I mean, it's an entirely different type of boating." The Forest Service supplied
horses for a trail ride up Sand Creek and a feel of the canyon-face
wilderness; Interior provided a helicopter, and Harvey arranged for
a float plane to land in the narrow canyon in front of his Willow
Creek camp, pick up the secretary, and fly him upriver to Brownlee
Reservoir so that he could get a proper feel for both the dammed
and undammed portions of the river.

Almost as gratifying as the success of the two Godfrey trips, for
the environmentalists, was the failure of the power companies'
single attempt to copy them. They invited Art Linkletter to tour the
canyon and report on it from the pro-power standpoint. "It was a
disaster," grins Harvey impishly, shaking his head. Well, maybe
not quite *that* bad, says Clem Stearns, but he admits that it was not
all it could have been. "That was one attempt which didn't work
out, just for some oddball reason," he recalls. PNPC had prepared
the ground well enough; they had a boat standing by to take
Linkletter up the canyon and had arranged for the taping of a series
of interviews with Governor Samuelson, and with a Hells Canyon
rancher, and with Stearns himself, and with the captain of the boat
that would transport them into the black depths of the gorge. But
Linkletter's plane was delayed in Boise, and he ran out of time.
"He didn't even get to Nez Perce," sighs Stearns. "He never even
got to see the Mountain Sheep site or the rest of the canyon." Then
the format of the TV program "Life with Linkletter" changed, and
the entertainer didn't even get a chance to air the little film footage
he had taken. Net cost: several thousand dollars. Net results: zero.

It is little wonder that the power companies chose to plan no more publicity trips.

The preservationists, on the other hand, with a more successful base to build on, continued to take celebrities and others into the canyon. Results of the continued trip program were mixed. HCPC board member Annette Tussing, a friend of Washington congressman Mike McCormack, took the congressman for a float trip down the canyon in the summer of 1971. McCormack had such a good time that he invited two other members of the House Public Works Committee, Patrick T. Caffery of Alabama and James Kee of West Virginia, to join him on a second trip the next summer. That trip was a little less pleasurable: The raft carrying Caffery and Kee capsized in the angry white maelstrom of Granite Creek Rapids, pinning the two congressmen and HCPC president Pete Henault underwater, and it was several anxious moments before they struggled free. Even then, the excitement wasn't over: The overturned raft, with the congressmen still clinging to it, was out of control, and there was another large rapid—Three Creeks—just downstream. McCormack's raft chased the runaway, caught it, and with the congressman himself at the oars managed to beach both craft on the Idaho shore, inches from the brink of Three Creeks. It was not an experience that the Public Works Committee would soon forget.

A similar trip by the House Interior Committee, on the other hand, was quite forgettable. It was midsummer, the canyon was hot and sultry, time was short, and most of the committee members were decidedly unimpressed. "Joe Skubitz, from Kansas, was disgusted" with the place, laughs Pete Henault, and he adds impishly, "You know—it wasn't flat. He couldn't see more than about a mile at a time, and it bothered him. . . ." Skubitz was later to become one of the chief Interior Committee foes of preservation for Hells Canyon.

iii

The moratorium bill passed the Senate but failed in the House; the National River bill was quietly sat upon by the leaders of both legislative bodies and failed even to get hearings. Both bills died with the close of the Ninety-first Congress and were reintroduced early in the Ninety-second, the moratorium as S. 448, the National River as S. 717. Sen. Mark Hatfield of Oregon signed on as a cosponsor of S. 448; since he and Senator Church were both ranking members of the Interior Committee, rapid and favorable action was virtually guaranteed. This was not necessarily pleasing to the preservationists. They had supported the moratorium bill in the Ninety-first Congress, somewhat reluctantly, as a stepping-stone to eventual protection. Since that time, however, a number of things had happened. The Oregon State Game Commission had published a study effectively dynamiting power company claims that their dams were a recreational asset to the Snake by showing that many, many more recreationists were using the free-flowing sections of the river than the impoundments, even though access to the free-flowing sections was considerably more difficult. There had been a great public outcry over the decimation of the lower Snake and Columbia salmon runs by dam-induced nitrogen narcosis. And Idaho voters had tossed out their prodam governor, Don Samuelson, and elected in his place a man named Cecil B. Andrus, an avowed environmentalist who had made dams in Hells Canyon a major campaign issue. Andrus had immediately written to the Federal Power Commission putting the state of Idaho on record in opposition to further dams in Hells Canyon, and—to the immense delight of the Hells Canyon Preservation Council—this freshman Democratic governor had induced veteran Republican governors Tom McCall of Oregon and Dan Evans of Washington to cosign the letter with him. Locally, the *Lewiston Tribune* had come out in favor of preservation; nationally, the *Washington Post* and the *New York Times* had adopted the same stand. Public opinion was clearly coming down strong for preservation, and the Preservation Council was in no mood to wait ten years. As Pete Henault put it in a letter to the council membership, in March 1971, "The Hells Canyon controversy has gone on for seventeen years, countless articles have been written, hearings have been held and hearings records piled up, the question has been debated in the Supreme Court of the United States, and it's getting just too hard to listen to those who tell us we should wait a little longer." So the weight developing behind the moratorium bill was not pleasing. But for the time being, at least, there seemed to be little that could be done about it.

That was how things stood for the next several months. The moratorium bill continued to advance; the National River bill continued to be denied even the courtesy of hearings. In the House, Al Ullman, announcing that his stand on dams was "modified," hemmed and hawed and finally came down hard in support of a House version of the moratorium, as introduced some weeks earlier by Idaho congressman Orval Hansen. He remained adamantly opposed to the National River bill, but he was no longer insistent that a bill be passed specifically allowing dams in the canyon: That, he said, he would leave to the Interior Committee to decide. This was encouraging—the man was coming along. However, he had a long way to go yet, and the Preservation Council and its friends were not yet ready to praise him freely.

In late May, with a floor vote on the moratorium bill imminent in the Senate and with his own National River bill still being held somewhere off in left field, Bob Packwood and his wife, Georgie, came out to Oregon and took a four-day Memorial Day weekend float trip through Hells Canyon with the leadership of the Hells Canyon Preservation Council. Brock Evans was there along with Pete Henault, and Boyd Norton; Pete van Guytenbeek, of Trout Unlimited; and Jack Hemingway, eldest son of author Ernest Hemingway and himself a prominent outdoor writer. They put in at the ramp just below Hells Canyon dam, in the deep, tight gorge, with the tall black walls looming thousands of feet above them on either hand. One night they spent between Wild Sheep and Granite Creek rapids, watching the shadow of the east rim creep down the great west wall of the canyon as the moon rose; another night they tied up at Salt Creek Bar, on the Oregon side, with the massive cliffs of Suicide Point blotting out the eastern sky. Packwood tried whitewater kayaking under the expert tutelage of the Idaho Environmental Council's Doc Blackadar and got dunked. Days, they drifted; evenings, they sat around the campfire, warmed equally by the flames and the fellowship, cursing dams and discussing strategy and tactics and means by which to stop them. The newspapers called the trip a publicity stunt, and perhaps it had originally been conceived that way; but if so, the magic crucible of the canyon had transformed it utterly, and those who were along know that there will never be another experience like it. "It was a blue-ribbon trip," says Bob Packwood today. "From the standpoint of friendship, of camaraderie . . . the water was high . . . . everything was green. . . ." And, summing the whole thing up with simple sincerity: "It was a high point of my life." Conservation leaders agree. "The experience was—unique," says Pete Henault. "Philosophically, we were a bunch of people who were all close together. And the wives were there, and it was a very emotional, intimate-type thing."

Back in Washington, renewed by the spell of those four perfect days in the canyon, Bob Packwood plunged vigorously into the problem of getting a fair hearing for the National River bill in the face of the immense political pressure behind the rival moratorium. It was painfully obvious by now that the normal procedural avenues of the Senate were not going to be adequate for that task. Packwood was not a member of the Interior Committee; Church was. Therefore, under normal conditions, Church's bill would move through committee and Packwood's wouldn't. Unless, that is, a way could be found to circumvent those normal conditions. And with his indignation at the dam builders who would make trips like the one he had just taken impossible prodding him, Bob Packwood found a way.

Quietly, over the next few weeks, he put together a list of cosponsors for the National River bill—senators from all over the country, from all parts of the political spectrum, their single common denominator being a willingness to attach their names to the cause of saving the deepest gorge on earth. George McGovern was on the list; so was Barry Goldwater. Edward Brooke and Edward Kennedy of Massachusetts, Walter Mondale and Hubert Humphrey of Minnesota, Hugh Scott of Pennsylvania, William Proxmire and Gaylord Nelson of Wisconsin—the roll of names reads like a Who's Who of the Senate. "I literally talked with them one at a time, asking each one of them to do me a personal favor and to add their name to this," Packwood recalls, and he adds, "That's the kind of effort that really does pay off in the Senate, where you personally go to another senator and say, 'Look, this is a good bill, I need your help, can you please let me put your name on this.' " He had assistance: Brock Evans spent most of that period of time in Packwood's office making phone calls, and Stewart Brandborg of the Wilderness Society and George Alderson of Friends of the Earth were also involved—but the principal weight fell on Packwood, and Packwood alone. It was slow, and it was time-consuming, but he persevered. And gradually the list grew.

The floor vote on the moratorium bill was scheduled for June 29, 1971—a Tuesday. A week beforehand, with his list of cosponsors grown to twenty-six, or a little more than one-fourth of the Senate, Packwood pulled his coup. He announced that he meant to offer an amendment to the moratorium bill on the Senate floor—an "amendment in the nature of a substitute," replacing the text of the moratorium bill, in its entirety, with the complete text of the National River bill.

It was a splendid move, and it achieved excellent results. The moratorium sponsors, their backs suddenly pressed against the wall by the enormous political weight of that list of cosponsors, were forced to negotiate, and within days a compromise had been worked out. Full-scale Interior Committee hearings were scheduled on the National River bill. And Packwood, his purpose accomplished, withdrew his threatened amendment. He had succeeded in getting the National River bill seriously considered—that was the important thing. Preservation had been shown to be a politically viable alternative, and it was no longer possible for the moratorium to destroy it. And since, at that point, there was not a snowball's chance in hell of passing either measure in the House, there was no sense in antagonizing Frank Church and Mark Hatfield any further.

Packwood has been strongly criticized, then and since, for the unconventional nature of this move. Such criticism does not bother him. "It was, in essence, going around the established procedures," he admits, but he adds quickly, "I'll say two things in defense. One, the issue of Hells Canyon had been heard and heard and heard, and studied and studied and studied; it wasn't like you were springing something brand-new on the floor of the Senate. Two, I had tried to use the procedures and had been rebuffed. So, I thought—I'll go around 'em."

iv

On Saturday, June 26—the day after the National River hearings were announced and Bob Packwood withdrew his threatened floor amendment to the moratorium—representatives of more than forty organizations, ranging from preservationist groups like the Sierra Club and the Hells Canyon Preservation Council all the way to commercial firms like Bumble Bee Seafoods, Inc., met in Lewiston to forge a new coalition dedicated to their common purpose of keeping further dams off the Snake River.

Although the proximity of these two events was striking, it was also largely coincidental. A meeting that large is not thrown together on a day's notice: It takes time. In the case of the Coalition to Save the Snake, the time involved works out to exactly four months, from February 26—when Bob Packwood first suggested, in a letter to Pete Henault, that the preservationists and the commercial fishermen should find a way to work together on this issue—to the June 26 organizational meeting. In between, most of the work was done by Lewis A. Bell, an attorney from Everett, Washington, who was active in a number of sports fishing clubs and had conceived of the coalition idea independently a few weeks after Packwood had written to Henault. It was Bell who suggested Jack Hemingway as the chairman of the new group, and it was Bell who talked Hemingway into taking the position. Details were worked out in meetings and phone calls in April and May among Bell, Henault, Hemingway, and Brock Evans, and the coalition was a chief item of discussion on the Packwood float trip over Memorial Day weekend. Finally, everything was in readiness: The invitations went out, the meeting was held, and the new coalition began enthusiastically planning for its first major appearance, at the National River hearings, now scheduled for mid-September. A young, curly-haired dramatics instructor named John Barker from Lewis-Clark State College in Lewiston showed up at that first meeting as a representative of the Northern Rockies chapter of the Sierra Club and ended up finding himself elected to the coalition's board of directors. Nothing much had been heard of John Barker before this, but that would soon change; from this point forward, he would be a pivitol figure in the drive to save Hells Canyon.

The promised hearings were held in Washington, D.C., on the sixteenth and seventeenth of September. Henault, Barker, Hemingway, and Evans all went back; so did Larry Williams of the Oregon Environmental Council, and HCPC founding members Boyd Norton, Jim Campbell, and Jerry Jayne, and Dale Storey of HCPC's Wallowa chapter. Former secretary of the interior Stewart Udall showed up to endorse the National River and to admit that he had been wrong when, as secretary, he had sought further dams in the canyon. Arthur Godfrey spoke briefly and forcefully of the need to prevent further "obscenities" such as the three existing Idaho Power Company dams.

Nevertheless, most preservationists left the hearing disappointed and with a feeling that they had, in the phrase of the Portland *Oregonian*, been sold down the Snake River. The handling of witnesses by the committee leadership, they charged, left little doubt that the hearing had been strongly biased against the bill from the beginning. This was most apparent in the amount of time various witnesses were allowed to testify. After timing the presentations and the question-and-answer sessions, Boyd Norton reported that Robert R. Lee, testifying for the Idaho Water Resources Board—a supporter of dams—had occupied the witness chair for an hour and a quarter, while Brock Evans stepped down after five minutes. Pete Henault was limited to thirty seconds less than Evans, giving a four-and-a-half-minute presentation that he later calculated had cost the membership of the Hells Canyon Preservation Council nearly ninety dollars per minute to deliver. And so it went.

The behavior of Frank Church was especially puzzling. The questions he directed toward witnesses who testified in favor of damming this stretch of the canyon clearly marked him as a preservationist; at times, as with WPPSS's Owen Hurd, for example, he was close to brutal in his cross-examination. Curiously, though, when preservationists themselves were in front of him, he attacked them even more strongly than he had the power-company witnesses. To Henault and Norton, in particular, he was bitter almost to the point of vindictiveness, and the Hells Canyon Preservation Council was left wondering, as they had been ever since he had refused to sponsor their bill, just which side he was on.

A further blow came with the publication of the hearings record.

Leafing through it, conservationists discovered to their intense dismay that two of their most telling pieces of testimony, John Barker's and Dale Storey's, had inexplicably been left out. Bob Packwood, as Barker puts it, "blew up," and an addendum was issued containing the missing testimony, but even so, it was difficult to convince the more ardent preservationists that the original omission hadn't been made on purpose.

The slighting of Barker's testimony was especially crucial, because the Lewis-Clark State College drama instructor and Coalition to Save the Snake board member had focused, to a far greater extent than any other witness during those two days of testimony, on a new and very potent threat to the integrity of Hells Canyon. A new enemy had come on the scene, an enemy far more subtle—and therefore far more dangerous—than the dam builders. Land speculators and developers were quietly moving into the canyon, surveyors' stakes were sprouting from the alluvial bars, maps of postage-stamp-sized tract home lots were being drawn up, and the great gorge, unbelievable as it may seem, was about to go down in the record books as the deepest subdivision on earth. Barker's testimony ignored the dam builders and concentrated on the developers, and in the process fired the opening salvo in what came to be known later as the Great Snake Land War. Nearly two years would pass before things could be brought under control and the dams could once again be awarded the position of center of attention.

12

The Great Snake Land War

The trouble began—to oversimplify things slightly—because the ranchers in Hells Canyon, who had never been overly successful to begin with, wanted to get themselves out of the increasingly unprofitable sheep business. At first, attempts were made to deal with this problem through consolidation; the smaller ranches disappeared as the bigger ones gobbled them up in an attempt to grow large enough to reach an economical operating size. Begun during the Depression, this process continued through the 1940s and the 1950s, and by the late 1960s it had gone just about as far as it could, with all private property between the mouth of the Salmon River and the site of Hells Canyon Dam in the hands of four large landowners: Ken Johnson, Lem and Bud Wilson, and the New Meadows Ranching Corporation, owners of the Circle C Ranch at Pittsburg Landing. Among them, these four controlled virtually every flat spot in the canyon, every beach and cove, every alluvial bar, to the point that it was impossible for a float trip to go through the gorge without camping on private land. Salt Creek Bar, where the Packwood party had camped, belonged to Lem Wilson; Ken Johnson held title to Saddle Creek, the official location of the world's record depth; Bud Wilson had virtually everything on the Idaho side south of Kurry Creek; and so it went. However, even combining holdings in this manner did not prove profitable, and the four landowners were forced to cast about for new ways to make money from their Hells Canyon holdings.

Ironically, it was the very success of the Hells Canyon Preservation Council that provided these landowners with their biggest opportunity. Earlier, with the threat of inundation by Nez Perce or Mountain Sheep Dam hanging over them, these properties had been practically worthless on the real estate market. By 1971, however, due largely to the council's work, that threat had receded. The governors of Oregon, Idaho, and Washington had come out against further damming of the Snake. Public opinion polls by Senator Packwood, congressmen James McClure and Al Ullman, and even by the Pacific Northwest Power Company itself had clearly shown that the vast majority of Northwesterners—up to 72 percent in one poll (McClure's)—wanted the canyon to remain undammed. Although senators Hatfield and Church continued to oppose the National River bill, they let the press know that they considered the chances that another dam would be built in the canyon exceedingly remote; Rep. McClure, gearing up to run for the seat of retiring senator Len Jordan, withdrew his prodam stand in the blinding light of those public opinion polls and began to hint that he was moving over to the preservationist viewpoint. At the same time, recreational use was increasing as more and more people heard about this tremendous gash in the earth between Oregon and Idaho and began to come into this remote and mountainous border country to see it for themselves. And this popularity, coupled with the reduced threat of inundation, left the Hells Canyon landowners holding some extraordinarily valuable pieces of property. Not too good for running sheep, maybe—but start thinking of them as vacation homesites and watch those cash register wheels start to spin!

To their credit, the landowners approached the Forest Service first to see if the government wished to buy their land and consolidate its holdings in the canyon. The government certainly did want to do so but there was a problem. Government regulations will not allow any federal agency to buy land at more than its appraised value. Appraised value typically lags far behind speculative value. Vacation tract home developers were therefore able to offer two and three times the top government price per acre and still stand to make a considerable amount of money themselves. And in a bidding game like that, the Forest Service inevitably was going to come out on the bottom.

The first sale to a developer and the subsequent subdivision took place a number of months before the September 1971 hearings on Packwood's National River bill, and it was the results of that deal that had drawn John Barker's wrath in the testimony that had been left out of the hearings record. It was well below the mouth of the Salmon, and it didn't involve any of the four landowners of the main canyon, but it was pretty bad nonetheless. The location was Wild Goose Rapids, five miles above the Grande Ronde, the site of the proposed China Gardens reregulating dam for the Nez Perce project and of the Nez Perce fishing operation that Lewis and Clark's men had visited when they discovered the canyon in 1806. Any development there at all would be in poor taste; this one was particularly bad because in addition to a gross lack of historical perspective, it exhibited certain elements of land fraud. Buyers were promised river frontage, and they got it, but in many cases it turned out that what was purchased was not a beach or a building site but a cliff face rising vertically out of the river for several hundred feet. Even if you managed to pin a house to the wall there would be no way to get to the river and no means of arranging drinking water or sanitary facilities. Barker was still fuming about the whole thing when I talked to him five years later. "They've sold off twenty-eight lots," he snorts, "all over five acres. Each one has about 120 feet of frontage. They run *clean* to the top of the mountain! And they're just, you know, rocky hillsides. I don't even think you could run cattle on that land. It's not even your normal open-sloped bunchgrass hillside; it's just a pile of rocks."

By the time the addendum containing Barker's missing Wild Goose Ranchos testimony had been printed, it was early 1972 and there were substantial rumors that the events at Wild Goose Rapids were about to be repeated upstream on the property of the two Wilsons. Within a few weeks, those rumors had taken the first step toward reality with the listing of more than 10,000 acres of prime canyon benchlands with an Idaho realtor for an asking price of $350 per acre. At the same time, negotiations between the landowners and the Forest Service appeared to have broken down completely due to a failure of the Forest Service's money supply. The Federal Office of Management and the Budget had just taken a hatchet to the Land Conservation and Development Fund—used for Forest Service land purchases—reducing it from a budgeted $30,000,000 to $11,000,000. Bob Packwood was furious. "They're talking turkey with out-of-state developers from as far away as Texas," he fumed to the press, adding that "if this type of activity is allowed to proceed unheeded, we will soon have a nicely subdivided and commercially developed riverfront along our magnificent Snake." Hatfield and Church, in a move that was extremely heartening to Northwest conservationists, agreed, and they both teamed up with Packwood in a previously unprecedented show of solidarity before the Senate Appropriations Committee to seek the addition of $4,000,000 to the pole-axed fund specifically earmarked for purchase of lands in Hells Canyon. Was there any significance in this newfound solidarity? Can the threat of honky-tonk development be credited with doing something that the Hells Canyon Preservation Council had been trying, and failing, to do for five years—getting the Idaho and Oregon senatorial delegations to move in a unified manner toward preservation? "I think that's a fair statement," says Bob Packwood today, looking back at it. "Because, at that stage we were starting to move to the place where we *knew* there wasn't going to be a dam built, that there wasn't going to be any development. And the problem became, now, what do we do to make sure nothing is disturbed until we get this bill finally passed." At last, under the threat of the imminent loss of this land, things began to fall into place.

The leadership of the Appropriations Committee was impressed. "We'll find the money somewhere," Chairman Alan Bible of Nevada assured the three northwest senators, and he was as good as his word. When the appropriations bill cleared the Senate on June 29, the Hells Canyon funds were in it.

Unfortunately, this did not mean that the problems were over. The Forest Service was still up against that regulation requiring them to pay no more than the appraised value for any land they purchased. While the owners grumbled at the delay, a new appraisal was made, and in mid-September of 1972 the Forest Service made public its offer based on that appraisal. The amount: $150 per acre, less than half the asking price.

Lem Wilson had had enough; he was, as he told the press, "disgusted." He sold his sheep, engaged a team of surveyors, and—rather than sell out to an out-of-state developer—moved ahead to subdivide and develop the land on his own. He told the newspapers he would be selling lots "as soon as possible." An alarmed Pete Henault got on the phone and extracted a promise from Wilson to notify the HCPC before any sales took place. That defused the situation somewhat, but it was still inflammable—as was proved a short two months later, on Thanksgiving Day, 1972, when the smoldering vacation-home issue blew up in everybody's face.

ii

It was a phone call from Pete Henault to Lem Wilson that sparked the conflagration.

Henault was working on a new bill to replace the now-defunct National River bill. "During the election process that fall," he recalls, "when Senator McClure was running for office, Frank Church approached us and said, 'OK, it looks like the time is right.' And he met with us during the summer recess in late August or early September and asked us to write a bill. We called in the environmentalists from Oregon and the other parts of Idaho, and we all met with Frank Church in his office, and we dickered over the National River bill, spelling out what we wanted. His minimum requirement was that we had to give some guarantees to the irrigators in southern Idaho. And he said, 'I'll handle that part of the language, you guys can put all the other stuff in.' We talked about a wilderness core, with a recreation area, and he was agreeable to all of that. And it was out of that meeting that I started putting the draft together."

It was slow work. Henault was aware that one of the principal drawbacks of the National River bill had been the lack of consultation with anyone outside the environmental community during the drafting stage, and he was determined that it wouldn't happen with the new bill. He talked to everyone—the jet boaters, the irrigators, the archaeologists, the fish interests, the landowners, the Forest Service—anybody he could think of who might conceivably have some interest in the canyon, with the single exception of the dam builders. He took all those recommendations, and he sat down at his dining room table in Idaho Falls and went to work. And it was in the course of that work that he made a Thanksgiving Day phone call to Lem Wilson to make a routine check on some of the language pertaining to the rights of property owners and discovered that Wilson had sold eight subdivision lots in Hells Canyon the day before. They weren't just any old lots, either; they were at Salt Creek, the Packwood party's second overnight stop in 1971 and one of the loveliest alluvial benches in the canyon. Building houses there, Henault later charged, would be akin to building hot dog stands in a cathedral. The lots were tiny—100 by 200 feet each— and they were going for a tidy $5,000 apiece.

When he found out about the sale, Henault was furious. "I said to Lem," he recalls, " 'Lem, that really pisses me off. Because we had this gentleman's agreement that you wouldn't do anything before we talked about it.' And he took that as being kind of insolent from a young idiot and said he was going to go up and get in his airplane and come over here and give me hell. Said he'd *shot* people for less than that. Anyway, after that we calmed down and talked it over." Wilson promised that he would sell no more lots until December 4—then a little more than a week away. They hung up.

Henault went into action.

"I called Larry Williams right away. And Larry, in turn, called Jim Kadera of the *Oregonian*, and Kadera called me back, and I told him the background. And then Kadera called Lem Wilson. And this all happened within a couple of hours of my phone call, and the next day was page one headlines in the *Oregonian*. Just lucky for us, it turned out to be a quiet news day, so we got big coverage." Henault grins playfully. "And I guess that impressed the hell out of Lem Wilson."

After that hectic Thanksgiving Day, things moved much more quickly.

The Forest Service, for the first time, began speaking openly of condemnation. Congress had appropriated $4,000,000 specifically to purchase Hells Canyon land; it was therefore obviously the intent of Congress that this land be purchased, and if condemnation turned out to be the only way to get the job done there would be no hesitation in using that step. It would, however, have to be done quickly. "There is a sense of urgency about this," Forest Service negotiator Wade Hall told the *Oregonian*. "You never know if a high-powered outfit will come in, and the Lord only knows what will happen then." Hall was genuinely concerned: A veteran Wallowa-Whitman National Forest employee, he had been the agency's strongest internal voice in favor of preservation, with a record of propreservation recommendations going back to the 1920s. He also knew how to buck things up the chain of command: Though it was a holiday weekend, he succeeded in obtaining condemnation approval from Forest Service chief John R. McGuire in Washington, D.C., by the following Tuesday. After that, of course, the pressure was off. The actual condemnation proceedings would take some time, but the land was safe—no one else would buy it with the foreknowledge that the government was about to condemn.

The landowners were angry and disappointed. "I'm not against saving the area," fumed Lem Wilson, "But, dammit, we should get a fair price."

"A terrible precedent," lamented Dave Campbell of the Circle C Ranch. "We don't want to subdivide or anything else. We just want to run cattle. . . . If the government can condemn property like that for recreation, a person's deed isn't worth anything. Hell, they keep going like that, they could buy Sun Valley and turn it into a bird sanctuary or something." Aside from letting off a certain amount of steam, however, statements like these were of little consequence. The government was going to get the land; it was merely a matter of time. No sidetracks were possible.

The Declaration of Taking was signed by Assistant Secretary of Agriculture Robert Long on Friday, May 11, 1973. With the filing of that declaration in the district courts for Idaho and Oregon a few days later, title to the contested land passed to the Forest Service. The single remaining act of the drama was the determination of price, which would be done in local courts by local juries—a situation that tends to favor the original landowner. There was no exception to that rule here. The prices that were eventually awarded were more than twice the assessed valuation of the property, in the neighborhood of $1,000,000 for each of the four affected owners. That did a pretty good job of smoothing ruffled feathers and soothing hostile feelings. "Lem Wilson," laughs Larry Williams, "came out smelling like a rose on the whole thing. The Forest Service ended up paying extraordinary amounts of money for this land that really wasn't worth anything unless it was part of a larger ranch." Or, to put it in John Barker's slightly more picturesque language: "Shit, they've been awarded the moon!"

13

A Meeting of Minds

By late 1972 the new protection bill for Hells Canyon was proceeding quite nicely. The National River concept was pretty well defunct: At Frank Church's suggestion, the name Hells Canyon National Recreation Area had been appropriated from an abortive exploitation bill that Al Ullman had introduced in 1970 in answer to the National River, and would now serve the cause of preservation, as it had recently done in the Sawtooth Mountains of central Idaho. The Hells Canyon Preservation Council was not too happy with the name ("It's like calling the Notre Dame Cathedral the Notre Dam Recreational Hall," moaned one board member), but they accepted it as a necessary step toward gaining Frank Church's support and therefore passage of the bill.

In November Rep. Jim McClure was elected to the Senate to replace retiring senator Len Jordan and immediately announced that he was ready to work with the council and with Senator Church toward finding a preservation bill that they could all support. "I want you to go back to Idaho Falls and kick that Pete Henault in the kneecap!" he told HCPC secretary Dick Farman in his Washington, D.C., office, insisting that Henault had misrepresented his position and that he had been ready to work with them toward preservation all along. The council had reams of evidence to the contrary, but it quickly covered them up and issued an apology. The important thing was not defense of pride but defense of Hells Canyon, and it would do little good to pick a quarrel with McClure when they should be welcoming him aboard.

The situation was somewhat different in the case of the bombshell that Al Ullman dropped in mid-December. The Oregon congressman, who had built his original political power base on his support of big dams in Hells Canyon—but who could read the public opinion polls as well as anyone—announced that he had undergone what he calls today "a gradual change in values" and that he was about to introduce a brand-new *anti*dam bill that would, in addition to banning further dams in the canyon, create what he called the "Hells Canyon National Forest Parklands"—a 750,000-acre reserve straddling the canyon and containing a large wilderness study area (the two faces of the canyon plus the Seven Devils) along with provisions for a major scenic highway along the Oregon rim. That the former head of the Hells Canyon Development Association would author such a bill astonished many observers; but an even bigger surprise was in store. It came eight weeks later, on February 9, when the Oregon Environmental Council's Larry Williams issued a statement that amounted to a full-scale broadside blast at Ullman's Parklands bill, clearly designed to blow the whole thing out of the water and sink it without a trace. *"No* legislation is better than the Ullman proposal," Williams wrote in March 1973 in the OEC's magazine, *Earthwatch Oregon.* "The OEC staff has .reviewed the proposal and finds it totally inadequate to provide any meaningful protection to the region."

> . . . The administration, protection and development of the Parkland is left *entirely* up to the discretion of the Secretary of Agriculture and he is directed to administer the area under the rules and laws applicable to the National Forest System. In our judgement, the area deserves something more than multiple use management. . . . The establishment of a boundary around the Hells Canyon area and directing them to continue with the same management does not provide sufficient safeguards against the gradual degradation of this area. The en-

couragement of "industrial tourism" is not an acceptable goal
for the future of Hells Canyon.

Williams's action not only took Ullman by surprise, it caused a
bit of a stir in the environmental community as well. "Everybody
kinda thought Williams was not right on the ball on that, as I
remember," says John Barker, adding, "We were *delighted* [with
the Ullman bill] over here." Why did Williams make that move?
Why did he risk alienating Al Ullman—whose support was going to
be absolutely necessary if any bill was to eventually pass the
House—by blasting him out of the water the moment he made his
first positive move toward preservation? In sponsoring an antidam
bill, Ullman had repudiated his original power base among prodam
people and had thus taken a step that required a considerable
amount of political courage. Shouldn't conservationists have been
praising him instead of hitting him over the head?

"There were reasons for it," says Williams, leaning back in his
swivel chair in the "new" Oregon Environmental Council office, a
converted Victorian house on a side street just off the Interstate 5
freeway in downtown Portland. The flag draped across the wall
behind him, a large bandanna handkerchief with a "Save Hells
Canyon" bumper sticker emblazoned upon it, was made by folk
singer Pete Seeger on a trip through the canyon with Williams in
the summer of 1972. "It appeared that the bill had been written by
the Forest Service staff and did not reflect the environmentalists'
ideas of what a bill should say. It didn't have many controls over
what the Forest Service could do to the area. We found it completely unacceptable. It was just as good as not having any legislation at all, except that maybe it would stop the dams. But moratoriums were rampant, and that wasn't the main issue. The issue
was to protect the area as a whole. And what we *didn't* want was
for a bill to go through that would just stop dams and then take all
the pressure off preserving the area. Now, at that time, the Senate
was looking at introducing legislation—new legislation—that
would be more acceptable to it than the current Packwood bill.
And there was a possibility that they would introduce legislation
identical to what Ullman had introduced, if they didn't hear any

great complaints about it. So we had to convince the Senate some way that it was not the bill we would support.

"It's a calculated risk you take. If the bill is unacceptable, and you can't live with it, then you either have got to say, 'We wash our hands of it, no dice,' or you've got to say, 'Well, maybe we *can* live with it.' And it just was not acceptable."

How did Ullman take it? Williams grins. "Al Ullman," he says with deliberate understatement, "was not *happy* with our reaction to his piece of legislation. But the experience we've had with him in the past is that he responds to rather determined pressure. He responds well; he doesn't go off and sulk, as many congressmen and senators might do. If you don't like what they're doing, they take you off their list forever and never speak to you again. He isn't that kind of guy. He's a guy who is politically astute, who knows from where you are coming, and why you're doing what you're doing. He was naturally very unhappy with my criticism of his bill, thought it was unjustified—but that's the name of the game. Instead of going off and pouting, he responded well. And I think that says a lot about the kind of guy he is."

The risk, in other words, paid off; the ploy worked. Al Ullman, after his initial anger, agreed that yes, perhaps his bill was not all it should be and could be modified. And the senatorial delegation from the two states—which could have taken the easy way out and simply introduced Ullman's bill, intact, as their compromise legislation—set that possibility aside and continued their talks based on Pete Henault's draft bill. Even Senator Hatfield, who had announced emphatically that he liked Ullman's language and would introduce it in the Senate, stayed with Church, Packwood, and McClure in the negotiating sessions toward a separate Senate bill. Larry Williams, by his carefully and coldly calculated "reckless" act, had assured that the deepest gorge on earth would not simply be undammed and forgotten but would have a chance to get a mandate for the kind of full care and attention that it deserved and so desperately needed.

The talks among the four senators went on all through that spring of 1973. They were extensive, careful, wide-ranging talks. Pete Henault's draft bill was torn apart, rewritten, and pasted back together, not once but many times. "Numerous staff meetings were held to try to define the boundaries,'' says Church's administrative assistant, Mike Wetherell. ''Whenever an impasse was reached . . . . the senators would work out details. This process assured that the bill would have the best possible chance of survival. The efforts made between the staff and the senators—involving long hours, innumerable sets of maps, and at least a hundred or more revisions in language—resulted in an extremely well thought out bill.'' Most of this was done without direct conservationist input. ''There were drafts that would go around,'' says one who was closely involved at the time, ''and we would make efforts to change things in the draft, and try to get them as close to what conservation groups had in mind as possible.'' And he adds, ''A number of those ideas didn't make it into the bill at that time, but have gotten into it since.''

A major thrust of the rewriting was to make sure that the bill that was eventually introduced could gain enough support from Al Ullman to find its way through the House. The way that this was done was simply to adopt certain concepts from Ullman's environmentally unacceptable preservation bill, couched in language that the environmentalists could live with.

Final agreement was reached on the bill in mid-July; and on July 23, 1973, Pete Henault's bill, as modified by senators Packwood, Church, McClure, and Hatfield, with input from the Sierra Club, the Wilderness Society, the Hells Canyon Preservation Council, and many others, was introduced into the United States Senate. Frank Church gave the introductory speech; the bill carried the sponsorship of all four Oregon and Idaho senators, with the explicit support of the governors of both states. It had begun to look as though finally the long battle might be just about over.

ii

By the time the new National Recreation Area bill—S. 2233, known colloquially as the ''Four Senators Bill''—was dropped in the Senate hopper in the summer of 1973, there had been some significant changes in the leadership of preservation groups in the Northwest. Pete Henault was no longer heading the Hells Canyon Preservation Council: His job at the National Reactor Testing Station had been terminated, and he had found new employment in Seattle, with—curiously enough for an antidam activist—Seattle City Light, the city-owned electric utility. He had therefore resigned his HCPC post, which had been taken over by former council vice-president Dick Farman ("I guess," laughs Farman today, "I was the only one still standing.") Similarly, Jack Hemingway was no longer head of the Coalition to Save the Snake: That position had passed to John Barker, under the new title of executive director. Barker kept it alive, but it never did fulfill its original promise. Forty separate organizations representing more than a million and a half people represented a tremendous amount of potential power, but they also presented a problem of coordination that simply proved insurmountable. The coalition did not exactly fail, but its role remained minor.

Far more important than the new personalities in command of the HCPC and the coalition was the change in leadership that had taken place in the Sierra Club. Brock Evans was no longer head of the northwest office but had moved to Washington, D.C., to take over the position of Washington representative from the ailing Lloyd Tupling. Evans had been a highly committed and extremely effective voice for the preservation of Hells Canyon, and northwestern conservationists wondered what effects his leave-taking would have on the future of the great gorge. They needn't have worried. Evans's replacement quickly proved that he was not only as committed to the canyon as Evans had been but that his grasp of the political processes necessary to get a preservation bill through Congress was, if possible, even greater than that of his predecessor. In choosing Douglas W. Scott to head its northwest office, the Sierra Club had made one of the wisest employment appointments of its sixty-year history.

Doug Scott is a small, slightly built individual with a boyish grin topped by a thick shock of curly black hair that gives him the appearance and the commanding presence of a slightly underaged choirboy. Opponents and friends alike, however, discover rapidly that this innocent appearance is deceptive in the extreme. Scott is one of the most politically shrewd men in the United States, with an extraordinary memory and a mind that cuts through to the core of a difficult problem like Alexander's sword going through the Gordian knot. He is also an absolutely mesmeric speaker—a skill, it turned out, that would prove highly important. For Hells Canyon, suddenly, the name of the game seemed to be public hearings—and more public hearings—and still *more* public hearings.

Kicking off this sudden flurry of solicited public input was the Oregon Water Resources Board, which held a series of meetings in various parts of the state in the latter part of November 1973, seeking comments on a proposed rewording of the official Water Board policy statement in regard to Hells Canyon. The then-current policy read: "Utilization of these waters of the Snake and Imnaha Rivers for power production, flood control, recreation, wildlife, navigation, and fish life will represent the highest public benefit to the State of Oregon." The board had before it a resolution that the two words *power production* be deleted from that statement. This would bring the Water Board into line with Gov. Tom McCall's public statements on the issue and with the results of the Packwood and Ullman constituent polls, and it was likely that the change would be made, but first the board wanted to take its own very thorough pulse count of citizen opinion. Hearings were scheduled for Pendleton and Enterprise; for Medford, in the southwestern corner of the state; for the population centers of Eugene and Portland; and finally, by specific request, for the Vale-Ontario region at the canyon's upstream end. The Pacific Northwest Power Company sent Hugh Smith to represent it; he trotted around the state on the heels of the board, appearing at every hearing and presenting essentially the same statement to each, a performance that seems a bit astonishing coming from a man of Smith's political acumen and which failed to endear him to the board members who had to sit through it six times. "It infuriated many of us," recalls board member Frank MacGraw, a geography professor at Southern Oregon State College in Ashland. "It was about 180 degrees removed from reality." No reason has surfaced for the dismal inadequacy of the power company's effort, but it seems likely that they simply were not yet concerned enough to do better. Pacific Northwest Power, Smith has explained to me since, was still convinced that the central issue was the Federal Power Commission proceedings, where the company was clearly winning. That was a serious miscalculation. The Federal Power Commission had long since become peripheral; the real issue was, and had been for several years, in Congress. The power companies were pouring their primary energies down the wrong funnel, and it would be the better part of a year before they would come to the sudden, belated recognition that this was so.

Close on the heels of the Water Resources Board meetings came the Senate field hearings on S. 2233, the "Four Senators Bill," held in LaGrande, Oregon, and in Lewiston, Idaho, on December 7, 8, and 9, 1973. Conservationists, still smarting from the beating they had taken at the National River hearings, found to their delight that attitudes in the Senate had altered considerably in the two intervening years. "I was *amazed*," says John Barker, grinning with delight at the memory of the Lewiston phase of those hearings. "You couldn't call the hearing anything except absolutely slanted to our side." The LaGrande phase was similar. Bob Packwood, who is not a member of the Interior Committee and who had been treated as a virtual outsider at the National River hearings, found himself entrusted with the hearings chairmanship this time around. Lead testimony was presented not by the power companies but by Doug Scott of the Sierra Club. ("I was a little nervous," Scott recalls, "because my hair was fairly long. But I felt better once I discovered that Hugh Smith's hair was longer than mine.") Of the 221 witnesses who spoke on the three hearing days, only 81—less than 37 percent—were opposed to the Hells Canyon National Recreation Area bill, and most of these qualified their opposition to make it clear that they were opposed to dams, too, that they simply thought S. 2233 took in too large an area, and they would not be opposed to a similar bill limited to the river and the two faces of the canyon. First public opinion had turned; now the Senate had turned. The only question marks remaining were the House of Representatives, and the brand-new and little-tested commitment of Al Ullman to canyon preservation.

iii

Shortly after the Senate field hearings, there came, for the first and last time in the history of the preservation effort, open violence.

Late in 1973, Floyd Harvey, who had been relatively inactive since the Arthur Godfrey/Burl Ives/Walter Hickel extravaganza of 1970, had begun planning a similar trip for the summer of 1974. This time, in addition to Godfrey, he had invited Environmental Protection Agency director Russell Train and former attorney general of the United States Elliot Richardson. Harvey hoped that the publicity weight of Richardson's presence in the canyon would help push S. 2233 to enactment during the 1974 congressional session. It might well have done so, too, but no one will ever know. The trip never took place. Sometime on or about midnight on the evening of January 31, 1974, a person or persons—the facts are not officially known—broke into Harvey's camp at Willow Creek in the depths of the canyon, stole $500 worth of fishing tackle, poured acid over much of the metal fixtures and equipment, chopped up the radiator of the power plant, and retreated, leaving behind burning bags of charcoal briquettes in each of the seven buildings. Two of the buildings, including the main lodge, caught fire and burned to the ground. Floyd Harvey, insurance broker and jet boat operator, founder of Hells Canyon Excursions, Inc., and acknowledged father of the Hells Canyon preservation movement, went out of business.

Harvey is virtually certain that he knows who lit the match at Willow Creek, but he has met only frustration in his attempts to have that identification proved in court. The crime took place in Idaho County, Idaho, and was therefore subject to what one state attorney general's office staff member has called "that infamous Idaho County law." The deputy district attorney for the county was the stepson of Harvey's chief rival in the jet boat business and has, Harvey charges, delayed and hindered the prosecution of the arsonist. The chief suspect—another business rival, with an alleged arson record—has refused to be fingerprinted for comparison with prints found on the broken glass of the burned-out lodge. One key witness—a sheepherder who was in the Willow Creek area on the night of the arson—was threatened with death if he testified before the Grand Jury, and has since fled the Hells Canyon country in fear for his life. As this is being written, on a cold January Wednesday three years later, the statute of limitations on the arson is about to expire, with no action due to be taken. I have seen much of

Harvey's evidence, and it is good. The case against the suspect is plain, and there are clear indications that evidence has been suppressed, "lost," and delayed, by certain state and county officials whose sympathies are known to lie with the dam builders. Floyd Harvey is a broken and bitter man, and the image of justice in America has taken a plunge from which, for Harvey's friends, it is likely never to recover.*

iv

With the LaGrande and Lewiston field hearings out of the way, the Senate Interior Committee scheduled a final hearing for Washington, D.C., on April 23, 1974. Conservationists fully expected that this would be the last Senate committee step, clearing the way for floor action in the Senate and committee action in the House. They were wrong. The next day, Doug Scott was dictating an "urgent and confidential" memo to conservation leaders throughout the Northwest. "On the basis of soundings in recent weeks," he wrote, "our expectation had been that the Forest Service would come in with a reasonable position. . . . Surprise! They got unplugged. The Deputy Chief showed up to say that they had no position at all, were preparing their own alternative position. Whereupon the whole thing adjourned for sixty days." Suddenly, everyone's timing was off by two months, and the result was virtual chaos.

"That sixty-day delay," Scott remembers, "infuriated everybody. It wasn't necessary. But worst of all, that delay in passage in the Senate delayed any start of action in the House. We finally got House action, and we got into November of '74, we were in committee, we had the votes—but November is too bloody *late*." There was action in the House, all right, but it was not the kind of action the preservation forces wanted. The power companies and their

---

*There is a happy ending to this story. With his criminal case bogged down and going nowhere, Harvey instituted civil damage proceedings against the arsonist and his two companions—and won! As the galleys for this page were being edited, word was received that one of the three men, Keith Flugstad, had been ordered to pay $1.75 million in damages and costs. Proceedings against the other two, David Gilkey and Bruce Oakes, are still pending at this time.

friends had suddenly awakened to the fact that they were about to lose, and they were flexing an awesome set of political muscles.

When did this realization come to Pacific Northwest Power? When did it first begin to look as though the bill would pass and the dams would fail? Ask Hugh Smith that question, and you get a straightforward answer: "When Al Ullman showed up in a markup on his bill and made it clear that he was going to have a bill passed. Until that day, we were winning. We lost on that day." PNPC and WPPSS had long since given up on the Senate and were counting on stopping the bill in the House, where they were still holding out hope that their old ally, Al Ullman, had not really deserted them but had only done so for the sake of appearances. "The mere fact that he introduced the bill," Smith points out, "was no political indication that he proposed to get it passed. But when he showed up at the markup session and publically presented strong support for the bill, what happened was that for the first time in the entire history of this case there was not only a member of the House, but an *influential* member of the House, who wanted to pass it. Up till then, nobody on the House side gave a damn." Suddenly, it was apparent that somebody *did* give a damn, somebody whose congressional district was involved, and who—because a striptease dancer named Fanne Fox had just jumped into the Potomac Tidal Basin, to the great embarrassment of veteran Arkansas congressman Wilbur Mills—was about to inherit the vast powers of one of the most important committee chairmanships in Congress: the House Ways and Means Committee. And for the dam builders, the name of the game had suddenly become Stop Al Ullman, using any means necessary short of mayhem and dismemberment.

By this time, conservationist forces were solidly unified behind Ullman's bill. Once he had gotten over his initial peeve at Larry Williams's highly negative reaction to his bill, the Oregon congressman had moved in a genuine spirit of compromise to delete or alter many of the sections of the bill that environmentalists were displeased with. At the same time, the environmentalists had made some compromises, as had the four Northwest senators whose National Recreation Area bill was currently the chief preservationist vehicle. To all of the principals, preserving the canyon had become far more important than nit-picking details.

Against the great political weight of this new spirit of cooperation, compromise, and harmony among preservationists and congressional leaders in both houses, the newly awakened power
companies had two principal weapons. One was time, or rather the
lack of it, purchased for them by that sixty-day hearing delay the
Forest Service had brought about earlier in the year. The other was
a sympathetic congressman with the parliamentary skill necessary
to convert that lack of time into a defeat for the bill: Craig Hosmer
of California, number two ranking Republican on the House Interior Committee and a longtime foe of environmentalists whose
mastery of delaying tactics was legendary (he had once held up a
bill he disliked for six days on the House floor itself, where action
normally takes place in a matter of two hours or less). Hosmer was
retiring at the end of his current term, so he had no political axe to
grind and could freely and unhesitatingly use any procedural delaying maneuvers that he could think up, and when he announced to
the press on November 21, the day before the scheduled subcommittee vote on the Hells Canyon bill, that he would use "whatever
tricks are at my command" to keep it from passing ("My objection
to it is that if these environmentalists are allowed to lock up the
country, the people aren't going to be able to eat or keep warm or
anything"), conservationists knew that they were going to be in for
a rough battle. "It's pretty desperate," moaned Larry Williams,
who had flown into Washington with Doug Scott, to be there for
the final lobbying push. Political reporters, sensing a story, pricked
up their ears. They would not be disappointed.

Of the actual battle, which began the next day, Doug Scott remarks, "I remember being angry for a considerable amount of
time, but I don't remember, I guess, all the details." Hosmer used
the old technique of repeated quorum calls, the same tactic that had
defeated the high Hells Canyon Dam bill in a House committee
twenty years earlier. Congressional committees normally operate
without a quorum present, but this may be done only by unanimous consent of those present; if the demand for quorum is made,
even by just one member, the committee may not proceed to business until the demand is fulfilled. A committee quorum is a simple
majority; in this case, with a committee membership of twenty-
five, the necessary number would be thirteen. Al Ullman, furious at

Hosmer's intervention and more determined than ever to pass a preservation bill, worked desperately to muster those thirteen warm bodies. Assisted by fellow Oregonian John Dellenback, a Republican supporter of the bill and the only member of the state delegation on the Interior Committee, Ullman made numerous calls attempting to locate the scattered committee members. Scott, Williams, and Brock Evans did the actual footwork. "The Rockefeller confirmation hearings had been going on for the vice-presidency," Scott recalls. "Two of the members of the Interior Committee were also on the Judiciary Committee, which was holding those hearings. Brock and I ran over and got them out—we had to get by the Secret Service and everybody to get into the back room and get hold of these two congressmen and get them to come over, and they did, and somehow they got there faster than we did, and we were running. I well remember the sprint that Commissioner De Luga, the delegate from the Virgin Islands, put on, coming up three flights of stairs to get there in time, and the chairman of the full committee, Mr. Haley, who is not a young man, made tracks that were astonishing, and all of these people assembled in the room." A count was taken. There were fourteen congressmen present—one more than the required quorum.

Congressmen Joe Skubitz (Kansas) and Teno Roncalio (Wyoming) walked out.

"Al Ullman had come over," Scott continues, "and was standing where Teno had to go right by him to get out of the room. And Al put the arm on him. He said, 'Teno, can't you stay in here?' And Teno was obviously *highly* uncomfortable, but he said he couldn't, he had a personal commitment. So he ducked out and went and hid in the back room, and Skubitz was out in the hallway. I went by him—I don't think he knows me from Adam—and he asked me if the quorum call was still under way, and I said, 'Well, you know very well that it is, Mr. Skubitz, and if you went back in there'd *be* a quorum, and we could proceed democratically.' " But Skubitz remained unmoved. Subcommittee chairman Roy Taylor stalled while Ullman and Dellenback tried desperately to round up just one more friendly face. They were unsuccessful. The subcommittee was forced into early adjournment, and the next day began the Thanksgiving recess.

The backers of the bill tried again after Thanksgiving, but their course continued to be, in John Dellenback's words, "very, very uphill." At every turn, they ran into a Hosmer-induced stone wall. Mostly these were repeated quorum calls, but there were some other tricks used too. Rep. Joe Skubitz, acting for Idaho congressman Steve Symms—a conservative Republican and an opponent of the bill who had been elected to Jim McClure's old seat in the First District when McClure had become a senator—proposed an "amendment in the nature of a substitute" that would replace Ullman's bill with what amounted to the old Jordan-Church moratorium, its time span now reduced to four years. It was voted down by one slim vote. Hosmer sought to have the votes of the delegates from Guam and Puerto Rico thrown out on the grounds that they could not vote on floor action in the House; this was ruled invalid on the basis of precedent allowing them a vote in committee action. When these tactics failed, though, there was always the quorum call to fall back on. Hosmer's cronies would walk out; the committee, denied a quorum, would have to adjourn. The California congressman was in high good spirits. "It's choo-choo season," he said, referring to the hectic rush of the last few days of Congress. "I'm just trying to keep the cowcatcher on." A weary, angry John Dellenback blamed the whole mess on multiple committee assignments, which made it virtually impossible to assemble half the membership of any one committee at any one place at any one time. But pointing to the problem, of course, did not solve it. The quorum—and the bill—continued to fail.

On December 11, a Wednesday, the full Interior Committee stepped in, voting 22 to 7 to bypass the subcommittee vote and bring the Hells Canyon bill directly to full committee consideration. It was a desperation move, and there was little chance it would succeed. Before the Hells Canyon bill on the committee agenda loomed the Bureau of Land Management Organic Act, an enormously complex and controversial measure that was, Dellenback complained, "like a cork in a bottle. Until we clear it out of the way, or drop it, everything else will just back up behind it." It would be possible to take up the Hells Canyon bill out of order, but to do so would be just as difficult as mustering a quorum in the subcommittee, if not more so. And there was still Craig Hosmer to deal with.

"Believe me," the Californian declared, "you have laid a nestful of broken eggs on this Hells Canyon issue. You are headed for the rocky shoals of parliamentary procedure." He threatened a filibuster and at one point actually began one, shouting down all others who tried to speak and continuing until he was gaveled angrily into silence by committee chairman James A. Haley of Florida. Finally, on December 17, with adjournment due on December 20, the backers of the Hells Canyon bill gave up the struggle and allowed their bill to die. Hosmer and the dam builders had prevailed; no Hells Canyon Act would survive the Ninety-third Congress.

14
Victory!

Although the games Craig Hosmer played managed to kill the Hells Canyon bill for the 1974 legislative session, the end result of his efforts seems to have been to strengthen the preservationist position. "I don't think Hosmer did his cause a whole lot of good," says the Preservation Council's Dick Farman, "and maybe it even helped us in the end." Doug Scott concurs. "That bill," he says, "died in a way that angered people on the Interior Committee. That's not a tactic that's appealing to anybody's substantive judgment on the issues; that's saying, 'If I can keep my guys out of the room, the majority will not be able to work its will.' So we went in, of course, in January, in the very first days of the new Congress, and secured the cosponsorship of almost a majority of the committee to the Ullman bill. The bitter taste of the Hosmer efforts was still in their mouths, and so they agreed at that stage to become cosponsors. So when the bill was introduced the first day, H.R. 30, it came in with a highly impressive percentage of the committee, demonstrated tangibly by their cosponsorship. And that was very important."

The significance of this great weight of cosponsorship was not lost on the power companies. Up to and all the way through 1974, they had continued to cling to the hope that the National Recreation Area bill could be permanently defeated, leaving the fate of

Hells Canyon solely in the hands of the Federal Power Commission, which seemed fairly certain to grant a license to build one or more dams. Now, however, they could see that this was no longer a realistic hope. Some sort of bill was going to be passed. Their job—if they were ever going to build those dams—was not to defeat the bill as a whole but to see to it instead that the bill as passed contained a loophole big enough to drive a cement truck through. They would have to amend, not kill.

And thus, almost out of desperation, was born the dam builders' last weapon—a device so brilliantly conceived and so carefully worked out that the sheer genius of it continues to be admired today, even by its enemies. By means of a few minor changes—a few words here, a few words there—the bill could be altered so that the prohibition against dams applied *only to the downstream half of the canyon.* The entire remainder of the legislation—the wilderness and wilderness study areas, the National Recreation Area, the planning mechanisms, the roads and trails—all would be left intact. From the Imnaha down, the river would remain free-flowing; it would be stipulated that the Nez Perce and Mountain Sheep damsites should be left forever untouched. But from the Imnaha up—in the deepest and most spectacular portion of the canyon—dam building would still be allowed. That would mean that the Pleasant Valley-Low Mountain Sheep dam combination, PNPC's original 1954 plan, could be constructed.

An amendment incorporating the minor changes in language necessary to bring about this "compromise" fifty-fifty split of the canyon was drawn up early in 1975 and prepared for introduction by Congressman Teno Roncalio of Wyoming. Roncalio's association with this cause remains somewhat of an enigma. A liberal Democrat with a good environmental voting record on most issues—he received a solid 67th percentile rating from the watchdog League of Environmental Voters for 1975—the Wyoming representative is not normally found voting in favor of dams. At the same time that he was leading the House fight against Hells Canyon, for example, he was siding with the antidam forces on other water issues of national importance such as Lock and Dam 26 on the Mississippi River and the destructive Dickey-Lincoln Project in Maine. "When it first became apparent to us that he was going to oppose the [Hells Canyon] legislation,'' says Dick Farman, ''we got in touch with quite a few people in Wyoming, and they were absolutely astounded at his position. He's been good on everything else relative to environmental things, but on this one issue he's just absolutely been unyielding. People in Wyoming exerted a tremendous amount of pressure on him and discussed it with him, and he just wouldn't give them any good excuse for his behavior. As of this day, I don't know if any of us knows what the real motivation for his position was. It's been quite frustrating.'' Whatever its cause, Roncalio's position on Hells Canyon was a tremendous boon to the dam builders. Dam advocacy on the part of a militantly prodevelopment congressman like Craig Hosmer or Steve Symms could be dismissed with a wave and a what-else-can-you-expect; dam advocacy by a congressman with a 67 rating from the LEV could not be so lightly passed over. Undecided congressmen—the majority on nearly every issue, right up till the final vote—would have to consider Roncalio's position seriously.

There was also another approach being tried to stop the Hells Canyon bill, although the power companies were carefully not having anything to do with it. This was an attempt by Idaho congressman Steve Symms, supported by fellow Idahoan George Hansen, to replace the National Recreation Area legislation with a bill calling for a moratorium—the old Jordan-Church approach, now down to three years—coupled with a National Recreation Area *study*. Symms, a fruit rancher who is listed in the official *Congressional Directory* as an ''Individualist Republican,'' was not considered a serious obstacle to the legislation even though the Idaho portion of the canyon lay in his district. ''Symms,'' one prominent environmentalist assured me some time prior to the final vote, ''is no threat. He's simply too far out from the average crowd.''

While the Hells Canyon preservation forces did not take Symms seriously, this almost proved to be a mistake. When it came down to the wire, Symms was able to muster a considerably higher percentage of strength than had been thought possible. Like Samson in the temple, he very nearly brought the whole thing crashing down.

After a House subcommittee hearing in April, action on the Hells Canyon issue seemed to slow down to a plod and a grind. "What did we do in 1975?" asks HCPC president Dick Farman. "Kept our fingers crossed, I guess." "The whole story of 1975," adds Doug Scott, "has just been the dogged efforts to get through the procedural hearings and get a day scheduled, and find a room, and hold a markup, and all of that, and it takes longer than one wishes it would take." The Senate, which had passed the bill the previous session, got its part of the act done in early June, slipping the legislation through without a dissenting vote. (This performance was less impressive in reality than it appears on paper. "There were four senators on the floor," says Hugh Smith disgustedly, "and they went through the formality of taking a vote.") The House, despite the efforts of Washington congressman Lloyd Meeds, who had taken over the job of committee manager for the bill, continued to drag its feet. There were markups and more markups. Friends of the canyon began to wonder once more if they would ever reach the end of the road.

In late August came a serious setback. Citing growing national energy needs, Oregon congressman Bob Duncan—a Portland Democrat who had signed on as a cosponsor of the Ullman Hells Canyon bill in January—announced that he "probably would vote no" when the legislation reached the floor. "I've been looking things over," he told the *Oregonian*, in an interview published on Friday, August 22, "and I'm not satisfied, with the energy crisis we've got right now, that we ought to lock up those two dams." He did not immediately withdraw his name from sponsorship, but it was no longer possible to say accurately that the Oregon delegation was wholly behind the bill even if there *was* a piece of paper saying that they were. If Duncan teamed up with Roncalio, there could be trouble.

By October 31, the day that the full House Interior Committee voted its approval of H.R. 30 and sent it out for a floor vote, it was quite apparent that the Duncan-Roncalio bond had indeed been forged, and knowledge of this fact precipitated a minor crisis of uncertainty. What path should the bill take from the committee to the floor? There were two possibilities, each of which presented some problems. One route, the standard itinerary for most House legislation, would involve taking the bill through the Rules Committee, obtaining a program (known as a rule) for floor consideration, and then taking both to the floor itself, where first the rule and then the bill itself would be voted on. This would have the advantage of allowing passage by a simple majority of those present and voting, but the disadvantage of allowing amendments to be offered on the floor. The other route, called the suspension calendar, is a method by which certain "privileged" committees—Interior among them—may bypass the Rules Committee and take legislation directly to the floor. No amendments are allowed under suspension, which would eliminate the possibility that Bob Duncan could offer the Roncalio Amendment for a vote of the full House membership. But the suspension calendar carries a risk, too. Passage must take place not by a simple majority but by a two-thirds vote. A one-vote margin is sufficient to establish a simple majority, but in the 435-member House of Representatives a two-thirds majority can require a winning margin of as much as 145 votes. And that is a great deal harder to obtain.

"Our view of that," says Doug Scott, "was that the guys who were our advocates in Congress wanted that bill every bit as badly as we did. So this was really their decision, about how to go. At one point they pretty well decided they were going to take it on suspension, and then they backed off, and then it got delayed for one reason or another, and finally Congressman Taylor, the subcommittee chairman, as I understand it, was the decisive factor in saying, 'No, let's take it through Rules.' And so they made the decision." It would go to the Rules Committee on the eighteenth of November. Floor action, it was anticipated, would follow a few days later.

So it was planned. But "The best laid schemes o' mice and men," says Robert Burns, "Gang aft a-gley."

ii

The morning of November 18 found the opposing forces widely scattered. Brock Evans was in New York City giving a speech; Hugh Smith was in his Portland office working on something entirely unrelated to Hells Canyon; John Barker was in Lewiston, teaching his classes and entertaining, as he put it later, "a feeling of void, because the thing was just sort of out of our hands at that point." Al Ullman's mind was occupied with the growing confrontation between Congress and the president over the tax reform bill for which he, as chairman of the House Ways and Means Committee, had chief responsibility. The press was busy covering the debate over whether or not Congress should bail New York City out of debt, which was expected to come to a vote that afternoon. Nobody was paying a great deal of attention to the scheduled Rules Committee action on H.R. 30; the results of that action were largely a foregone conclusion anyway. The real battle, everyone knew, would come when the bill reached the House floor several days hence.

In Seattle, Doug Scott rose at his usual time, ate a leisurely breakfast, and prepared for what he confidently expected to be a normal day. Hells Canyon was the farthest thing from his mind; in fact, he admits, "By the time all this transpired, I quite completely forgot that the Rules Committee was going to be taking up the bill that day." He locked his front door, threw his briefcase into his Volvo station wagon, and got ready to drive the four miles along Sandpoint Way to his office. That was when he discovered the flat tire. Cursing a little, he wrestled the spare to the ground and rummaged around till he found the jack and the lug wrench. The lugs were frozen. Scott worked at them ineffectually for a while, then threw the wrench to the ground in exasperation and went back into the house to call fellow Seattle environmentalist and Hells Canyon crusader Dale Jones, head of the local Friends of the Earth office. Jones had also forgotten about the Rules Committee action. He came right out. "And so," says Scott, "we were out at my house for most of the morning, working on this damn car. I had absolutely and totally forgotten, and in fact there was some chance I might have just stayed home that day and worked at home." *For want of a nail . . .*

By 10:30, however, Scott and Jones had the spare tire under control, and slightly under a half hour later they were walking into the Sierra Club office on University Way—tired, disheveled, a little grimy, and distinctly out of sorts. The phone was ringing as they came through the door. One of the staff people answered it while Scott hung up his hat and coat. She listened a moment, then handed the receiver across the desk to him. "It's for you," she said. "Person-to-person from Washington."

Scott took the telephone, glared at it a moment, and put it to his ear. "Doug Scott speaking," he said.

"Doug," said the voice on the other end, "this is Lloyd Meeds. I'm calling from outside the Rules Committee rooms. They've just granted a rule on Hells Canyon."

Hells Canyon. Rule. Omigod, yes! What kind?

"One-hour open," said Meeds.

Any trouble?

"A little." Meeds proceeded to relate a capsule version of the Rules Committee hearing. Symms had been there, violently attacking the Ullman bill, and some of the members had been listening to him. A vigorous challenge could be expected on the House floor, where several weakening amendments were sure to be offered. Meeds thought that they'd better start getting the word around to all members of the House, to make sure they knew how large a constituency there was in support of the bill. They had two days to do it—floor action had been tentatively scheduled for the twentieth.

"Tentatively" wasn't firm enough for Scott, who was having alarming visions of the need to accomplish three weeks' worth of work in forty-eight hours. "When will we know for certain?" he asked.

"Well," said the Washington congressman, only half joking, "I think we'll know for *certain* just about an hour before the bill actually comes up. Hang on a second, Doug—here's somebody I have to talk to." There was a pause, the sound of a receiver rattling, and then Scott, still holding onto his end of the 3,000-mile-long telephone line, distinctly heard a voice in the background say, "Lloyd, how about bringing up your bill this afternoon? We're not going to do the New York debt bill."

Meeds immediately returned to the phone. "Did you hear that, Doug?" he asked.

"Yeah," said Scott, a little dazed.

"What do you think?"

Scott took a deep breath and plunged. "Sounds good to me," he said. "What do *you* think?"

"Sounds good to me, too." said Meeds. "Let's do it."

They hung up. Scott rubbed his ear, ran his fingers through his thick mane of black curly hair, and went to the extension phone in his private office. There were a staggering number of calls that would have to be made in the next hour or so, to congressmen, congressional staff people, and environmentalists in Washington and all over the country. But there was also this: The bill's opponents would have at least as big a job in front of them, and *they* didn't know about it yet. The only people who knew anything so far were he, Meeds, Mike Reed, Dale Jones, and the others who had been listening with him in the Seattle office. But to take advantage of this slight edge, he would have to move extraordinarily fast.

He picked up the phone and started dialing.

iii

Across the hall from the Rules Committee rooms, within the walnut-paneled walls of the largest legislative assembly hall in the world, the United States House of Representatives had already been in session for nearly two hours. It was the day for the private calendar; and, after the prayer (delivered by a visiting priest from the Bronx), the reading of the journal (dispensed with by unanimous consent), the delivery of messages from the president and the Senate, and the ritual of the first quorum call (391 out of 435 members present), the thirty-four private bills for that day were called up, one at a time. Members with no private bills in the hopper began drifting quietly away to lunch or to meetings or back to their offices to dig into the mounds of paper work that always seem to be awaiting any congressman. Gradually, the floor became almost empty.

Scott: *"All that hoo-rah about the tax bill was in progress that morning, too. And Congressman Ullman was nowhere to be found. But the first call I made was to his office, and I alerted his staff man, Bill Ullberger, who wasn't aware of all this, that the bill was going to come up that afternoon—assuming Mr. Ullman and Mr. Taylor agreed. Meeds was calling them. And in very short order the decision was firmly made. . . ."*

The private calendar ground down to the last bill. Now the principal business of the afternoon could get under way, beginning with reports from the House-Senate Conference Committees on bills that had passed both houses, had gone into conference to get their differences ironed out, and were now ready for reapproval in their amended forms. There were five of these. Activity on the first three followed quite a standard format: debate by the few members who happened, for one reason or another, to have remained on the floor; a call for the vote; the ringing of bells throughout the House side of the Capitol, the House office buildings, the House cafeteria, and a few nearby restaurants, announcing the vote; and a tidal wave of congressmen flowing into the House chamber for the vote, then ebbing back out again, flow, ebb, flow, ebb, flow, ebb, all through the first part of the afternoon.

Scott: *"So during that period of time I called the Sierra Club's office in Washington and got hold of Chuck Clusen. And Chuck dropped everything and did a masterful job of organizing people in the Sierra Club office, and the Friends of the Earth office, and a few other people to sit down and systematically telephone the several hundred members of the House who are affiliated with the Environmental Study Conference, which is an internal organization of members of the House who are interested in the environment, and who have their own whip system to alert each other to urgent things that are coming up. I think there are one hundred and seventy of these people. And—between all the secretaries and everybody in the Sierra Club office, and these other groups—every one of those offices was called, to alert them that this unscheduled bill was coming up that afternoon, and would they please be sure to vote for it, and get over there on the House floor. And I called personal friends in the Congress, and we did a fair amount of calling—we called every Northwest congressman, to make sure they got over there to help defend the bill, all the ones that were cosponsors. To do such things as to show up and be at the doors, so as the average member of the House walked into the chamber there was somebody standing at the door saying, 'This is a good bill, vote for it.' Something as simple-minded as that. Which is a very important thing."*

Rep. Steve Symms, to his credit, was remaining on the floor between votes, stubbornly resisting the ebb and flow of the congressional tide. He had let the first three conference reports go by
without much comment; but the fourth concerned a bill to which he
was strongly opposed, and on the fourth he swung into action.

The bill bore the unwieldy title of Extension of the Federal Insec-
ticide, Fungicide, and Rodentcide Act (H.R. 8841). It was taken
up—as is usual for a conference report—under suspension of the
rules. Suspension is commonly decided upon by a simple voice
vote, but it is the privilege of any member to demand a vote by
teller. Symms so demanded. The bells announcing a teller vote rang
through the House, and a small intertidal wave of congressmen
who had nothing else to do at the moment washed into the well of
the House chamber and prepared to be counted. The final tally
showed that 123 members had voted, less than 29 percent of the
House membership (compared to a 95 percent vote on roll calls that
same afternoon). It also showed that Symms had lost badly, 106 to
17. Debate began under suspension; but it had proceeded only a
minute or two when Symms, nursing his wounds and mentally
roughing out the blistering speech he was about to give denouncing
H.R. 8841, was startled suddenly to hear the words *Hells Canyon.*

Hells Canyon? How did *that* get in here?

The speaker had been Thomas P. ("Tip") O'Neill, the large,
ruddy, popular House majority leader, who had asked for and
received the unanimous consent of the House to speak out of turn
in order to give the legislative program for the remainder of the
day. He had reminded the members that they were currently on
H.R. 8841 and explained that this would be followed by the conference report on SJR 121, Quarterly Adjustments of Support
Prices for Milk, and then (matter-of-factly) by H.R. 30, establishing the Hells Canyon National Recreation Area. At this point he
was interrupted by John Rousselot of California, a ranking
member of the Committee on Banks and Currency, who wanted to
know what had happened to the New York Debt bill. The interruption gave Symms time to collect his thoughts, and as soon as
Rousselot was finished, the gentleman from Idaho was on his feet.

"Mr. Speaker," he demanded, "Would the gentleman tell me
what it was he said about the Hells Canyon bill? Was it the rule or
the legislation?

"We intend," answered O'Neill calmly, "to bring up the rule *and* the legislation."

"Today?"

"Yes, today."

"We will actually have the legislation today?"

O'Neill aimed an acid look in the direction of the Idahoan. "Following the quarterly adjustments of support for prices of milk," he explained, with exaggerated care, "we would consider the Hells Canyon bill, having cleared it with the Committee on Rules and having cleared it with the leaders of the committee. We do hope to be through at a reasonable hour. I suppose that will be sufficient for the gentleman to go through with his daily routine of trying to prevent legislation coming up. . . ."

Symms subsided, but his mind was racing. He had a maximum of two hours, and probably considerably less, to rally the opposition to Hells Canyon. And he was needed on the floor! Well, the floor would just have to do without him for a moment. He slipped into the cloakroom and picked up the telephone.

iv

There were thirty-five people on the floor—about 8 percent of the House membership—when the historic final debate on the Hells Canyon bill got under way late that afternoon. Environmentalists seated in the gallery could spot a number of familiar figures. Al Ullman and Lloyd Meeds were both there; so were subcommittee chairman Taylor and—significantly—the chairman of the full Interior Committee, James Haley. On the debit side, Symms was still stubbornly planted in his seat; he had been joined by Hansen and Roncalio and by Del Clawson of California, who had been a principal spokesman against the bill in the Rules Committee. Bob Duncan was at his desk looking grim; but so was the other Portland-area congressman, Les AuCoin, who had remained an ardent supporter of the bill and who therefore might be able to blunt Duncan's drive. All in all, the division of major forces looked about equal. It was hard to say what would happen.

Debate began with a call for the rule by Richard Bolling of Missouri, a fourteen-term veteran of the House and a longtime

Rules Committee member, who delivered an impassioned little speech in defense of the bill. He was followed by Clawson, speaking for the Republican minority on the Rules Committee, and what Clawson said was a bit of a surprise. He opposed the bill, he had always opposed the bill, he would continue to oppose the bill, but in the interest of justice he thought it high time for a vote on the thing. The rule should be adopted, he said, in order "to allow the House to work its will on H.R. 30."

He sat down. George Hansen got up. He objected "strongly" to adoption of the rule. Consideration of this measure was premature. No field hearings had been held in Idaho. The bill was being forced on his constituents without any opportunity for them to express their will. King George III had lost an awful lot of tea for a similar offense. . . . It was a regular three-ring circus of a speech, and it was a circus man that answered it—crusty old James A. Haley of Florida, chairman of the House Interior Committee, formerly of Ringling Brothers, Barnum & Bailey in Sarasota. "I have heard about Hells Canyon," he drawled, "for twenty-three years that I have been in Congress. If all the hearings were put together in one place I think we would have a good-sized boxcar full of papers on those hearings because we have explored this thing upstream and downstream and sideways and everything else. I do not know what good an additional hearing would accomplish."

Bolling called for the rule. It was adopted on a voice vote, without even a test of the two-thirds question. In the gallery, the observers breathed a sigh of relief. The final obstacle had been overcome; at last the bill could stand or die on its own merits.

Now the House resolved itself into the Committee of the Whole House on the State of the Union, a parliamentary maneuver that alters the rules of debate slightly in order to expedite the process of producing legislation. The Speaker leaves the chair, and another House member—in this case, Murphy of Illinois—takes the rostrum. The mace, symbol of House authority, is moved from its tall green pedestal to a low white one in front of the Speaker's desk. And in addition to these window-dressing alterations, there is one significant change: The size of a quorum is reduced from 218 to 100. This makes it far more difficult for foes of a bill to obstruct the legislative process by repeated demands for a quorum.

The Committee of the Whole is maintained for purposes of debate only; to vote on a bill, the House resolves itself back into regular session. However, amendments may be offered during the committee session. If defeated there, they are dead; if passed, they may be brought up again during the final vote, after the Committee of the Whole has been dissolved.

Debate on a bill is further defined, of course, by the rule which has been adopted for it. In the case of the Hells Canyon bill, this was a standard form known colloquially as a "one-hour open," providing for an hour of debate divided equally among Republicans and Democrats, thirty minutes for each party. Control over the way those thirty minutes were allocated would be in the hands of two men: Parks and Recreation Subcommittee chairman Roy Taylor for the Democrats, and the subcommittee's ranking minority member, Keith Sebelius, for the Republicans. Following the hour of general debate, amendments would be in order under the so-called five-minute rule, during which debate may proceed for no more than ten minutes, five in support and five in opposition. This ten-minute limitation, however, is more apparent than real. Any member can circumvent it by moving to "strike the last word"—in other words, by offering a trivial amendment of his own that would give him five additional minutes to speak. No rule of germaneness governs the "striking of the last word"; the five minutes so obtained can thus easily be applied to debate of the principal amendment under discussion.

The general debate got under way. There were few surprises. Nonpartisanship was apparent from the beginning, as Sebelius, representing what was nominally the minority position, used his opening statement to present a defense of the bill that was, if anything, stronger than that given by Taylor a few minutes previously. "I am not in favor," Sebelius emphasized, "of losing for all time the very last of any of our superlative natural resources, and I believe that is what this bill would constitute, if it were amended to permit dams to be constructed within the Hells Canyon." He zeroed in specifically on the Duncan-Roncalio position:

> Now Mr. Chairman, there is an amendment which will probably be offered today, and it was offered before and fully

debated and finally rejected by the committee, which is labeled as a compromise. Now I caution my colleagues, that this amendment is no compromise. It is the amendment which is vigorously sought and endorsed by the power interests, and they would be extremely gleeful over its adoption. That in itself should tell you that it does not represent a compromise.

Lloyd Meeds took the floor to explain the trade-offs in resources that the bill would represent. Hansen made an attempt to get him to talk about the possibility of a "1978 moratorium." Meeds had heard quite enough about moratoriums, and he lost his temper. "I don't know of any 1978 moratorium," he snapped. "There was a moratorium proposed in the Senate. The Senate has twice repudiated that moratorium by the passage of the legislation before us, so there *is* no moratorium. We have run out of moratoriums. We have run out of time. It is time *now* to make up our minds about preserving this area!"

The Hansen–Meeds exchange essentially marked the end of serious colloquy; for, though general debate went on for another half hour, there were no more sparks flying. Most of the time was devoted to extended speeches by Symms and Duncan in defense of their separate amendments, which were yet to be offered; Symms, in particular, was so long-winded that three times he had to ask his colleagues for extra time, moving even the sympathetic George Hansen to remark, in a sidelong reference to Symms's adamant antiwelfare stance, that this was "the first time I have ever seen the gentleman in the well on the dole." Al Ullman managed to get in the last word, with a concise, moving statement of the reasons for the bill, summing up the years of battle, of study, and of indecision in three short final paragraphs that deserve to be quoted in their entirety:

Mr. Chairman, I think we crossed the bridge of damming this section of the river a long time ago. I came to the conclusion five years ago that there never would be a dam built in this stretch of the canyon. Subsequently I reached the conclusion that it would be totally impossible from almost any point of view, whether it be economic or whether it be from the point of view of the conservation interests of the nation. I came to a later conclusion that even if the dam *could* be built, it should *not* be built.

The highest and best use of this vast and spectacularly beautiful area is to allow this free-flowing river to remain in its present state in this tremendous canyon, and we should save it for America's posterity. That is what this bill does.

Mr. Chairman, I strongly oppose the amendment which will be offered by the gentleman from Idaho. This area has been studied to death. We are now at the point of decision, and it is time to make a final disposition of this area and adopt this bill.

That was the end of the general debate. It was time to proceed to the amendments.

The Symms Amendment came first. It was debated briefly and heatedly and then brought to a vote by division of the House, a procedure in which the members literally stand and are counted. The bells don't ring, and only those who happen to be on the floor—or who can hustle in from the cloakroom—are able to vote. "It was scary," recalls Doug Scott. "They had more horses standing around, relatively, than we did." The amendment was defeated, but only by a slim five-vote margin—far closer than had been expected, and much too close for comfort. As Duncan got up to present the "compromise" amendment, Meeds and Ullman were seen scurrying off the floor toward the phones in the cloakroom; for the next several minutes they were busy calling supporters of the bill, and by the time Duncan's amendment came to a vote some fifteen minutes later, the margin of victory had swelled to a comfortable sixteen votes. By this time the chamber, for the first time since the call of the roll on the previous bill, contained a quorum, and the size of it continued to swell steadily as more and more members continued to pour through the doors. In the gallery—and on the other end of a hot phone line in Seattle—the environmentalists could scarcely contain their elation. The two amendments were both dead; all that was left was the up-or-down vote itself, and the outcome of that had never been in any real doubt.

Now the final roll-call vote began, winding down through the alphabet. When it ended twenty minutes later, even the environmentalists, who had expected to win, were staggered by the lopsidedness of their victory. The final score: 342 in favor, 53 against. What Brock Evans was already calling "the greatest conservation battle of our time" had ended with a smashing success.

Over the main door of the House chamber, on the inside where the members can see it as they sit in session, there is a large plaster shield with a quote engraved on it. The words are attributed to Daniel Webster, and they begin, "Let us develop the resources of our land, call forth its powers. . . ." Passing out of the chamber after the vote, Steve Symms and Bob Duncan might have glanced up at that shield and chuckled a little at the irony of what had just happened under the auspices of that hoary exhortation. But there is no record that either of them did.

Epilogue:
Return to the River

At slightly past seven o'clock on the morning of the first day of spring, March 21, 1976, Lewiston physician Dave Spencer backs his big boat trailer expertly down the ramp at Hellsgate Marina on the city's western waterfront and launches his sleek aluminum jet boat onto the backwater of Lower Granite Dam. My wife and I climb aboard. We are bound for Rush Creek Rapids at the foot of Hat Point, beyond the official head of navigation and as far up Hells Canyon as power boats can normally go.

It is three months, less ten days, since President Gerald R. Ford—in one of his last official acts of 1975—signed the Hells Canyon National Recreation Area into law, marking the end of the controversy that had swirled around the deepest gorge on earth for nearly three decades. That signature came late on New Year's Eve, midway through the congressional Christmas recess and after a ten-day delay that left conservationists biting their fingernails. Doug Scott explained the genesis of that delay to me the day before it was resolved. The bill the House had passed on November 18 had been sent to the Senate for repassage, to bring the Senate- and House-passed versions into conformity with each other; but instead of simply approving the House changes, as it had been expected to do, the Senate—under Sen. Jim McClure's prodding—had made a

few further changes of its own. That meant that the House had to
re-repass the legislation. ''People were worried, at that stage, about
pocket veto possibilities,'' Scott told me, referring to the ability of
presidents to allow a bill to simply die without signature during a
congressional recess. ''So they were trying to think of a way to sit
on the bill through the Christmas holidays and not have it go up to
the president till January, when he couldn't have that opportunity.
Now, right about that stage the 1975 tax reform bill was in a *big*
mess, and of course Congressman Ullman was running the tax bill.
And it looked like the Congress was going to be staying in *pro
forma* sessions right on through the holidays, which meant that
there wouldn't be the pocket veto possibility. And so they picked
the bill up off the House calendar one day, and passed it, and sent
it on to the White House. That same day, a compromise on the tax
bill was worked out, and the Congress *did* adjourn.'' The Hells
Canyon bill was left dangling. Ten tense days had gone by. And
then, finally, on New Year's Eve, at almost the last possible legal
moment, that signature had come.

All this is behind us now, on this March morning on the river.
The air is still and fresh, and the surface of Lower Granite Reservoir is glass smooth beneath a high, delicate overcast. The canyon
beckons. It is going to be a glorious day.

A short distance below the Grande Ronde we strike little
Limekiln Rapid, our first white water. It is not much—John Barker
has referred to it earlier as ''a little splashy water''—and the big
boat handles it easily, climbing through the waves and foam and
hidden rocks to the calmer water above in a very few minutes. Even
these small rapids, however, can be dangerous. Speeding upriver
beyond the upper lip, Dave and his friend Ernie Duckworth discuss
the tragedy that occurred the summer before at Limekiln when a
girl tried to ride through it on an inner tube, without a life vest, and
upset and was lost. Ernie points out ''Dead Man's Eddy,'' a large
backwater where the bodies of those drowned further up the canyon are supposed, by local legend, to collect. For a short time, the
boat throbs upstream in silence.

Beyond the Grande Ronde, the canyon proper begins; the walls
climb steeply to higher and higher rims, the river whitens. Beaches

and gravel bars alternate with long sections of rocky narrows where the cliffs plunge directly into the water. After a few miles of this, we come out of a narrows around a long, slow curve to the right and see before us, stretching from shore to shore across the river, something that looks like a low white wall that churns and thunders as we approach. This is Wild Goose Rapids, lowest major rapid on the river and a place of much history. Beside this "very considerable fall" stood the Nez Perce fishing village that Lewis and Clark's men visited; above it, set firmly in a flat rock face on the Washington side, is the great iron ring that once anchored the steamer *Imnaha* as she winched herself upriver toward Eureka Bar. High on the walls paint splotches frown down on us, marking the height of the proposed China Gardens Dam—now outlawed— which was to have been the reregulating facility for the discredited Nez Perce project. And on a tiny shelf next to the calm water above the rapid, at the base of a tall, incredibly steep face of black rock, nestle a few forlorn-looking A-frame cabins. Wild Goose Ranchos. The starting point of the Great Snake Land War. Dave throws his boat at the rapid, fighting his way up, following the navigation markers set out by the Army Corps of Engineers. The deck shudders and churns; waves slap the sides, spray flashes from the prow. Slowly we gain headway, crest out, slip over the lip into the calm above.

And so the day proceeds. There are benches and beaches; there is white water; there are long, gloomy narrows where the boat, reduced and humbled by the immensity of its surroundings, threads the base of a steep-sided V whose walls seem to rear upward almost to the end of sight. We pass through the immense, echoing cathedral of the Nez Perce site, cruise slowly above the grave of the *Imnaha* at Mountain Sheep, pay our respects to the souls of the dead Chinese miners at Deep Creek Bar. There is a side trip up the Salmon River to its lowest rapid, the photogenic Eye of the Salmon, and there is a long pause on the shore opposite Eureka Bar, gazing at the great, forever unused stamp mill foundation and at the powerful little river pouring out of its cleft in the rock just upstream. Ernie points out the remains of the steamboat landing below the Imnaha Rapids, and of the old road that hugs the base of the cliffs from the landing to the abandoned townsite, a half mile distant.

Dave uses this stop to tell us of the political problems sport fishermen such as himself must put up with in Hells Canyon. The good fishing holes, it seems, are no respecters of state lines; some are in Oregon, some in Idaho. Dave must therefore buy two licenses. "I used to buy only an Idaho license," he says, "but some of my favorite holes are in Oregon. I'd fish them anyway, but whenever I heard a jet boat coming I'd have to jump in *my* boat and rush over to the Idaho side. Just in case it was the game warden. It got so the cost of the extra license was worth it for peace of mind."

The canyon walls climb higher and higher as we go upstream. Waterfalls cascade down them; flowers grace them with their bright beauty. There is saxifrage, buttercup, fritillaria. We spot a brodiaea lily at the Chinese Massacre site. Prickly-pear cactus sprouts from every conceivable surface.

At about 2:30 in the afternoon, we round the corner at Johnson's Bar and the great wall of Hat Point, whitened two-thirds of the way down with spring snow, looms over us. Ahead is Rush Creek Rapids. We are at the wild heart of the canyon, the lower end of the deepest and narrowest section and the farthest point upstream that we will be able to reach.

Maneuvering carefully in the choppy, whitecapped water below the rapid, Dave brings the boat to shore on a small piece of sand and the rest of us scramble out. A thorough tie-down is necessary here; the swift water could easily send the boat careening away downstream, wrecking it and stranding us. Dave holds the prow against the beach with the motor while my wife and I help Ernie secure the bow line around a large rock and pile others along its length. Then he cuts the motor and joins us on shore. The boat swings and bobs at the end of its tether, but it holds. We move along the boulders lining the shore to the edge of the angry water. An otter scurries off at our approach and hides under a glistening wet stone. The rapid thunders.

Rush Creek is awesome. Here the whole body of the powerful Snake is confined to a steep, boulder-choked chute perhaps eighty feet wide. Great, thick pours of water thunder over the stones in all directions. Waves dance and crash into each other, breaking backward as the swift river flows out from underneath them. Over by the Idaho shore, a great sloping hole yawns big enough to swallow a cabin cruiser. Masses of deceptively smooth water pour into it and climb out the other side; the hole is perpetually changing, but its size and location remain constant. The shudder and thud and express-train roar of falling water is overwhelming. Rush Creek is considered a Class IV rapid, on a scale of six. In the seventeen miles further to Hells Canyon Dam, there are larger ones yet: Granite Falls, Wild Sheep—Class VI each—but we will not see them this trip. Very few men go beyond Rush Creek Rapids in jet boats. Ernie has done it. Dave has tried, in the boat we came upriver in today. The hole caught him. Pieces of his original windshield still lie on the bottom of the Snake River.

This is what the downstream dams would have covered with water: the challenge of the Snake, the power of it, and the overwhelming beauty. The dam builders would have replaced it with a flat reservoir, far easier to boat on, it is claimed, and thus a recreational enhancement. Is this true? Ernie shakes his head. Reservoirs are easier boating only in the calmest of weathers. In a good healthy breeze, a reservoir will kick up waves large enough to swamp an unwary boater; on running water, the wave patterns seldom change, even in a strong wind. Twice as many boaters go up the open Snake from Lewiston, he says, as go down the Lower Granite Reservoir from the same launch sites.

For the moment, this rapid is the center of the known universe. Beyond it, like an explosion of space, is the great, enveloping canyon; and beyond the canyon, the distant and irrelevant world. That is the proper order of things; that is how they should be. Standing beside Rush Creek and breathing its spray, I remember the words Bob Packwood spoke to me the week after the National Recreation Area Act was finally signed into law. "It's one of those very rewarding things in life," he said, emphasizing his words with powerful thrusts of his hands, "where you work and you work and you work on something, and you *get* it. So often you work on something, and you get *half* of it, and you accept it, and you feel a bit frustrated, but—you know—you accept it. But this is one, that—I guess, as you look back on your career—you can really feel very, very satisfied.

"Hells Canyon is unique. Everybody says, 'Well, this is unique, or unusual,' but Hells Canyon is *genuinely* unique. And there *is* nothing else like it.''

Bob Packwood is right. Hells Canyon is unique, irreplaceable, priceless. It is beyond value. And those who have set it aside, undammed, in this age of power shortages, have performed a deed of sacrifice and generosity for which all future generations who come to measure themselves against this river and the deepest gorge on earth will forever remain profoundly grateful. Do the power companies understand this, even yet? Is anybody listening?

And we climb back in the boat and go away from Rush Creek, back down the river, out of the deepest gorge on earth, back to the standard-size objects of our everyday and unimportant lives.

Appendix: Your Visit to Hells Canyon

Travel in Hells Canyon is not easy. The traveler must come prepared for heat, dust, rattlesnakes, and—to reach the rim viewpoints—lingering summer snow and some of the worst roads in North America. But though the difficulties are great, the rewards match them. There are flowers; there are Indian pictographs and mining relics; there are spectacular rapids and sky-topping vistas; and there is always, permeating each moment of each day, the magnificent and overwhelming presence of the deepest gorge on earth. And the situation is changing—for the better. As this is written, management plans for the Hells Canyon National Recreation Area are still in the formative stage, but it can be predicted almost without question that an early result of those plans will be improved access to viewpoints on the Oregon rim, probably with a major visitor center to replace the current primitive facilities at Hat Point. There may also be paved access to the river itself near the midpoint of the canyon, made possible through improvements in the currently existing primitive roads to Dug Bar in Oregon and Pittsburg Landing in Idaho.

This brief guide reflects the state of Hells Canyon travel as of the spring of 1977.

GETTING THERE

Hells Canyon lies roughly at the center of a ten-thousand-square-mile triangle with apexes at Boise and Lewiston, Idaho, and at Pendleton, Oregon. Travel around the perimeter of this triangle is primarily by Federal highway: U.S. 95 on the east, U.S. 12 on the north, and Interstate 80N on the west. Travel within it is something else again. Roads are few and far between; most are unpaved, and even the paved routes are likely to be narrow, winding, and slow. The best of these are the state highways, of which there are four: Washington 129/Oregon 3 (south from U.S. 12 at Clarkston, Washington, signed to Enterprise, Oregon); Oregon 82 (east from Interstate 80N at LaGrande, Oregon, signed to Enterprise); Oregon 86 (east from Interstate 80N at Baker, Oregon, signed to Halfway); and Idaho 71 (west from U.S. 95 at Cambridge, signed to Brownlee Dam). Oregon 82 and Idaho 71 converge at Oxbow Dam, where they are met by an Idaho Power Company road (open to the public), which snakes its way twenty-two miles on downriver to Hells Canyon Dam and currently forms the only paved access route to any part of the gorge. It is thus the best way to get a quick look at the place if you are in a hurry, but be warned that "quick," as used here, is relative; allow at least half a day from the time you leave either Cambridge or Baker and the time you return. For access to any other view of the canyon, allow at least a full day—although a somewhat less-than-satisfactory glimpse may be had of the downstream end by leaving Washington 129 at Asotin and following an unimproved county road thirty miles or so upriver to the mouth of the Grande Ronde, for a total elapsed time of perhaps two hours from U.S. 12.

THE WEST RIM

The west rim access points offer the classic views of Hells Canyon: the meadows, the sky, and the great gulf falling away into the blue depths and rising again in the middle distance to the jagged, snow-flecked peaks of the Seven Devils Mountains. From most points, the river itself cannot be seen, and the canyon seems truly bottomless. So, unfortunately, do the chuckholes on the access roads. Driving this country is not for the timorous; it requires strong nerves, good tires, and a suspension system that can take a beating. But the rewards, for the well prepared, are great.

Best known of the west rim viewpoints is Hat Point Lookout, reached over a combination of county and Forest Service roads from the town of Joseph, Oregon, on state highway 82 in the Wallowa Valley. The first thirty miles of the Hat Point road, from Joseph to the tiny hamlet of Imnaha, are paved; the twenty-four remaining miles from Imnaha to the lookout are narrow, rough, and tortuously crooked. Check your suspension system, your gas gauge, and your tires before setting out, and be prepared to take it *slowly*. Along the way there are impressive views of the Imnaha Canyon at Five Mile Overlook and Granny View and a splendid first view of Hells Canyon at Saddle Creek Observation Site, where the Forest Service maintains a picnic area. The last six miles, from Saddle Creek to Hat Point itself, are along the rim, but you will not see the river until you reach the lookout and gaze down on Johnson Bar and Rush Creek Rapids, three airline miles away and nearly six thousand feet below you. There are more picnic tables here and, nearby, a small campground. A branch road a mile before the lookout leads two miles north to a trailhead; Sommers Point is fourteen trail miles beyond this point, almost all of it along the rim. Another trail leaves the access road near Saddle Creek and traverses the rim southward for twenty spectacular miles to McGraw Lookout. A third trail, beginning directly at Hat Point, descends six corkscrew miles down Smooth Hollow to the river at the mouth of Saddle Creek; the first half mile of this trail offers an excellent taste of Hells Canyon hiking, with minimal effort, through meadows with some of the most spectacular displays of wildflowers to be found anywhere.

Easier to reach than Hat Point, but with somewhat less spectacular views, is Buckhorn Point, on the lower portion of the rim north of the Imnaha River. Buckhorn is reached by forty-five miles of mostly level driving over back roads from Enterprise. Obtain instructions and a map from Forest Service offices in Enterprise, Joseph, or Wallowa, and follow signs to Zumwalt, Thomason Meadow, and Buckhorn Springs. A progressively worse road, with progressively better views, leads north from Buckhorn Point along

Cemetery Ridge, and trails descend to the river along Cherry and Eureka Creeks.

Two other west rim viewpoints are reachable by car: McGraw Lookout and Buck Peak, less than two miles apart and both located near the end of a rough nine-mile-long Forest Service road beginning near Ollokot Campground on the upper Imnaha River (accessible either from the north, through Joseph, or from the south, up North Pine Creek from the vicinity of Oxbow Dam. In either case, the Forest Service road number you want is 393). This is the southern terminus of the west rim trail and overlooks the reservoir behind Hells Canyon Dam, an artifact that unfortunately tends to tame the view somewhat. But the canyon wall views are among the most spectacular anywhere.

THE EAST RIM

The view from the east rim of Hells Canyon is less well known than that from the west. It is also higher, wilder, and in many cases far more spectacular. In fact, the ultimate canyon view in the United States is probably that from Dry Diggins Lookout, seventeen miles by road and another nine by trail out of Riggins, Idaho, midway between Boise and Lewiston on U.S. 95. The river is 6,400 feet down—straight down—and the canyon's depth is emphasized by the flatness of the far rim, seen here where the old remnant Snake River Plateau is at its broadest. And, as if this vista of broad plateau, great canyon, and distant angry river were not enough, there is also, close at hand to the south, rearing up like a new planet being born, the jagged gray mass of the Seven Devils. There is little wonder that those who have been to Dry Diggins swear that it is worth any amount of torture just to stand on the edge of that abyss for five minutes.

You can't drive to Dry Diggins, and there is nothing quite like it accessible by car. The nearest match is probably Sheep Rock, an overhanging rock shelf a vertical mile above the waters of Hells Canyon Reservoir quite near the dam. To reach Sheep Rock, leave U.S. 95 at the little town of Council and drive forty miles of good quality gravel road to Cuprum, then fifteen miles further over a "road" that is even lower standard than the one to Hat Point (passable by passenger cars, but just barely). Nearby are two inferior overlooks, Horse Mountain and Kinney Point, and several trailheads for lakes in the southern half of the Seven Devils.

A spectacular view, but one in which the canyon seems distant and incidental, can be had from Heavens Gate Lookout, a mile and a half by a good quality road above Windy Saddle and Seven Devils Lake—the trailhead for Dry Diggins Lookout—on Forest Service Road 517 out of Riggins.

THE RIVER, NORTH: JET BOATS

The north portal of Hells Canyon may be glimpsed by taking a gravel road south from Asotin, Washington (six miles south of U.S. 12 via Washington 129), thirty miles along the west bank of the Snake to the mouth of the Grande Ronde River. Penetrating any further requires a boat. If you have your own craft, you may launch it at the Grande Ronde or at any one of a number of boat ramps in the Lewiston-Clarkston-Asotin area. Do not do so, however, unless you are familiar with the difficulties and dangers of white-water boating. The upper limit for outboards is Wild Goose Rapids, five miles into the canyon. Jet boats can and do go much further: Skilled operators occasionally climb all the way through the canyon to the tailrace of Hells Canyon Dam—though this is likely to be prohibited in the near future under use regulations being established for the Hells Canyon National Recreation Area. The official upper limit of navigation is Johnson Bar, ninety miles above Lewiston and within sight of Hat Point and Dry Diggins lookouts. A number of commercial firms in the Lewiston-Clarkston area run one- and two-day excursions via jet boat to Johnson Bar: The fact that you are sitting at ease in a comfortable seat the entire way upriver and back on one of these tours detracts little from the excitement of the flying spray, throbbing boat deck, awesome scenery, and heart-in-mouth sensation each time the boat strains to reach the crest of one of the thundering surges of white water they call "little" rapids on the middle Snake. Write to the Lewiston Chamber of Commerce for a current list of Hells Canyon jet boat tours.

THE RIVER, MIDWAY: TRAILS

Stout cars and stout-hearted drivers may reach the banks of the Snake River at two points midway in its course through Hells Canyon. These two points, Dug Bar in Oregon and Pittsburg Landing in Idaho, also happen to be the northern terminal points for the east and west bank water-level trails through the canyon.

To reach Dug Bar, leave the Hat Point road at Imnaha and proceed down the Imnaha River on Forest Service Road N422. The first eighteen miles of this road, to Imnaha Bridge, are fairly good quality; the last four, over Cactus Mountain and down to the river's edge, are called "road" only by courtesy. At Dug Bar you will find garbage cans, pit toilets, and a large wooden sign on the riverbank proclaiming this as the site of Joseph's Crossing, though most authorities believe that the actual crossing took place at the mouth of Big Canyon, several miles downstream. The west-side trail, which begins here, terminates fifty miles upstream at the mouth of Battle Creek, five miles below Hells Canyon Dam. Hikers on this trail should be prepared for long detours away from the river and up the canyon wall, and for encounters with heat and with rattlesnakes. The views, however, are constantly spectacular. This is the access route to the site of the Chinese Massacre, five trail miles south of Dug Bar at the mouth of Deep Creek.

Pittsburg Landing lies at the end of Forest Service Road 493 out of White Bird, Idaho, via Malthorn Saddle and Kurry Creek. This road is even rougher than the Dug Bar access route, but it is also more rewarding. Downstream a short distance is the spectacular site of the now-outlawed Pleasant Valley Dam; upstream is the beginning of thirty miles of high-standard trail terminating at Brush Creek, a mile and a half below Hells Canyon Dam. This is a far better trail than the one on the Oregon side, and stays closer to the river. Side routes branch off at most of the major streams and offer access to the high lakes of the Seven Devils, between ten and twenty trail miles away. The combination of this trail and its branch route up Granite Creek is probably the finest wilderness experience available in Hells Canyon country.

THE RIVER, SOUTH: FLOAT TRIPS

Unlike most approaches to Hells Canyon, the drive into the canyon to the south requires no special mountain-driving gymnastics. Though the road is rather twisty, it is well paved, two lanes wide, and mostly level, following the shore of Hells Canyon Reservoir to the Idaho Power Company's dam at Hells Canyon Creek. Thus large motor homes may safely proceed directly into the profoundly deep and narrow trench that turned back Benjamin Bonneville and Wilson Price Hunt and drowned Jean Baptiste Prevost. But we have paid for the privilege. Though the great walls of the canyon are as steep and tall and awesome as ever, the rapids are silent. Water skiers speed above the grave of Copper Ledge Falls, where the *Norma* and the *Shoshone* almost wrecked; the greatest white water of the Snake is gone forever.

Hells Canyon Dam is the put-in place for float trips through Hells Canyon; these trips take four days to run the entire length of the gorge, from the dam to the mouth of the Grande Ronde River. There is one day of exciting river-running to below Granite Falls, followed by three days of quiet drifting and easy rapids, a situation that causes some veteran river-runners to scoff that the Snake is "built backwards." A list of commercial float operators is available from the Lewiston Chamber of Commerce or the Wallowa-Whitman National Forest headquarters in Baker, Oregon; or you may run the river in your own craft if you first obtain the required float permit from the Forest Service.

There are also commercial jet-boat tours from Hells Canyon Dam down to Wild Sheep Rapids, a distance of six miles; and hikers who can arrange boat transportation to the trailheads at Battle and Brush Creeks often use Hells Canyon Dam as a jumping-off point for beginning the long hike through the canyon on either the Oregon or Idaho side trails.

THE MINES AT EUREKA BAR

The site of the old mining camp at Eureka Bar, doomed by the sinking of the steamer *Imnaha* in 1903, may be reached by trail from the Imnaha Bridge on the road to Dug Bar. The trail follows the Imnaha River six miles from the bridge to the river's confluence with the Snake; Eureka Bar begins at this confluence and extends downstream for half a mile or more. Look for the site of the old steamboat landing at the downstream end of the bar and climb to the great, never-used stone foundation for the stamp mill on the canyon wall above the old townsite.

IN THE FOOTSTEPS
OF CAPTAIN BONNEVILLE

Strong hikers with a sense of history may follow almost precisely the route taken by Benjamin Bonneville in 1834 on his nearly disastrous exploration of the canyon. Take the twelve-mile-long west bank road along Hells Canyon Reservoir, from Copperfield through Homestead to the road's end at Copper Creek (the site of vanished Copper Ledge Falls); continue on trail 1890 two miles further along the water's edge to the mouth of McGraw Creek and an intersection with trail 1879, which should be followed up the creek to McGraw Cabin and on across the canyon face until it rounds the corner of the McGraw Creek Divide, about six miles from the trailhead. You are now standing at approximately the site of Bonneville's first-night camp away from the river (see chapter 2). To follow his route along the canyon face and over the rim to the Imnaha, continue on trail 1879 to its junction with 1884 at Spring Creek; then keep to 1884 to Squaw Creek and a junction with trail 1789. Follow 1789 as it crosses the head of Thirty-Two Point Creek and climbs to the rim; walk the rim north to Saulsberry Saddle along an old mining track, turn west onto trail 1777, and descend Summit Creek to the Imnaha River. Allow five to seven days for the trip, which took Bonneville two weeks through heavy snow.

FOR FURTHER INFORMATION

Further information about roads, trails, float trips, jet-boat tours, and lodging, may be obtained from the following sources:

Wallowa-Whitman National Forest
P.O. Box 907
Baker, Oreg. 97814

Lewiston Chamber of Commerce
Ponderosa Lewis Clark Motor Inn
Lewiston, Idaho 83501

Nez Perce National Forest
319 East Main
Grangeville, Idaho 83530

Payette National Forest
Forest Service Building
McCall, Idaho 83638

Baker Chamber of Commerce
P.O. Box 69
Baker, Oreg. 97814

Enterprise Chamber of Commerce
Enterprise, Oreg. 97828

Grangeville Chamber of Commerce
221 West Main
Grangeville, Idaho 83530

Council Chamber of Commerce
Council, Idaho 83612

Bibliography

BOOKS

Bailey, Robert G. *Hells Canyon*. Lewiston, Idaho: R. G. Bailey Printing Company, 1943.

Baldwin, Ewart M. *Geology of Oregon*. Eugene, Oregon: University of Oregon Cooperative Bookstore, 1964.

Clark, Ella E. *Indian Legends of the Pacific Northwest*. Berkeley, California: University of California Press, 1963.

Cleland, Robert Glass. *This Reckless Breed of Men*. New York: Alfred A. Knopf, Inc., 1950.

Congress and the Nation, 1945–1964. Washington, D.C.: Congressional Quarterly Service, 1965.

Dicken, Sam. *Oregon Geography*. Eugene, Oregon: University of Oregon Cooperative Bookstore, 1965.

Eckman, Leonard C. *Scenic Geology of the Pacific Northwest*. Portland, Oregon: Binsfords & Mort, 1962

Fogle, Cornelia, ed. *Sunset Travel Guide to Oregon*. Menlo Park, California: Lane Publishing Company, 1976.

Froman, Lewis A., Jr. *The Congressional Process*. Boston: Little, Brown & Co., 1967.

Gulick, Bill. *Snake River Country*. Caldwell, Idaho: Caxton Printers, Ltd., 1971.

Haines, Francis. *The Nez Perces*. Norman, Oklahoma: University of Oklahoma Press, 1955.

Holbrook, Stewart H. *The Columbia*. New York: Rinehart & Company, 1956.

_____. *Far Corner*. New York: Macmillan & Company, 1952.

An Illustrated History of Union and Wallowa Counties. Western Historical Publishing Company, 1902. Facsimile edition pub. Ann Arbor,
Michigan: University Microfilms, 1970.

Irving, Washington. *The Adventures of Captain Bonneville*. The Works
of Washington Irving, vol. 11. New York: P. F. Collier & Son, 1904.

_____. *Astoria*. Portland, Oregon: Binsfords & Mort, n.d.

Johnson, Allen, ed. *Dictionary of American Biography*. New York:
Charles Scribners' Sons, 1929.

Jordan, Grace. *Home Below Hells Canyon*. New York: Crowell, Inc.,
1954.

Jordan, Jim, ed. *Western Campsites Directory*. Menlo Park, California:
Lane Publishing Company, Sunset Books, 1972.

Josephy, Alvin M., Jr. *The Indian Heritage of America*. New York:
Alfred A. Knopf, 1969.

_____. *The Nez Perce Indians and the Opening of the Northwest*. New
Haven, Connecticut: Yale University Press, 1965.

_____. *The Patriot Chiefs*. New York: The Viking Press, 1961

LaFarge, Oliver. *A Pictorial History of the American Indian*. New York:
Crown Publishers, Inc., 1956.

Lewis, Meriwether, and Clark, William. *Journals*. Ed. Reuben Gold
Thwaites, 1904. Modern edition pub. New York: Antiquarian Press,
Ltd., 1959.

McArthur, Lewis A. and McArthur, Lewis L. *Oregon Geographic Names*.
4th ed. Portland, Oregon: Oregon Historical Society, 1974.

Moser, Don. *The Snake River Country*. New York: Time-Life Books,
1974.

Norton, Boyd. *Snake Wilderness*. San Francisco: Sierra Club Books,
1972.

Oregon, End of the Trail. 4th rev. ed. Portland, Oregon: Binsfords &
Mort, 1951.

Parker, Samuel. *Journal of an Exploring Tour Beyond the Rocky Mountains*. Ithaca, New York: Mack, Andrus, & Woodruff, Printers,
1838.

Reservoirs, Problems, and Conflicts. Corvallis, Oregon: Water Resources
Research Institute, Oregon State University, 1969.

Ross, Alexander. *Fur Hunters of the Far West*. London, 1855. Modern ed.
edited by Kenneth Spaulding. Norman, Oklahoma: University of
Oklahoma Press, 1956.

Sandoz, Mari. *Beaver Men*. New York: Hastings House, 1964.

Schuster, Alvin, ed. *Washington: The New York Times Guide to the Nation's Capital*. Washington, D.C.: Robert B. Luce, Inc., 1967.

Scott, Harvey W. *History of the Oregon Country*. Cambridge, Massachusetts: Riverside Press, Inc., 1924.

Smith, Warren, D. *Scenic Treasure House of Oregon*. Portland, Oregon: Binsfords & Mort, 1941.

Sunset Travel Guide to Idaho. Menlo Park, California: Lane Publishing Company, 1969.

Swanton, John R. *Indian Tribes of the Pacific Northwest*. Seattle: Shorey Book Store, July 1974.

Weaver, Warren, Jr. *Both Your Houses: The Truth About Congress*. New York: Praeger Publishing Company, 1972.

PERIODICALS

The Daily Tidings. Ashland, Oregon, 1973–1975.

Evans, Brock. "Hells Canyon on the Snake." *Sierra Club Bulletin*, September 1968.

_____. "Success at Hells Canyon." *Sierra Club Bulletin*, April 1976.

Foote, Jeff. "Hatfield-Ullman Bill 'Completely Unacceptable' . . . and Here's Why." *Earthwatch Oregon*, March 1973.

Frome, Michael. "Must This Be Lost to the Sight of Man?" *Field and Stream*, July 1969.

"A Great Victory on Hells Canyon." *Sierra Club National News Report*, November 21, 1975.

"Hells Canyon." *Life*, August 1, 1969.

"Hells Canyon—A Great Victory." *Sierra Club National News Report*, September 19, 1975.

"Hells Canyon Bill Signed into Law." *Sierra Club National News Report*, January 9, 1976.

"Idaho Power Company." *Electrical West*, August 1962.

James, Richard D. "Long Battle Over Dams on the Snake River Seems about to End in Victory for Environmentalists." *Wall Street Journal*, July 29, 1975.

Leopold, Luna B. "Landscape Esthetics." *Natural History*, October 1969.

Lewis, Anthony. "How the Supreme Court Reaches a Decision." *New York Times Magazine,* December 1, 1957.

Lewiston Morning Tribune. Lewiston, Idaho, 1903; 1968–1976.

Livingston, D. C. "Certain Topographic Features of Northeastern Oregon and Their Relation to Faulting." *Journal of Geology*, vol. 36, no. 8.

Neuberger, Richard L. "The Deepest Canyon on the Continent." *Travel,* May 1942.

_____. "Hells Canyon, the Biggest of All." *Harpers,* April 1939.

The New York Times, January 1915.

Norton, Boyd. "The Last Great Dam." *Audubon,* January 1970.

The Oregonian (Portland, Oregon). June 15, 1907; December 1914–January 1915; October 1948–present.

Raisz, Erwin. "The Olympic-Wallowa Lineament." *American Journal of Science,* vol. 243-A.

"Steamboat Down the Snake." *Idaho Yesterdays,* winter 1961–1962.

Swanson, Earl H. "Anthropological Resources of the Middle Snake." *Idaho Yesterdays,* winter 1968–1969.

"A Victory Celebration!" *Earthwatch Oregon,* December 1975.

"We Still May Save Hells Canyon." *Argus,* August 16, 1974.

Wheeler, Harry E. and Cook, Earl F. "Structural and Stratigraphic Significance of the Snake River Capture, Idaho–Oregon." *Journal of Geology,* November 1954.

GOVERNMENT DOCUMENTS

Bessey, Roy F. *The Public Issues of Middle Snake River Development.* State of Washington Division of Power Resources, Bulletin no. 9.

Department of the Interior Resource Study of the Middle Snake. United States Department of the Interior, April 1968.

Draft Environmental Impact Statement, Middle Snake River Project No. 2243/2273, Idaho–Oregon–Washington. Federal Power Commission, Bureau of Power, February 1975.

Haas, James B. *Fishery Problems Associated with Brownlee, Oxbow, and Hells Canyon Dams on the Middle Snake River.* Fish Commission of Oregon Investigational Report Number Four, January 1965.

"Hells Canyon National Recreation Area." Recreationists' brochure. United States Forest Service, Department of Agriculture, July 1976.

Hells Canyon National Recreation Area Interim Recreation Management Plan. Payette, Wallowa-Whitman and Nez Perce National Forests, United States Forest Service, Department of Agriculture, July 1976.

OREGON REVISED STATUTES

Review Report on Columbia River and Tributaries. Seattle District, U.S. Army Corps of Engineers, October 1, 1948.

United States Congress. *Congressional Record.* 1952–1957; 1970–1975.

_____. House of Representatives. Interior Committee Hearings on Hells Canyon Dam. H.R. 5743, 82nd Congress, 2nd Session.

_____. House of Representatives. Interior Committee Hearings on Hells Canyon National Forest Parklands and Hells Canyon National Recreation Area, H.R. 2624 and H.R. 15798, 93rd Congress, 2nd Session.

_____. House of Representatives. Interior Committee Hearings on Hells Canyon National Recreation Area and Hells Canyon National

Recreation Area Study. H.R. 30, H.R. 1630, and H.R. 5394, 94th Congress, 1st Session.

_____. House of Representatives. Committee Report Number 94-607, 94th Congress, 1st Session (Interior Committee Report on H.R. 30, the National Recreation Area bill).

_____. *Official Congressional Directory.* 91st Congress.

_____. Senate. Interior Committee Hearings on Middle Snake River Moratorium. S. 940, 91st Congress, 2nd Session.

_____. Senate. Interior Committee Hearings on Hells Canyon-Snake National River. S. 717 and S. 448, 92nd Congress, 1st Session.

_____. Senate. Interior Committee Hearings on Hells Canyon National Forest Parklands and Hells Canyon National Recreation Area. S. 657 and S. 2233, 93rd Congress, 1st Session.

Public Law No. 94-199. United States Statutes. Establishes the Hells Canyon National Recreation Area.

CORPORATE DOCUMENTS, BROCHURES, AND PAMPHLETS

Environmental Statement, Middle Snake River. Pacific Northwest Power Company/Washington Public Power Supply System, July 1971.

"Fun Country." Idaho Power Company recreationists' brochure, undated.

Great Mountain Country of the West. Pacific Northwest Power Company/Washington Public Power Supply System, February 1971.

Hells Canyon Summary. Idaho Power Company, May 1957.

Smith, Wendell E. *Where Did All the Salmon and Steelhead Go?* Idaho Power Company, July 1976.

Summary of Federal Power Commission Decision Regarding Snake River Development. Idaho Power Company, November 1955.

"Welcome to the T. E. Roach Hells Canyon Development." Idaho Power Company recreationists' brochure, undated.

UNPUBLISHED MATERIALS

Anderson, Gary; Witty, Ken; Holubetz, Terry; Welsh, Tom; and Reid, Will. *An Evaluation of Recreational Use on the Snake River in the High Mountain Sheep Dam Impact Area.* Lewiston, Idaho: Report to the Oregon Game Commission and the Idaho Fish and Game Department, April 1970.

Brock Evans Papers. University of Washington Library, Seattle.

Gunsolus, Robert T. *A Report of Events and Observations Related to Fish Passage Problems at Oxbow Dam in 1958.* Report to the Fish Commission of Oregon, August 4, 1959.

Major Activity Dates, Pacific Northwest Power Company. Pacific Northwest Power Company, Spokane, Washington, February 1976.

Northwest Office, Sierra Club. Working Files. Seattle.

Northwest Public Power Association Records. University of Washington Library, Seattle.

A Report on Recent Fish Passage Problems at Oxbow and Brownlee Dams. United States Department of the Interior Fish and Wildlife Service, Washington, D.C., December 1958.

Statement of Idaho Power Company and Morrison-Knudsen, Inc. Presented to Robert D. Holmes, Governor of Oregon, Salem, Oregon, September 16, 1958.

OTHER SOURCES

Austin, Judith, Idaho Historical Society, Boise, Idaho. Correspondence, 9/76–1/77.

Barker, John, Coalition to Save the Snake. Interview taped at Lewiston, Idaho, 12/23/75; also correspondence, 1/76–4/77.

Brown, Bob, Idaho Power Company, Boise, Idaho. Correspondence, 9/76–12/76.

Farman, Dick; Jayne, Jerry; and Slansky, Cyril, Hells Canyon Preservation Council. Interview taped at Idaho Falls, Idaho, 2/7/76.

Harvey, Floyd, Hells Canyon Excursions, Inc. Interview taped at Lewiston, Idaho, 12/23/75; also correspondence, 1/76–4/77.

Henault, Pete, Hells Canyon Preservation Council. Interview taped at Seattle, Washington, 12/30/75.

Hurd, Owen, Washington Public Power Supply System. Interview taped at Sun City, Arizona, April 10, 1976; also correspondence, 1/76–4/77.

Meeds, Lloyd, United States Representative from the State of Washington. Correspondence, 4/76–5/76.

Packwood, Bob, United States Senator from the State of Oregon. Interview taped at Medford, Oregon, 1/7/76.

Pitney, Bill, Oregon Fish and Wildlife Commission. Correspondence, 9/76–11/76.

Scott, Doug, Sierra Club. Interviews taped at Seattle, Washington, 11/7/75 and 12/29/75.

Smith, Hugh, Pacific Northwest Power Company. Interview taped at Portland, Oregon, 2/13/76.

Stearns, Clem, Pacific Northwest Power Company. Interview taped at Spokane, Washington, 3/24/76; also correspondence, 2/76–4/77.

Ullman, Al, United States Representative from the State of Oregon. Correspondence, 11/75–1/77.

Warman, Don, United States Forest Service. Interview taped at Portland, Oregon, 2/13/76.

Wetherell, Mike, aide to United States Senator Frank Church from the State of Idaho. Correspondence, 1/75–11/76.

Williams, Larry, Oregon Environmental Council. Interview taped at Portland, Oregon, 2/12/76.

Witty, Ken, Hells Canyon Preservation Council. Untaped interview at Enterprise, Oregon, 7/30/76; also correspondence, 7/76–9/76.

Index